MAO PAPERS

MAO PAPERS

Anthology and Bibliography

edited by JEROME CH'EN

London

OXFORD UNIVERSITY PRESS

NEW YORK   TORONTO

1970

Oxford University Press, Ely House, London, W. 1

GLASGOW   NEW YORK   TORONTO   MELBOURNE   WELLINGTON
CAPE TOWN   SALISBURY   IBADAN   NAIROBI   DAR ES SALAAM   LUSAKA
ADDIS ABABA   BOMBAY   CALCUTTA   MADRAS   KARACHI   LAHORE
DACCA   KUALA LUMPUR   SINGAPORE   HONG KONG   TOKYO

SBN 19 215188 6

PRINTED IN GREAT BRITAIN BY
STEPHEN AUSTIN AND SONS LTD., HERTFORD.

For Mary

Contents

Plates

Foreword

Some years ago when I came across the 1944 and 1947 editions of Mao's *Hsüan-chi* ('Selected Works', hereafter *HC*), the temptation to collate these with their post-revolution editions was too strong to resist. In the inclement winter weather of north England in 1965 the work of textual comparison was done. Then my university generously gave me a grant to study in the Far East, where at the Toyo Bunko and the libraries of Todai and Keio in Tokyo I was fortunate enough to have further opportunities for comparing Mao's essays and statements in the currently available editions with the *Chien-fang chou-k'an* ('Liberation Weekly'), *Chien-fang jih-pao* ('Liberation Daily'), and *Ch'un-chung* ('Masses'). This work was continued during my sojourn at the Hoover Library at Stanford, the Library of Congress, and the East Asian Library of Harvard. My friends in Hong Kong, Japan, and the United States of America selflessly helped me to locate other, hitherto unpublished or little known writings by Mao. Some of our discoveries were made by others who have since published them in Hong Kong and Japan. For instance, there are the *CCP Documents of the Great Proletarian Cultural Revolution 1966–67* and *The Case of P'eng Teh-huai* (Hong Kong: Union Research Institute, 1968) and Nakajima Mineo's translation of *Mao Tse-tung ssu-hsiang wan-sui!* ('Long Live Mao Tse-tung's Thought!') in the *Chuo Koron*, July 1969. In October 1969 the American Consulate in Hong Kong brought out an English translation of the same collection as Nakajima's.

These three recent collections came to me early in 1968, together with some other material of which there was a volume of Mao's statements and essays with its title page torn away. They are all Red Guard publications as the State Department told the press (*Time Magazine*, 12 December 1969). Some of the pieces in these collections appear in my book, *Mao*, published by Prentice-Hall in May 1969; some of the others are included in this compendium.

I chose to arrange Mao's writings and statements in this volume according to their literary genres and within each category in their chronological order. This is merely a device to help my readers in locating a piece they may want to refer to more conveniently. I am aware that some of the pieces are important pronouncements and others have only biographical significance. They cover, however, a wide range of subjects and a long period of time. Any other classification may therefore be impossible or clumsy.

In translating these pieces, I have endeavoured to preserve their original flavour, sometimes even at the expense of readability in English. Where jargonistic Chinese is used, the translation is correspondingly jargonistic. After all Mao does frequently think in jargon, although he is capable of outdoing Mr. Khrushchev in using colloquialisms and folk-tales.

My annotation does not go beyond short biographies and brief explanations of terms and events; no attempt is made on the scale of Professor Wittfogel's study of Mao's lecture on dialectical materialism, Professor Schram's of Mao's essay on physical training, or even my own commentary on the Tsunyi Resolutions. To give historical and political annotation is to change an anthology like this one into many short monographs. Since the pieces are simply included rather than selected schematically, this volume can hardly follow the style, say, of Schram's excellent *Political Thought* or even of Mao's *Selected Works*.

It was with almost an antiquarian's interest that I collected Mao's instructions as the Cultural Revolution developed. To this day I am still not sure why Mao chose to use only this terse and peremptory form of communication throughout 1966–9. His great age and failing physical strength, the rapidly changing situation, and the preoccupation of his erstwhile secretaries such as Ch'en Po-ta may have been reasons for this choice instead of longer expositions. The instructions themselves undoubtedly played an important role in the Cultural Revolution. To have them collected together and arranged in chronological order, may, in my view, help the reader to understand the traumatic events in China in those years.

Finally, the bibliography in two versions is the expanded form of a version in Japanese I prepared for the *Kikan Toa*,

Tokyo, August 1968. It differs from this earlier effort in two respects—it includes the pieces discovered in 1967 and gives information on existing English translations of Mao's other writings.

Bibliographical work is seldom rewarding, for it is only occasionally complete and perfect. The sins of commission and omission of any bibliography become apparent often as soon as it is published. If my bibliography has any virtue, I think it is fuller than any of the others I have consulted. It includes a fair number of items ascribed to Mao on no higher an authority than my own guess. The guess is made on two grounds—the importance of the subject matter which suggests that only a man of Mao's stature could have tackled it, and the stylistic features as discussed in my essay on his written style. I have decided to leave out all the edicts and ceremonial statements signed by Mao alone or jointly with his colleagues. For instance, as the chairman of the Soviet Republic of China in the 1930s, he promulgated many decrees with his deputies, and after 1949 he made many speeches on the occasion of receiving the credentials of ambassadors and issued many orders of appointments and dismissals. As chairman of the People's Republic of China, he sent many congratulatory messages to other governments and communist parties. It seems to me pointless to incorporate them in the bibliography.

I would like to express here my sincere thanks to Mr. John Ma of the East Asian Library of the Hoover Institution, Mr. K'ai-hsien Liu of the Harvard-Yenching Library, and Mr. Eric Grinstead formerly of the British Museum and now in Copenhagen, for their help in locating some of the pieces translated below. With the editorial staff of my publishers I have enjoyed many pleasant and useful sessions of discussion over this and other manuscripts. They have gently restrained me from doing too much violence to their language. To Professor Takeuchi Minoru of the Toritsu University of Tokyo I owe a special debt. Without his kindness and meticulous scholarship, this anthology and bibliography would contain many more mistakes than it does and would lack many essential details. To my wife who checked the manuscript and made many invaluable suggestions for improvement this volume is affectionately dedicated.

January 1970   J.C.

Mao's Literary Style

There can be no doubt that Mao Tse-tung received in his youth a more than adequate training in Chinese classics, so much so that whenever he wanted to make a veiled criticism or to express his sentiments through a classical parallel, he had ample facility to do so. Many examples of this kind can be found in his poems, the most impressive one being his reference to an essay by Mei Sheng, 'Ch'i-fa' (Seven Advices)[1], when writing to admonish Chang Wen-t'ien during the Lushan Plenum of the Central Committee of the CCP in 1959.

This classical training left a deep imprint on Mao's manner of thinking; in the case of his reference to Mei Sheng, he obviously thought first of 'Ch'i-fa', which he had read forty years before, and only afterwards of Pavlov, Engels, Kautsky, and Stalin. The training also conditioned his literary style. His early writings, such as his letter to Miyazaki Toten, the fragments of his diaries, notes, and correspondence, and his essay on physical training in 1917 bear witness to this.[2] Before the vernacular style movement (*pai-hua-wen yüng-tung*) of 1919, Mao, like many others, still wrote in the classical style (*wen-yen*).

The May the Fourth Movement meant more than the promotion of the vernacular; it also saw the introduction of many European writings. The arduous task of translating Ibsen, Wilde, and others inevitably affected the styles of the Chinese translators and readers. Reading such works as *Thus Spake Zarathustra* in the original also influenced the styles of many writers, as, for example, Lu Hsün's *Madman's Diary*. Consequently the literary styles of this vintage can be characterized by three essential ingredients—the temptations of europeanization, the persistence of classical expressions, and the experimentation in colloquialism. As metals are mixed to produce various

---

[1] *The Case of P'eng Teh-huai*, Document 40, pp. 325–7 and 493–4.
[2] Cf. my bibliography p. 163.

alloys, so the proportions of these three ingredients produced different styles; the stamp of individual authors could be seen in the way they combined these ingredients according to their personal strengths, weaknesses, and predilections. Since the Peking dialect was, as it is still, regarded as the standard spoken language, writers of southern origins were more restricted in their use of colloquialism for fear of seeming obscurantist; they consequently relied more on the classical heritage and europeanization for literary expression. Lu Hsün from Shaohsing in Chekiang was an outstanding example of this and Mao was another.

Literary merit and scholastic solidity were often given equal weight according to traditional ways of evaluating a Chinese scholar; the May the Fourth Movement did not quite eradicate this practice. In order to gain a wide hearing, a writer still had to argue his points not merely cogently but also readably. Every scholar therefore had to have some interest in pure literature and display his literary propensity, if not brilliance, at some stage and on some occasions in his career. Mao's interest in literature is shown through his poems. His statements and instructions on literature and art are, however, another matter altogether and I shall discuss them presently. Had he had enough leisure in the early 1920s, he might have availed himself of that time for reading and experimenting with writing in modern literary forms. But right from the beginning of the May the Fourth Movement he was involved in its political work—the founding of the CCP, the organization of its Hunan branch, the provincial politics of Hunan, and the alliance with the KMT. Because of this lack of opportunity, Mao's knowledge of modern literature, Chinese as well as foreign, does not seem to have gone much beyond Lu Hsün.

According to Mao himself, during the May the Fourth period his style was greatly influenced by Ch'en Tu-hsiu.[1] This statement remains somewhat hard to substantiate from his writing alone. Comparing Mao's style with that of Ch'en, one may safely point out two features common to both authors. First, both of

---

[1] R. Payne, *Mao Tse-tung, Ruler of Red China* (London, 1950), pp. 58–9, quoted in my *Mao and the Chinese Revolution* (Oxford Paperback, 1967), p. 66. Ch'en was the dean of the faculties of arts at the Peking National University, editor of the influential *New Youth*, and the first secretary-general of the CCP.

them tackle their subject matter at the very beginning of their essay; neither of them liked preambles or leisurely introductory sentences—a stylistic imperative to most other writers. This direct approach to subject matter makes the style of Mao and Ch'en markedly different from the 'eight-legged', stereotyped style of the CCP leaders trained in Moscow. Second, in 1919 both authors began to use the vernacular to express more complicated ideas or to describe more complex situations. It is just as difficult to visualize how Ch'en could have written his 1919 essays for the *New Youth* magazine in the literary style and yet preserve their punch, as to imagine how Mao could couch his famous Hunan Report of 1927 in parallel 'four or six character sentences'. Although Mao learnt a straightforward and unadorned vernacular style from Ch'en, the latter none the less was more europeanized and, as one of the leaders of the new literary movement, disciplined himself more rigorously in using the new style. As a consequence, the writings of the older Ch'en after 1919 showed less classical influence than those of the younger Mao. For instance, Ch'en evinced no aversion to the use of the colloquial conjunction, *ho* ('and' or 'with'), whereas Mao preferred the more traditional *yü*, *chi*, or *t'ung*. Each time when Mao wrote for the communist official organ, the *Guide Weekly*, his editor, Ch'en, had to take the trouble to alter his conjunctions.[1] Being more europeanized, Ch'en could sometimes burst out in long strings of adjectives like these:

The new era and new society we envisage are honest, progressive, active, free, equal, creative, beautiful, good, peaceful, co-operative, hard working, joyful, and totally happy. We wish that the hypocritical, conservative, negative, inhibitive, stratified, traditional, ugly, evil, war-stricken, hostile, lazy, frustrating, and unhappy phenomena will diminish and finally disappear.[2]

Mao has never permitted himself to write in this fashion; nor has he indulged in Ch'en's type of haranguing sentimentality:

Countrymen! Patriotic students! Members of the Diplomatic Association! We have failed, almost 90 per cent failed, in our relations with Japan! Our failures are not confined to the Shantung Question only! Oh, how sad the present situation, but the situation after the

---

[1] See, for instance, 'The bitter sufferings of the peasants in Kiangsu and Chekiang and their movement of resistance,' the *Guide Weekly*, no. 179, p. 25.

[2] *Tu-hsiu wen-ts'un* (Hong Kong, 1965 ed.), I, p. 366.

destruction of our country will be ten, hundred, thousand, and myriad times sadder![1]

This self-imposed restraint was also due to Mao's temperament.

Mao's other mentor in the May the Fourth period was Li Ta-chao whose writings Mao read with relish. But perhaps because of his antipathy to Li's clear but pedestrian style, Mao is not known nor can be detected to have been influenced by Li's literary idiosyncrasies, except in one respect. Li's description of the living conditions of the miners in T'angshan[2] in a down-to-earth style of short crisp sentences seems to have set an example for Mao's Hunan Report on the conditions of the peasants in the early 1920s up to 1926. Otherwise, Li was ponderously meandering, always beginning his essays with general, commonplace introductions. While dealing with current affairs of some urgency, he demonstrated an easy excitability in this manner:

Gentleman, hurry up, go to work!

Victory! Victory! Victory of the Allies! Surrender! Surrender! Surrender of the Germans!

The new era has come! The new era has come!

Young people! Hurry, to the villages![3]

Mao has never screamed like this.

1920–7 was the first phase of Mao's career as a writer in the vernacular style with the same three ingredients—europeanization, the classical heritage, and colloquialism—at his disposal. In his case, there was more classical heritage than europeanization; hence his style was admirably clear but unfashionable when compared with, say, those of Lu Hsün and Chou Tso-jen which were enriched and refined by a high density of classicism and europeanization, or with Hsü Chih-mo and Wen I-to who were sophisticated and tenderized by Englishism. Mao was, generally speaking, formal and stiff, tentative and considerate, timid in using Hunan colloquialism except in his Hunan Report. Still, the proverb, 'pick up a stone and smash it on one's own feet',

---

[1] ibid., II, p. 619.

[2] In the *Mei-chou p'ing-lun* ('Weekly Review'), no. 12, 9 March 1919.

[3] The last sentence of 'The common man's victory', the *New Youth*, V, no. 5, 15 November 1919; the first two sentences of 'The victory of Bolshevism', the *New Youth*, V, no. 5, 15 November 1919; the first sentence of 'The new era', in the *Mei-chou p'ing-lun*, no. 3, 5 January 1919; and the last paragraph of 'Youth and villages', in the *Ch'en-pao* ('Morning Post') 20–23 February 1919.

made its appearance in his short comment on the 'Peking coup d'état and the merchants'[1] to become now a part of the national language. Even his Hunan Report lacked the freedom and confidence, lucidity and biting irony which he was to acquire at the beginning of the 1940s.

The second phase of his writing lasted through the civil war years and the Long March from autumn 1927 to autumn 1935. Under conditions of siege, it can be imagined that he did not have much chance to read, nor much leisure to polish his prose. His official statements (e.g. his speeches at the first and second national congresses of the Soviet Republic of China), rural surveys (e.g. those on Ts'aihsi, Ch'angkang, and other places), and the resolutions of the Tsunyi Conference drafted by him[2] show a popularization of his written style. The sentences became shorter and crisper, allusions less, and classical structures infrequent. None the less, he would not use such colloquial conjunctions as *ho* and *ken* and such emphatic adverbs as *hen* ('very'). Even the vernacular genitive, *ti*, was used no more frequently than its classical equivalent, *chih*. His attempt at popularization in this period is understandable, for he was then writing for a less educated audience of peasants and soldiers and a cadre rising from them.

In Yenan the situation was vastly different. The anti-Japanese war from 1937 onward preoccupied Mao's attention as most of his writings in the last years of the 1930s were on the political and military strategies of the war. The war itself and the united front between the KMT and CCP meant that the suppression of left-wing publications was somewhat relaxed; books on Russia, Marxism-Leninism, the world communist movement, and the CCP were openly sold in Shanghai, Wuhan, and later Chungking. Some of these books were sent to Yenan where, according to Edgar Snow,[3] Mao engaged himself in avid reading. He read Marxian philosophy and wrote on it and on

---

[1] In the *Guide Weekly*, nos. 31–2, 11 July 1923.

[2] See my translation and commentary on the resolutions in the *China Quarterly*, no. 40, October–December 1969.

[3] This is reported in Snow's *Red Star Over China*. See also K. A. Wittfogel, 'Some remarks on Mao's handling of concepts and problems of dialectics,' *Studies in Soviet Thought*, III (4 December 1963). For a most exhaustive study of Mao's writings on philosophy in the late 1930s, see Takeuchi Minoru, 'Mo Takuto "mujunron" no genkei nitsuite,' (the original form of Mao Tse-tung's 'On Contradiction'), in the *Shiso*, April 1969.

strategic problems. When he was writing on the latter, he drew on his own and the Red Army's experiences and was always on top of his subject. His style was therefore free and lucid, although his simultaneous reading in philosophy had its impact—the use of opposites, hence of parallel sentences and even parallel paragraphs, is pronounced. On the other hand when he was drafting his philosophical lectures, he had to refer to books translated from Russian into stilted Chinese and in the process his fluency gave way to laboriousness, except at places where he was illustrating the general 'laws' with examples from Chinese history. The subject lent itself to europeanization, and Mao's essays on contradiction or practice show an exceptionally high degree of europeanization and read like translations.

An important event took place in Mao's life in 1939–40: he met and fell in love with Lan P'ing (now better known as Chiang Ch'ing)—a film starlet who followed many other writers and artists to work in Yenan, turning the place into a centre of cultural activities.[1] She first taught drama at the Lu Hsün College of Art and then was transferred to the secretariat of the Military Commission of the CCP presided over by Mao himself. Shortly after their marriage, Mao began to show an increasing interest in modern Chinese literature and art.

To be sure, Mao read Lu Hsün after the latter's death in 1936 as his speech on the writer in 1937 shows.[2] However, neither this speech nor his other writing before 1939 bears the stamp of Lu Hsün's stylistic influence. It does not indicate his interest in artistic and literary matters in a broader sense either. The belated awakening of this interest in 1939 may have been stimulated by his deep antipathy towards the stereotyped, long winded, and highly europeanized styles practised by his comrades in the CCP and the left-wing writers fashionable in the 1930s. If Mao wanted to combat these trends, the publication of Lu Hsün's *Complete Works* in 1938 may have given him an opportunity to study the author in detail and his meeting with Chiang Ch'ing may have aroused his interest in art and literature in general.

[1] Chung Hua-min (pseudo.), *Chiang Ch'ing cheng-chuan* (A true story of Chiang Ch'ing) (Hong Kong, Union Research Institute, 1967), pp. 17–23. The title itself harks back to Lu Hsün's 'True story of Ah Q'.

[2] See below, pp. 12–14.

Reading Lu Hsün changed Mao's own style. In his less formal writings, he now introduced his arguments with a short and casual paragraph like the following:

The publication of this material has been delayed until now, but [in the meantime?] the Hsünwu Survey was lost.[1]

or

I propose that we should reform the method and system of study throughout the Party. The reasons are as follows.[2]

Mao had never introduced his essays in this way before; this was Lu Hsün's manner—especially for prefaces. Lu Hsün also inspired a great deal of combativeness and sarcasm in Mao's style. From reading him, Mao seems to have realized that the repeated use of a colloquial or classical phrase could add force to an argument, drive a point home, or make an essay flow better. As Mao was then engaged in a fierce campaign against the 'dogmatists' in the party and their long-winded essays, Lu Hsün's prose style was ideal for the task. From Mao's 'On new democracy' of 1940 onward, with the help of Lu Hsün and his own growing stature in party and national politics, his literary style was gradually freed from its earlier stiffness, formality, and diffidence, although it had never been stodgy.

Let us take a few examples from his writings of the early 1940s to illustrate this point.

There are many people who 'the moment they alight from the official carriage' [a classical phrase] make a hullabaloo, spout opinions, criticize this and condemn that; but, in fact, ten out of ten of them will meet with failure. For such views or criticisms, which are not based on thorough investigation, are nothing but ignorant twaddle. Countless times our Party suffered at the hands of these 'imperial envoys', who rushed here, there and everywhere.

(*SW*, III, p. 13)

Generally speaking, in the last twenty years we have not done systematic and thorough work in collecting and studying material on these aspects, and we are lacking a climate of investigation and study of objective reality. To behave like 'a blindfolded man catching sparrows,' or 'a blind man groping for fish,' [both being common

---

[1] *HC*, III, p. 809, 'Preface to the "Rural Survey"'. This sentence appears in the Central China edition, 1941, but is deleted from the *HC* new editions.

[2] *HC*, III, p. 815, or *SW*, III, p. 17.

sayings] to be crude and careless, to indulge in verbiage, to rest content with a smattering of knowledge—such is the extremely bad style of work that still exists among many comrades in our Party, a style utterly opposed to the fundamental spirit of Marxism-Leninism.

(ibid., III, p. 18)

When making speeches, they indulge in a long string of headings, A, B, C, D, 1, 2, 3, 4, and when writing articles, they turn out a lot of verbiage. They have no intention of seeking truth from facts, but only a desire to curry favour by claptrap. They are flashy without substance, brittle without solidity. They are always right, they are the Number One authority under Heaven, 'imperial envoys' who rush everywhere.

(ibid., III, p. 21)

Books cannot run. You may open them; you may shut them. Nothing in the world is easier than that, much easier than a chef doing cooking, easier still than a butcher slaughtering a pig. Pigs do run, if you want to catch them. [laughter] They cry, when you kill them. [laughter] But a book lying on the desk neither runs nor cries. You can do whatever you like with it. Is there anything in the world easier than handling a book?

(HC, 1944 ed., V, pp. 47 ff. This paragraph is
deleted from the new editions. Cf. 1952 ed., III, p. 838)

Sometimes his irony went too far:

To this type of people, we should candidly say: 'Your dogmas are utterly useless. Permit me to be rude—they are less useful than dog shit.' We know that dog shit can fertilize land and human shit can feed dogs. What's the use of dogmas?

(ibid., this paragraph, too, is
deleted from the new editions. Cf. 1952 ed., III, p. 842)

Lu Hsün gave a shape to Mao's venom against Wang Ming, the 'flashy' and 'brittle' 'imperial envoy' from the Third International, and his fellow 'dogmatists'. In the years of the Rectification Campaign Mao was as devastating as his literary mentor. But unconsciously, perhaps, memories of his reading on literary matters in the May the Fourth Movement period came back to mind. Hu Shih's 'Eight Don'ts' (*pa pu chu-i*) of 1919 were now paraphrased into Mao's 'Eight Indictments' against the stereotyped party writing.[1] He had only six substantive

---

[1] These are to be found in 'Oppose stereotyped party writing,' 8 February 1942, *SW*, III, p. 64.

points to make; yet he made up eight to remind his audience that this was no less significant a campaign than Hu's against the use of the classical style almost a quarter of a century earlier.

The Yenan period (1926–47) highlighted by the Rectification Campaign of 1942–4 was the third phase in Mao's stylistic development. The Campaign was launched because, among other things, (a) the influence of Moscow over the CCP had reached its nadir while Russia was pre-occupied with the war against Hitler, and (b) there was a lull, as it were, in the Chinese war against Japan. In these circumstances, Mao and his comrades could shift their attention from war to disciplinary matters. Later, the surrender of Japan, peace negotiations between the KMT and CCP, and resumption of the civil war after V-J Day once again led Mao and his party away from intellectual problems. Probably Mao did not go back to reading again until the division of the two lines of leadership[1] and lessening of his duties in matters of State after 1950. But by then he was approaching 60 and was never again to write very much. From what he did write—'Selections from the introductory notes in the *Socialist Upsurge in China's Countryside*' and the three major statements since 1956 ('The ten great relationships,' 'On the correct handling of the contradictions among the people,' and 'Sixty points on working methods')[2]—one can detect no significant change in his literary style.

What are the features of Mao's written style before 1949? One limits one's period of inquiry this way because it is futile to ascertain the style of Mao's more recent writings which have either been drastically edited or not edited at all, even by the author himself. The edited and polished pieces, as those in the *Selected Readings*, cease to bear the hallmark of Mao; the unedited and unpolished drafts put out in print by the Red Guards during the Cultural Revolution are too rough and crude to be comparable with the essays in the old editions of the *HC*. Even for the 1920–49 period, an answer to this elusive question is by no means easy to find. However, if a more or less viable

---

[1] J. Ch'en, *Mao* (N.J., Prentice-Hall, 1969), p. 96.

[2] *Selected Readings*, pp. 341–9; J. Ch'en, *Mao*, pp. 65–85; *Selected Readings*, pp. 350–87, and below, pp. 57–76. The two essays in the *Selected Readings*, like all Mao's writings after 1950, are drastically edited.

answer can be found, then one should be able to decide on the authorship of some of the essays attributed to Mao and others which hitherto remained anonymous. By collating the texts of Mao's writings in the old and new editions of the *HC*, one comes to the following conclusions.

Some common usages of words

1. conjunctions:

   a. And: *chi*, *t'ung*, and *yü* (*Mathews*, 468, 6615, and 7615. Hereafter only the numbers are given) are always preferred by Mao to the more colloquial *ho* (2115). He uses *ho* as 'with' more often, but seldom uses *ken* (3330). Take 'The tasks of the CCP in the period of resistance to Japan' of 3 May 1937 for instance:

	OLD EDITIONS	NEW EDITIONS
chi	6 times	2
ho	none	54
ken	none	none
t'ung	1	1
yi-chi	none	1
yü	63	7

   b. But: *tan* (6038) is preferred to *tan-shih* (6038:13)

2. pronouns:

   No distinction is made between *t'a* (5961:1 not 2 and 3) and *t'a* (*t'o*, 6439) in the old editions. In the new editions, however, the former is used as a personal and the latter an impersonal pronoun.

3. verbs:

   a. *chiang* (656) is preferred to *pa* (4829) when a verb is used in its intransitive form. See *HC*, 1962, II, p. 415, l. 1 and p. 508, l. 8 and III, p. 838, l. 14. (This and the rest of the references to the 1962 edition do not mean that readers can actually find the usages under discussion but rather the places where the 1962 edition differs from earlier, pre-revolution editions. The differences can be verified by the reader by collating with any of the old editions. I use this method of reference on the assumption that old editions are not easily available to most of my readers.)

b. *hui* (2345) is preferred to *chiang* (656) for the future tense. See *HC*, 1962, II, p. 729, l. 3 and III, p. 1038, first paragraph.

c. verb+*yü* (7643) form is preferred to verb+*lai* (3768) or verb+*ch'ü* (1594). See *HC*, 1962, II, p. 460, section (50), where several *yü* would be replaced by *lai* or *ch'ü* by a younger writer.

d. *kan* (3235, to do) is preferred to *tso* (6776).

4. adverbs:

a. Mao seldom uses *ti* (6198) to transform an adjective into an adverb. See *HC*, 1962, II, p. 333, ll. 10 and 16. In the latter instance, he uses *ti* (6213) instead.

b. In expressions like *chin-k'o-neng* (as far as possible), he uses *chin* (1083) instead of the modern form of *chin* (1082). See *HC*, 1962, II, p. 405, last paragraph.

c. *yüeh . . . yüeh* (7699) is preferred to *yü . . . yü* (7932) when he says 'The more . . ., the more . . .'. In the essays I have collated (*HC*, 1962, pp. 371, 374, 419, 427, 446, 508, 766, 837, 907, 940, 1,059, 1,093, 1,148, 1,161, 1,203, 1,485, and 1,507), only on two occasions does Mao use *yü . . . yü* (*HC*, 1962, pp. 891 and 1,040). I shall come back to the authorship of these two passages presently.

d. *hen* (2094) is seldom used; he prefers such expressions as *fei-ch'ang* (1819:26)

Some common usages of phrases

OLD EDITIONS	NEW EDITIONS
hsiao tzu-ch'an chieh-chi (petty bourgeoisie)	*ch'eng-shih hsiao tzu-ch'an chieh-chi* (urban petty bourgeoisie)
pi-ju (for instance)	*p'i-ju*
yü-chou-kuan (view of the universe)	*shih-chieh-kuan* (view of the world)

OLD EDITIONS	NEW EDITIONS
ying-tang (should, must, necessary)	*pi-hsü*
ssu-shih nien-tai (the 1930s)	*san-shih nien-tai*
yen-yü (language)	*yü-yen*
1925–27	1925–1927
shortened forms of names	full forms of names
Chao	Chao Heng-t'i
Ma-Le-*chu-i* (Marxism-Leninism)	Ma-k'e-ssu Le-ning
	chu-i
chiao-mai (694–4325, proud and arrogant)	*chiao-man* (694–4334)

Some usages of punctuation

commas and full stops in quotes	commas and full stops outside quotes
frequent use of commas and less frequent use of full stops	more frequent use of full stops
commas between three things: A, B, C	commas between three things: A, B C
punctuation sometimes appearing at the top of a line	punctuation never appearing at the top of a line.[1]

These are the more definite characteristics of Mao's style. What do they amount to? Let me take his famous essay, 'On the protracted war', as an example to demonstrate the meaning of the exercise. As printed in the *HC*, 1962 edition, it runs from p. 429 to p. 504. There are these noteworthy points, having restored the essay to its original form:

p. 429   *hen* 3 times
   432   *ho* once
   433–6 a long quotation from his interview with Edgar Snow, obviously not translated by himself:
          hen 3 times
          ho 3 times

---

[1] For instance, on *HC*, 1962, pp. 402 and 404 the editors even cut out a word in each case to avoid having a punctuation at the bottom end of a line.

p. 446   *ho* twice
          yüeh . . . yüeh . . . yüeh
    448   *ho* once
    449   *ho* once
    452   *hen* once
    460   verb+*yü* several times
    461   *ho* once
    464   in the forties (now altered to 'in the thirties')
    474   *hen* once
    477   *ho* once
    487   (94) almost entirely in the classical style
    492   *chiao-mai* twice
    493   *ho* once
    497   *ho* once
    499   *ho* once
    500   *ho* once
    503   *ho* once in a quotation

Except for the first page and the quotations, this essay bears all the personal idiosyncrasies of Mao's style and can be accepted as written largely by him. The deviation from his style on p. 429 and perhaps also on p. 446 may have been due to the alterations made by Liu Shao-ch'i, Ch'en Yün, K'ang Sheng, or Chang Wen-t'ien.[1]

Let me take another example—'The Chinese revolution and the Chinese communist party', written in December 1939, which runs from p. 615 to p. 646 in the 1962 edition of the *HC*. The editor's note on p. 616 says that it was written by Mao and a few others. Its features in its old editions are as follows:

p. 615   *ho* once (This sentence does not appear in the old editions.)

---

[1] According to Mao's bodyguard, this is how Mao wrote this famous essay. For the first two days Mao did not sleep at all, working continuously by the light of a pair of candles and sometimes forgetting his meals. When he was tired he freshened himself up with a hot face-flannel. On the fifth day he was visibly thinner, ate even less, and his eyes were blood-shot, yet he went on writing. On the seventh day he was so engrossed in his work that he did not notice that the fire was burning a hole in his right shoe until his toes felt the pain. . . . It was not surprising that he had a headache on the eighth day and was unable to eat or sleep. . . . However, he went on working until the ninth day when the essay was completed. He checked it through before passing it on to Liu Shao-ch'i, Ch'en Yün, K'ang Sheng, and Chang Wen-t'ien for their criticism. See J. Ch'en, *Mao and the Chinese Revolution*, p. 209.

p. 617   *hen* once and *ho* once
618   *hen* once and *ho* 4 times
619   *ho* once
621   *ho* twice
624   *ho* once
625   *ho* 4 times and *hen* once
628   *ho* once
629   *ho* twice
630   *ho* once
632   *ho* once
633   *ho* twice
637   *ho* twice and *hen* 4 times (This passage on urban petty bourgeoisie is deleted from the new editions.)

From this brief study, one may suspect that the first section of this essay (pp. 615–26) was not written by Mao who drafted the rest of the essay, with the paragraphs on the urban petty bourgeoisie heavily edited by his collaborators. The urban petty bourgeoisie has always been a square peg in the Marxian doctrinal round hole, hard to fit in. Mao, lacking experience in working among urban intellectuals and other 'petty bourgeois' groups, had to have his collaborators' help in putting him right, hence the drastic revision of these paragraphs. The significance of this finding is that the famous passage on irredentism, of land but not necessarily of people, on p. 622 (falling between pp. 615 and 626), although having Mao's approval before publication, cannot be attributed to him, and that his analysis of the groupings in the urban petty bourgeoisie was not shared by the comrades who co-operated with him in writing this essay.

Even more interesting are his famous essays on the Rectification, 'Oppose the stereotyped party writings' and 'The talks at the Yenan Forum on literature and art', the first of which, written in February 1942, has these characteristics:

1. the tendency to use the impersonal *t'a* to mean both 'it' and 'they' (not *t'a-men*), begun in 1941, was continued.

2. the use of *ho* and *hen* in the *HC*, III compared with the old editions are to be found

    p. 852   *ho* once

p. 853   *hen* once
         ho once
   855   *ho* once
   856   *ho* 5 times
   857   *ho* twice
   858   *ho* once
   859   *ho* once
   861   *hen* once
   863   *ho* once (in a quotation).

The only stylistic inconsistency occurs on p. 856 when Mao was discussing the second indictment against the stereotyped writings.

But the talks at the Yenan Forum show different features:

p. 870   *hen* twice
   872   *hen* once
         yen-yü instead of *yü-yen* as in the new editions
   874   *hen* 3 times and *ho* 3 times in 3 sentences
   875   *hen* once and *ho* twice
   876   *ho* 3 times
   877   *hen* once
   878   *ho* once
   881   *ho* twice
   882   *ho* once in an exceedingly europeanized sentence which begins with 'tso-wei' (as) and uses the noun phrase, 'chieh-chien' (reference) as a verb.
   883   *ho* once
   884   *ho* twice
   887   *ho* once
   890   *yü* . . . *yü* twice, instead of his usual '*yüeh* . . . *yüeh*' in a highly technical passage on literature.
   893   *ho* twice
   894   *ho* once
   895   *ho* twice in a highly europeanized passage
   896   *ho* once
         Ma-Le *chu-i* in contrast to Ma-k'e-ssu *chu-i* in the new editions
   897   *ho* 3 times

As Mao was not versed in modern literature, it was probable that these two essays, more noticeably the latter, like many of his other writings on political matters, had been given to his close comrades for comment before they were published or delivered in public. In Yenan at that time, Mao had Chiang Ch'ing, Chou Yang, and Ch'en Po-ta at his elbow for consultations on intellectual, especially literary and artistic, matters. The passages showing a stylistic inconsistency (e.g. on pp. 874, 876, 881–2, 891, 895, and 897) are probably the handiwork of either Chiang Ch'ing, Chou Yang, or Ch'en Po-ta.

Without going into detailed textual comparison but applying the same principles, one can at least doubt the authorship of two sections in the essay, 'On the coalition government': the last paragraph on p. 1,076 in the 1962 edition of the *HC* and chapter 5 from pp. 1,117 to 1,122. One can also attribute some of the anonymous writings published in the high official organs of the CCP to Mao such as the items marked with an asterisk in the bibliography below.

Of course the attributions made in my bibliography are not solely on stylistic grounds; the subject matter is considered as well. For instance, items 230, 278, 292, and 303, not to mention the statements by 'a Yenan person of authority' (Yenan *ch'uan-wei jen-shih*) on problems of great importance; they are the sort of statements which could appropriately be made only by a man of Mao's status. This suspicion is confirmed by the stylistic features of these statements, hence the attribution.

Now a few words on the editing of Mao's *HC* since 1949. The editors have made it clear in their note that the *HC* is incomplete and that because of their wide circulation the *Rural Survey* and *On Economic and Financial Problems* (*Nung-ts'un tiao-ch'a* and *Kuan-yü ching-chi ts'ai-cheng wen-t'i*) are omitted from the *HC*, except one piece from the latter. The editors must have had a vast collection of Mao's writings at their disposal when they made the selection for the *HC*. The incompleteness of the *HC* cannot therefore be ascribed to the destruction of Mao's writings by the KMT or losses through years of hard fighting and fleeing, as the editors say. Even the exclusion of the essays in the collection, *Rural Survey*, may not entirely be due to 'wide circulation'. Inevitably, the editors' policy of selection and exclusion would result in some of Mao's writings being preserved and circulated and others being forgotten; this the editors anticipated and made the selections with such consequences in view.

The *HC* as it stands includes Mao's writings of the 1926–45 period only. The exclusion of all his earlier writings is under-standable as they do not represent the views of a mature Marxist. From 1926 onward, Mao's writings of the following categories are left out of the *HC*: 1. all his poems; 2. all his sur-veys of rural China published in the *Guide Weekly*, *Red China*, and other official organs of the CCP which should have been easily available to the editors, with the exception of his Hunan Report; 3. all his speeches and reports on the work of the Chinese Soviet Republic; 4. his early statements on Japanese aggression pub-lished before the formation of the second united front in 1937; 5. some early texts on military strategy and philosophy; and finally, 6. letters and statements on ephemeral and unimportant subjects.

The reasons for the exclusion of his writings in categories 1 and 6 are obvious; the exclusion of category 4 is due to the doubtful judgement and prediction expressed in those essays; the exclusion of categories 2 and 5 is largely due to the quality of these pieces as pointed out by Professors K. A. Wittfogel and S. R. Schram—they are crude and immature. One is left to speculate on the reasons for the exclusion of category 3. Was the Soviet period a period in Mao's political life that he would rather forget? Did he then toe a political line which he did not whole-heartedly support?

Apart from these categories, there is another significant omis-sion—'The new stage' (*lun hsin-chieh-tuan*), Mao's first political report to the Central Committee of the CCP in October 1938. As I have said elsewhere[1] 'it not only showed uncertainty in political analysis but also contained a number of platitudes and mistakes'. Although this essay was circulated widely together with 'On new democracy' and 'On the protracted war' as the three important essays by Mao in the early 1940s, it was, accord-ing to Mao himself, 'criticized, challenged, and doubted' by his comrades.[2]

As to the deletions and alterations of Mao's writings in the new editions of the *HC*, these can be understood only in the light of the circumstances under which the *HC* was edited. For the celebration of the thirtieth anniversary of the founding of the CCP, the Party Centre must have decided to compile Mao's

[1] J. Ch'en, *Mao*, 1969, pp. 16 ff.   [2] ibid., p. 17.

HC as soon as they had settled the more urgent problems of state-making in 1949 and 1950. By then, the war with Japan had been over for several years, the civil war had been won, and the Korean war was at its height. In other words, the *HC* was edited in a period when the hatred of Japan had abated, realization of an eventual Sino-Japanese co-existence and co-operation had begun, a need for Russian co-operation in China's economic construction and the Korean war was strongly felt, and hostility to the USA was intense. This was the international environment. Internally, Chiang Kai-shek and the KMT had been driven to Taiwan and yet the antagonism between them and the CCP remained unmitigated. The CCP, while faced with the tasks of nation building and other affairs of State, had also to go through internal organizational changes and political reorientation. And Mao himself, having assumed his new position as Head of State of a major power, needed to present an image of dignity befitting such a role. He could no longer appear to behave, talk, or write in the same old casual manner. These considerations must have faced the editors of the *HC* with several dilemmas. The principal dilemma was the one between historical accuracy and political expediency, and they sacrificed the former.

In consideration for Mao's being the head of a major power and a candidate for a place in the Marxist-Leninist pantheon, rude and crude remarks (which should have appeared in *HC*, 1962, on pp. 15, 355, 838–9, 842, 876–7, and 897), woolly and superfluous passages (which should have appeared on pp. 96, 372, 512, 523, 565–6, 834, 836–8, 871, 880, 882–3, 885, 955, and 1,031), and doctrinally mistaken utterances (which should have appeared on pp. 17–18, 20–2, 97–8, and 566) were deleted by the editors. For political reasons, Mao's earlier, more conciliatory remarks on Chiang Kai-shek and the KMT were crossed out (e.g. on pp. 246, 360, 372, 376, 445, and 662). In order to secure Mao's image of infallibility, the new editions of the *HC* omitted all his wrong predictions (e.g. on pp. 246, 254, 354, 371, 465, and 1,037). Anything remotely complimentary to the USA, Britain, and France also had to go (e.g. on pp. 446, 496, 683, 1,077, 1,109, and 1,110) just as did anything even slightly uncomplimentary to the USSR (e.g. on pp. 453, 607, 859, and 1,108). In attempting to display familiarity with foreign affairs,

Mao had made several naïve or erroneous statements on the history or political affairs of other countries, and these now found no place in the *HC* (e.g. on pp. 480, 523, 690, 859, 883, 885, 959, and 1,067). However, the more significant and certainly more noteworthy omissions are his remarks: in favour of specialization by the members of the party; on the lack of activism of the masses; on the ten tasks of the CCP; criticizing Li Li-san; attacking the foreign (Russian, mainly) 'eight-legged' or stereotyped style; in favour of federalism in China. These should have been on pp. 93, 482, 509, 713, 843–4, 858, and 1,080 respectively, but were rejected by the editors of the *HC*.

The editors of the *HC* also made numerous emendations in all the texts included, most of which were stylistic improvements. It is impossible to give a list of all the alterations, but again the criteria for emendation were roughly parallel to those for deletion. For instance, wrong dates (e.g. on p. 250) are corrected, unflattering phraseology about peasant uprisings (e.g. on p. 619) is changed, and clowning (e.g. on pp. 678, 683, 709, 726, etc.) is stopped. However, one's attention is drawn to such alterations of doctrinal significance as Mao's advocacy of the sinocization of Marxism (deleted from p. 522), approval of recovery of territories which had never belonged to China (deleted from p. 622), confusion of communism with socialism (deleted from p. 830), and misunderstanding of Marx's analysis of the commodity (deleted from p. 839).

No one outside the inner core of the CCP seems to know who actually edited the *HC*; there is insufficient evidence for anyone else to hazard even a guess. According to the editors' note, Mao himself took a hand in polishing up his old essays. This may be so. But one may be more inclined to accept the possibility that the stylistic uniformity of the *HC* was the painstaking work of a lesser man than Mao. Whoever this man was, he did a splendid piece of work at the expense of some historical truth.

The *HC* is indispensable and invaluable, yet incomplete. For a better understanding of its great author, it is absolutely necessary to compile his collected (not selected) works in their original, undoctored forms with their historical background clearly set out. If this were at all possible, it would be a gigantic but immensely worthwhile undertaking, a task beyond the scope of the present volume and the ability of its editor.

ABBREVIATIONS

Anti-party Clique	*Fan-tang Chi-t'uan* or *P'eng Chang Huang Chou Fan-tang Chi-t'uan*, N.P. 1966
*	attributed to Mao Tse-tung (in the bibliography)
BBC/FE	British Broadcasting Corporation Monitoring Service, *Summary of World Broadcasts*, part 3, the Far East (extracts reprinted by permission)
BTA	Bulgarian Telegraph Agency
Ch'en Ch'eng	the Ch'en Ch'eng documents
CCP and CP	the Chinese Communist Party and communist party
CQ	the *China Quarterly*
Dates	The date of completion of an item of Mao's writing usually precedes the title of that item whereas the date of publication follows it.
DH	Conrad Brandt, Benjamin Schwartz, and John K. Fairbank, *A Documentary History of Chinese Communism*, Harvard University Press, 1962
FLP	Peking: Foreign Language Press
Hatano	Hatano Kenichi, *Shina Kyosanto Shi*
HC	*Mao Tse-tung Hsüan-chi* (Selected Works of Mao Tse-tung). When this abbreviation is not followed by a date of publication, it means any edition of the book published after 1951. The Roman numeral that follows it indicates the volume and Arabic numeral the *number of an item, not the pagination*. Users of the bibliography in this book are therefore advised to number the items in the table of contents of the *HC* at their disposal.

JC	Jerome Ch'en, *Mao and the Chinese Revolution*, Oxford University Press, 1965, paperback edition, 1967
JMJP	the *People's Daily*
KMT	the Kuomintang (the Nationalist Party)
LD	the *Liberation Daily*
Liberation	the *Liberation Weekly*
MTT	Jerome Ch'en, *Mao*, Prentice-Hall, 1969
NCNA	New China News Agency bulletin
NT	the anthology without a title
n. tr.	no translation in English.
PLA Daily	the *Liberation Army Daily*
PR	the *Peking Review*
PT	S. R. Schram, *Political Thought of Mao Tse-tung*, Penguin Books, 1969
Quotations	*Quotations from Chairman Mao Tse-tung*
R	roll number of microfilms
RC	the *Red China*
RF	the *Red Flag Fortnightly*
SCMP	Survey of China Mainland Press
SHWS	*Long Live Mao Tse-tung's Thought!*
SR	*Selected Readings from the Works of Mao Tse-tung*
SRS	Stuart R. Schram
SW	see *HC*
Wang, *Draft History*	Wang Chien-ming, *A Draft History of the Chinese Communist Party*, Taipei, 1965
WCHP	*Wen-hua Ta-ke-ming Wen-chien Hui-pien*, Hong Kong, 1968

PART I

WRITINGS BY MAO

translated and annotated by the editor

Letters

TO HAKURO TOTEN (Miyazaki Toten)[1]   April 1917
Asahi Shimbun, 3.7.1967

Dear Mr. Hakuro Toten,

We have long admired your integrity but regret not having had the privilege of your acquaintance. Even at this great distance your reputation is enough to inspire us.

Sir, you gave moral support to Huang[2] [when he was alive] and now mourn him with your tears. He is to be buried, and you have come across a myriad leagues of waves to bid him farewell at his grave. Your lofty friendship reaches as high as the sun and moon; your sincerity moves gods and spirits. Both are rare in this world, in the past as well as today.

Chih-fan and Tse-tung are schoolboys in Hunan who have acquired some knowledge of the classics and have disciplined their aspirations. We long to have an opportunity to meet you, to learn deportment and receive instructions from you. We shall feel extremely honoured if our request is granted.

Students at the First Teachers' Training College, Hunan
signed Hsiao Chih-fan
Mao Tse-tung

---

[1] (1870–1922), a Meiji *shishi* (extremist patriot) and supporter of the revolutionary activities of Sun Yat-sen and his comrades.

[2] Huang Hsing (1874–1916), a revolutionary leader and supporter of Sun Yat-sen, who was buried on 15 April 1917.

Comrade Lin Piao,

I entirely agree with your letter. One further point—of the three courses, 'cultural' education (cultivating the ability to read, reading books and newspapers, and writing) is the most important, the basic component. According to what you and your colleagues say, equal emphasis will be given to theory and practice, and 'cultural' tools are a part of the 'practice' which links up theory with practice. 'Cultural' tools can and should be used to link up the two. If the student, having learnt other things, can neither read books nor write, his future development after leaving the school will be limited. If you agree with me, then I think in the next four months there should be more 'culture' classes (reading, writing, and composition) in the second and third courses. My view is that these classes should be increased to a quarter or even one third of the total study hours (including home work) of a student. Please give your consideration to this problem. When the time comes for the periodic test, 'culture' will be an important criterion of judgement.

Salute!

[1] (1908–   ), born in Huangkang, Hupei, and was involved in the May 30th strikes and boycott in 1925 when he was a middle school student. After his military training at Chiang Kai-shek's Whampoa Academy in 1926, he served in the regiment commanded by Yeh T'ing and became a member of the CCP in that year. His promotion in rank was spectacular: regimental commander 1928, C.O. of the 4th Division of the Red Army in 1929, of the 3rd Red Army in 1930, and of the 1st Red Army Corps in 1931. After the Long March, he was in charge of the Red Army Academy, Yenan, which was to be renamed the Anti-Japanese Military and Political University, since 1936. When the war with Japan broke out, he was made the C.O. of the 115th Division of the 8th Route Army. He was wounded in 1939 and sent to the USSR for medical treatment. Back to Yenan in 1942, he was elected to the Central Committee, CCP, in 1945 and despatched to Manchuria after V-J Day. As the commander of the 4th Field Army of the PLA, he made outstanding contributions to the communist victory in the civil war and later led the Chinese 'volunteers' to fight in Korea. In 1955 Lin became a member of the powerful Politburo of the CCP and a marshal of the PLA. His appointment as the Minister of Defence to replace P'eng Teh-huai after the famous Lushan plenum of 1959 was an event of historic importance which prepared the way for Mao's Cultural Revolution and Lin's own progress to his present position. He is Mao's successor, according to the 1969 constitution of the CCP.

Old Comrade Hsü,

You were my teacher twenty years ago; you are still my teacher; you will continue to be my teacher in future. When the revolution failed and many members left the party, even defecting to the enemy, you joined [the party] in the autumn of 1927 and adopted an extremely active attitude. From then until now you have shown through a long period of bitter struggle greater positiveness, less fear of difficulty, and more humility in learning new things than many younger members of the party. 'Age', 'declining physical and mental abilities', and 'hardships and obstacles' have all surrendered to you, in spite of the fact that they have served as excuses for the timidity of many people. You know a great deal but always feel a deficiency in your knowledge, whereas many 'half-buckets of water' [people of superficial knowledge] make a lot of noise. What you think is what you say or what you do, whereas other people hide filthy things in a corner of their minds. You enjoy being with the masses all the time, whereas some others enjoy being without the masses. You are always a model of obedience to the party and its revolutionary discipline, whereas some others regard the discipline as a restraint for others but not for themselves. For you, it is 'revolution first', 'work first', and 'other people first', whereas for some others it is 'limelight first', 'rest first', and 'oneself first'. You always pick the most difficult things to do, never avoiding your responsibilities, whereas some others choose easy work to do, always shunning responsibilities. In all these respects, I admire you and am willing to continue to learn from you. I also hope that other members of the party will learn from you. I write this congratulatory letter to you on your sixtieth birthday with my wishes that you will enjoy good health and a

---

[1] (1877–1968) went to Japan and joined Sun Yat-sen's Alliance Society (T'ung Meng Hui) in 1912. Hsü visited France, Germany, and Belgium in 1920–3 as a student and a worker and also Russia to study at the Sun Yat-sen University in Moscow in 1928–30. At the age of 57 he joined the communist Long March. In 1945 he was elected to the Central Committee of the CCP and after the revolution he worked in the party's Department of Propaganda as its deputy head. All his life Hsü had worked in the field of education and propaganda.

long life, and continue to be a model for all the members of our revolutionary party and all the people.

Revolutionary salute!

TO THE KWANGSI REGIONAL PARTY COMMITTEE ON NEWSPAPERS

12.1.1958

SHWS

Comrades Liu Chien-hsün[1] and Wei Kuo-ch'ing,

Here attached for your reference are a few copies of local papers each one of which has its characteristics and is well edited. They are attractive to the reader and their contents are good.

Provincial newspapers are an exceedingly important problem which deserves careful study. A solution can be found in a few months if you work with the editors of the *Kwangsi Daily* ('Kwanghsi Jih-pao'), to study the format, news items, editorials, features on theoretical problems, and literature and art [supplements], and think and analyse [these] over and over again, and if you compare it with other provincial newspapers. Careful writing of editorials is extremely important work. This must be studied by you, by the head of the propaganda department, the secretary-general, and the editor-in-chief of the newspaper. It is imperative that the first secretary must have full authority in revising major editorials. The paper will help to organize, encourage, stimulate, criticize, and promote the work of all the people in a province. Would you like to give some thought to this problem?

[1] See below, p. 41. Liu was born in Shansi, 1908, a graduate of the Teachers' Training College, Taiyuan, and a member of the Sacrifice League during the Anti-Japanese war. At the beginning of the Cultural Revolution in 1966, he was the first secretary of the CCP Honan branch and concurrently the first political commissar of the military district of Honan.

Comrades of the Provincial, District, County, Commune, Brigade, and Team Levels,

I would like to discuss some agricultural problems with all of you.

The first is the production quota. When the south is planting rice the north is engaged in spring ploughing. The production quota must be realistic, regardless of the instructions issued by the higher levels. You should ignore them, and pay attention only to realistic possibilities. For instance, it is very good if there can be an increase of 100 or 200 catties per *mou* this year at places where the production was 300 catties per *mou*. To brag about 800, 1,000, 1,200, or even more catties [per *mou*] is sheer bragging. [Since what is bragged about] cannot be done, what is the good of bragging? Another instance, where 500 catties per *mou* were produced last year another increase of 200 or 300 catties per *mou* would be a great achievement. Generally speaking, it is impossible to expect more.

The second is the question of higher density of planting. Planting must not be too sparse nor too dense. But many young cadres and some inexperienced high-level organizations want only denser and denser planting. Some even say the denser the better. This is no good; it only arouses suspicion on the part of old and middle-aged peasants. It would be a good thing if these three groups of people would hold a meeting to decide on an adequate density. Since there is the production quota, the question of density has to be solved by the brigades and teams involved. Stiff and rigid orders from above are not only useless but also harmful. Such orders should never be issued. The provincial party committee can suggest a density for reference; it must not issue orders on this question. If the high-level organizations wish to find out an optimum density, they can arrive at a more scientific decision by a study of the metereological conditions, the location, soil, water supply, kinds of seeds used, and the standard of agricultural management based on the farming conditions of a district. It would be a good thing if a realistic standard density could be established in a few years.

The third is the question of food economy. This must be firmly grasped and rations are to be determined according to the number of people concerned. More food is consumed during the busy seasons, but less during the slack seasons; dry cooked rice is consumed during the busy seasons but half congee and half dry rice during the slack seasons. Other food-stuffs, e.g. potatoes, green vegetables, turnips, melons, beans, peas, and yams should be mixed with rice. This must be firmly under control. Every year, the three things—harvesting, storing, and consumption—must be controlled tightly and in time. No opportunity must be allowed to slip through the fingers, for opportunities once missed never return. There must be reserve grain which is accumulated year after year. After eight or ten years, food will never be a problem any more. In the next ten years, we must not talk big—to talk big is a dangerous thing. We must know that ours is a big country of 650 million people and food is our foremost problem.

The fourth is the question of cultivated area. The idea of less planting, higher yields, and greater crops is possible, but cannot be completely, even largely, fulfilled in the next ten years. It is generally impossible in the next three years when we must still follow the old policy of planting more. More planting at a low yield and less planting at a high yield should proceed at the same time.

The fifth is the question of mechanization which is the basic solution to our agricultural problems. Ten years may be needed—minor problems can be solved in the next four years; medium problems in the next seven years; major problems in the next ten years. In the next four years we must depend on the improvement in agricultural tools and semi-mechanized tools. There must be an institute of agricultural tools in every county, district, and province which will assemble scientists and technicians, experienced blacksmiths and carpenters, and also more advanced designs of agricultural tools in the county, district, or province. They must study, compare, and experiment on them and then improve upon them before manufacturing them in large quantities for popular use. When we talk about mechanization, we should also consider chemical fertilizers. More widespread use of them year after year is very important.

The sixth is the question of honesty. Production quotas depend on how much can actually be produced. One must not promise what cannot with effort be fulfilled. The 'Eight Character Charter'[1] must be applied to all the measures to increase production and none of the eight characters must be turned into a lie. Honest [persons] who dare to speak the truth are in the end good for the cause of the people as well as for themselves. But liars do harm to themselves and others. It must be said that some of the lies are squeezed out by a higher level which brags, oppresses its subordinates, and indulges in wishful thinking, making life difficult for those who are under it. In sum, we need high working morale, not lies.

Please, Comrades, consider the above six questions and for the sake of truth please let us know your different views. We are still not experienced enough in handling agricultural work, but our experience increases year after year. In ten years' time we shall gradually grasp the objective inevitability and then we shall have achieved a certain degree of freedom. What is freedom? Freedom is the understanding of the inevitable.

Compared with the high key sung by everybody at the moment, what I have said is certainly at a low key. My aim is truly to mobilize our enthusiasm in order to increase production. If the reality lies at a higher key and loftier goals are to be attained, I shall be regarded as a conservative. I shall be grateful for that and feel extremely honoured.

TO THE COMMUNIST LABOUR UNIVERSITY IN KIANGSI   1.8.1961
SHWS

Comrades,

I wholeheartedly support your venture. Your schools, including your primary and secondary schools, and universities, which follow the principle of part-time work and part-time study, hard work and hard study, thus costing the government nothing to run them, and which are situated on the mountain tops

---

[1] Water conservancy, application of fertilizer, soil amelioration, use of better seed strains, rational close planting, plant protection, field management, and tool reform. See C. S. Chen and Charles P. Ridley, *Rural People's Communes in Lienchiang* (Stanford: Hoover Institution, 1969), glossary.

and in the plains of the province, are good schools indeed. Most of the students are young people, but there may also be some middle-aged cadres. I hope in other provinces besides Kiangsi there will be schools of this type. Other provinces should send competent and knowledgeable comrades in responsible positions to Kiangsi to investigate your schools and to absorb your experience. At the beginning there must not be too many students. Their number can be increased later to 50,000 as now in Kiangsi. Moreover, the party, government, and people's organizations (e.g. trade unions, youth league, and women's associations) should also run their own schools on the principle of part-time work and part-time study. But there should be a difference [between] the work and study of your schools [and theirs]. Your work consists of agriculture, forestry, animal husbandry, and so on; your studies are [also] on these subjects. The schools run by the party, government, and people's organizations, on the other hand, should work in their own institutions and study cultural sciences, current affairs, Marxism-Leninism, and so on. They are quite different from you. The central organizations have established two schools. One was created by the military police corps which has been in existence for six or seven years. There the soldiers and cadres began by learning to read and write in the primary section, then they were promoted into the secondary section, and finally entered the university section in 1960. They felt happy and wrote me a letter. I shall have the letter printed and show it to you. The other was established last year (1960) by the party institutions in Chungnanhai [Peking] on the same principle of part-time work and part-time study. Its work means the work in the institutions, [and its students] include senior members of the staff, members of the manual staff, members of the liaison staff, members of the medical staff, members of the security staff, and others. The military police, on the other hand, is an armed force whose work is security, i.e. sentry duties and so on. It also goes through military training. Naturally its school is different from civilian schools.

The Communist Labour University of Kiangsi celebrates its third anniversary on 1 August 1961 and I was asked to write a few words for the occasion. It is a big occasion for which I have written the above.

Commemorative Writings

THE SECOND ANNIVERSARY OF AN WU-CH'ING'S MARTYRDOM

1929

SHWS

Young communists and non-communists who have brought new blood and new spirit to the revolutionary ranks are precious people. Without them the ranks can never be expanded and the revolution can never be won. However, their weakness lies in a lack of experience, and experience comes only from personal participation in revolutionary struggles. The inexperienced can become experienced if they begin from the lowest level and work steadily without a grain of dishonesty for several years.

INSCRIPTION FOR THE FOUNDING OF THE NORTH SHENSI PUBLIC SCHOOL   1937

SHWS (Excerpts)

We must educate a lot of people—the sort of people who are the vanguard of revolution, who have political farsightedness, who are prepared for battle and sacrifice, who are frank, loyal, positive, and upright; the sort of people who seek no self-interest only national and social emancipation, who show, instead of fear, determination and forwardness in the face of hardships; the sort of people who are neither undisciplined nor fond of limelight, but practical, with their feet firmly on the ground. If China possesses many such men, the tasks of the Chinese revolution can easily be fulfilled.

SPEECH AT THE MEETING CELEBRATING THE COMPLETION OF THE
BUILDINGS OF THE ANTI-JAPANESE MILITARY AND POLITICAL
UNIVERSITY   1937
SHWS

What I want to say to you, Comrades, is that, in short, the
success of this great enterprise is due to [our] overcoming difficulties and uniting with the masses. The experience of the
struggles in the past ten years, the cave [-buildings] you have
dug, and the future course of the Resistance War have proved
or will prove that if we continue to overcome difficulties and
unite with the masses we shall be ever victorious!

To overcome natural difficulties by defeating the loess and to
overcome military difficulties by defeating the Japanese bandits[1]
have something in common but quite a lot of differences. The
latter is harder and more arduous. Therefore in addition to
orienting oneself towards overcoming difficulties and uniting
with the masses, the Resistance War requires skills in strategy
and tactics, in mobilizing, organizing, and leading the masses,
and in winning allies.

You have now the spirit to overcome difficulties and unite
with the masses. If you can use your talents to develop from this
basis, it is entirely possible to defeat Japan and drive the
Japanese out of China.

ON LU HSÜN[2]   1937
(based on the *SHWS* edition with discrepancies in the
Wen Hsien edition added in parentheses)

SHWS   Speech at the Meeting Commemorating the First
              Anniversary of the Death of Lu Hsün held in the
              North Shensi Public School on 19.10.1939

Wen Hsien   Speech at the Commemorative Meeting in the
              North Shensi Public School

---

[1] '*k'e-fu huo-ti ti-jen chan-sheng Jih-k'ou*'—literally, 'to overcome live enemies and
defeat the Japanese bandits'.
[2] (1881–1936), born in Shaohsing, Chekiang, the best known and the most
sardonic of modern Chinese writers. See the references to him in the Introductory
essay.

Comrades,

Our main tasks at the present moment are those of the vanguard. At a time when the great national Resistance War is making rapid progress, we need a large number of activists to play the leading role [in it] and a large number of vanguards to find the path. Vanguards must be frank, positive, and upright people. They seek no self-interest, only national and social emancipation. They fear no hardships; instead, in the face of hardships they are determined and forever moving forward. Neither undisciplined nor fond of limelight, they have their feet firmly on the ground and are realistic. They are the guides on the road of revolution. In the light of the present state of the war, if the Resistance is the concern only of the government and armed forces, without the participation of the broad masses, we cannot be certain that we shall win the final victory. We must now train a large number of vanguards who will fight for our national liberation and can be relied upon to lead and organize the masses for the fulfilment of this historic mission. First of all, the numerous vanguards of the whole country must urgently organize themselves. Our communist party is the vanguard of national liberation. We must fight to the bitter end in order to accomplish our tasks.

Today we commemorate [the death] of Lu Hsün. We must first of all understand him and his place in the history of our revolution. We commemorate him not only because he was a distinguished writer but also because he, at the forefront of national emancipation, dedicated all his strength to the revolutionary struggle. (We commemorate him not only because he wrote well, becoming a great literary figure, but also because he was a vanguard for national liberation and gave tremendous help to the revolution.) Although he did not belong to the communist party organization, his thinking, action, and writing were all Marxianized. He showed more and more youthful energy as his life drew to its end. He fought consistently and incessantly against feudal forces and imperialism. Under despicable circumstances of enemy pressure and persecution, he struggled (suffered) and protested. In a similar way, Comrades, you can also study revolutionary theories diligently while [living] under such adverse material conditions [because] yuo are full of militant spirit. The material arrangement of this school is poor, but here we have truth, freedom, and a place to train revolutionary vanguards.

Lu Hsün emerged from the decaying feudal society. But he knew how to fight back against the rotten society and the evil imperialist forces of which he had had so much experience. He used his sardonic, humorous, and sharp (powerful) pen to depict the force(s) of the dark society (and of the ferocious imperialists). He was really an accomplished 'painter'. In his last years he fought for truth and freedom from the stand-point of the proletariat and national liberation.

Lu Hsün's first characteristic was his political vision. He examined society with both a microscope and a telescope, hence with precision and farsightedness. As early as 1936 he pointed out the dangerous tendencies of the criminal Trotskyites. Now the clarity and correctness of his judgement have been proved beyond doubt by the facts—the obvious fact that the Trotskyite faction has turned into a traitorous organization subsidized by Japanese special agents.

In my view, Lu Hsün is a great Chinese saint—the saint of modern China, just as Confucius was the saint of old China. For his immortal memory, we have established the Lu Hsün Library and the Lu Hsün Teachers' Training School in Yenan so that future generations may have a glimpse of his greatness.

His second characteristic was his militancy, which we mentioned a moment ago. He was a great steadfast tree, not a blade of wavering grass, against the onslaught of dark and violent forces. Once he saw a political destination clearly he strove to reach it, never surrendering or compromising half way. There have been half-hearted revolutionaries who fought at first but then deserted the battlefield. Kautsky and Plekhanov of foreign countries (Russia) were good examples [of this]. Such people are not infrequently found in China. If I remember correctly, Lu Hsün once said that at first all [of them] were 'left' and revolutionary, but as soon as pressure came, [they] changed and presented their comrades [to the enemy] as a gift. Lu Hsün bitterly hated this sort of people. While fighting against them, he educated and disciplined the young writers who followed him. He taught them to fight resolutely, to be vanguards, and to find their own way.

His third characteristic was his readiness to sacrifice himself, completely fearless of enemy intimidation and persecution and utterly unmoved by enemy enticement. With merciless pungency his sword-like pen cut all those he despised. Among the bloodstains of revolutionary fighters he showed his tenacious defiance and marched ahead while calling [the others to follow him]. Lu Hsün was an absolute realist, always uncompromising, always determined. In one of his essays he maintained that one should [continue to] beat a dog after it had fallen in water. If you did not, the dog would jump up either to bite you or at least to shake a lot of dirty water over you. Therefore the beating had to be thorough. Lu Hsün did not entertain a speck of sentimentalism or hypocracy.

Now the mad dog, Japanese imperialism, had not been beaten in water yet. [*Wen Hsien* does not have this sentence.] We must learn this Lu Hsün spirit and apply it to the whole country.

These characteristics are the components of the great 'Lu Hsün spirit'. Throughout his life Lu Hsün never deviated from this spirit and that is why he was an outstanding writer in the world of letters and a tough, excellent vanguard in the revolutionary ranks. As we commemorate him, we must learn his spirit. [We] must take it to all the units engaged in the Resistance War and use it in the struggle for our national liberation.

Reproduced from the fortnightly,
July (Ch'i-yüeh), March 1938

(This was Mr. Mao Tse-tung's speech at the meeting commemorating the first anniversary of Lu Hsün's death, held at the North Shensi Public School. I took these notes, but up to now have not sorted them out for publication. Mr. Mao had read and studied many of Lu Hsün's works. His speech is a penetrating analysis of the writer and has a special meaning to everyone who is engaged in the arduous struggle for our national liberation. The delay in its publication has not made it out of date.

Since I did not show Mr. Mao these notes when I was in Yenan, I myself must naturally take all the blame for possible omissions or distortions.

Ta-han (pseudonym))

We meet today to celebrate Comrade Stalin's sixtieth birthday. 'It has always been rare for a man to reach seventy' [as a Chinese proverb says]; in fact it is not easy even to reach sixty. But why do we send greetings only to Stalin? And celebrate his birthday this way? Not only in Yenan, but all over China, all over the world, anyone who knows that today is his birthday, anyone who is under oppression, is celebrating it. This is because Comrade Stalin is the saviour of all the oppressed. Who can be against or who can dislike celebrating his birthday? The oppressors, including, first of all, imperialists. Comrades, it is unprecedented for us to celebrate the birthday of a foreigner who is thousands of miles from us.

[Why?] Because he is the leader of the great Soviet Union, of the great Communist International, and of the liberation movement of mankind, and because he helps China to fight Japan.

The world today is divided into two antagonistic fronts—the imperialist front which oppresses mankind and the socialist front which is against oppression. Some people think the national revolutionary front in the colonies and semi-colonies lies between this division. However, since its opponents are imperialists, it must make friends with socialism and it must fall in the category of the anti-oppression revolutionary front. Chinese die-hards want to be prostitutes and chaste women at the same time by fighting the communists with one hand and the Japanese with the other, while describing themselves as 'neutrals'. But they will never succeed. If they do not repent, they will eventually become counter-revolutionaries. There must be, nevertheless, a master or commander of each of the two fronts. Who is the commander of the counter-revolutionary front? The imperialist, [Neville] Chamberlain. Who is the commander of the revolutionary front? The socialist, Stalin. Comrade Stalin is the leader of the world revolution. This is very important. The existence of Stalin among men is important. His existence makes things easier to handle. You all know that Marx is dead, Engels is dead, and Lenin is also dead. Apart from Stalin, who else can possibly command? How fortunate for our world to have the Soviet Union, the [Soviet] communist party, and Stalin, to make things easier to deal with. What does the commander of the revolution do? He enables everyone to have food, clothes, shelter, and books. To achieve all this, [the leader] must lead millions of people to struggle against the oppressors and win the final victory and this is precisely what Stalin does. In that case, would all the oppressed celebrate his birthday? I think they would and should. We celebrate it and support him and learn from him.

We learn two things from him—his words and his deeds.

The immense complexity of Marxism can be summed up in one sentence: 'It is justifiable to rebel.' For centuries people have been saying: 'It is justifiable to oppress or to exploit people, but it is wrong to rebel.' Marxism turned this thesis upside down. That is a great contribution, a thesis established by Marx from the struggles of the proletariat. Basing their action on this thesis, people have shown defiance, struggled, and worked for socialism. What has been Comrade Stalin's contribution? He has developed this thesis, Marxism-Leninism, to produce a clear, concrete, and lively theory of forming a revolutionary front to overthrow imperialism and capitalism and to create a socialist society.

[Stalin's] deeds are the materialization of his words. Marx, Engels, and Lenin did not build a socialist society but Stalin has. This is unprecedented in human history (lit. 'since the beginning of this earth'). Before the two Five-Year Plans, capitalist newspapers of all countries had said how desperate things were in the Soviet Union and how unreliable socialism was. What do they have to say now? Chamberlain is silenced; so are China's die-hards. They admit now that the Soviet Union has triumphed.

Apart from moral support, Stalin has given material aid to our Anti-Japanese War. Because of the successes of his deeds, Stalin has been able to give us many aeroplanes, guns, airmen, military advisers to work in various war zones, and loans. What other country has given us this kind of help? What other class? What other party? Who else? Who else apart from the Soviet Union, the proletariat, the communist party, and Stalin?

Now there are some people who claim to be our friends. But they belong to the category of Li Lin-fu of the T'ang dynasty.[1]

---

[1] For a reference to Li Lin-fu, see *SW*, II, p. 336.

Li Lin-fu was a man with 'honey on his lips but murder in his heart'. All imperialists are people with 'honey on their lips but murder in their hearts', and Chamberlain is a modern Li Lin-fu. Which of the imperialist countries have cancelled their special rights, e.g. right to station troops, right of consular jurisdiction and extraterritoriality, in China? None, except the Soviet Union.

In the past, Marxism-Leninism guided the world revolution; now, there is something more—[the Soviet Union] can give material aid to it. This is Stalin's contribution.

After this celebration, we should publicize this [contribution] to the whole country by explaining it to our 450 million people, so that they will understand that only the socialist Soviet Union, only Stalin, are China's good friends.

> Compared with the *Liberation Weekly* no. 95, p. 9,
> 30 December 1939 and *HC*, II, pp. 651–2 or
> *SW*, II, 335–6.

SALUTE THE APRIL 8TH MARTYRS[1]   1946

SHWS

Dear Comrades-in-Arms and Immortal Heroes,

In the last few decades you rendered your glorious service to the people. Now in dying for them your deaths are also glorious.

Your deaths are a clarion call to deepen the Chinese people's understanding of the CCP and to strengthen their determination to defend peace, democracy, and unity.

Your deaths are a clarion call to the whole party and the whole nation to unite in the struggle for a peaceful, democratic, and united China.

The whole party and the whole nation will carry on your unfinished tasks and continue to struggle till victory is won. They will never relax or shrink back from their effort.

---

[1] On 8 April 1946 the communist leaders, Ch'in Pang-hsien (Po-ku), Teng Fa, Wang Jo-fei, and Yeh T'ing were killed in an aeroplane crash and subsequently there was a commemorative meeting held in Yenan.

STALIN'S SEVENTIETH BIRTHDAY   21.12.1949
NT

Dear Comrades and Friends,

I am extremely happy at the opportunity of taking part in the celebration of Comrade Stalin's seventieth birthday.

Comrade Stalin is the teacher and friend of mankind and of the Chinese people. He has developed the revolutionary theories of Marxism-Leninism and made outstanding and extensive contributions to the world communist movement. In the arduous struggles against the oppressors, the Chinese people have been fully appreciative of the importance of Comrade Stalin's friendship.

On this great occasion, let me in the name of the Chinese people and the CCP congratulate Comrade Stalin on his seventieth birthday and wish him good health and a long life. Let me wish that our great ally, the Soviet Union, under the leadership of Comrade Stalin, be prosperous and strong. Let me applaud the unprecedented unity of the working class of the world under [the leadership] of Comrade Stalin.

Long live Stalin, the leader of the working class and the communist movement of the world!

Long live the Soviet Union—the bastion of world peace and democracy!

SUN YAT-SEN NINETIETH ANNIVERSARY   1956
JMJP, 13.11.1966 or *Jen-min Shou-ts'e*, 1957, p. 134

Commemorate the great revolutionary pioneer, Mr. Sun Chung-shan!

Commemorate his bitter struggle from the unambiguous position of a Chinese revolutionary democrat against Chinese reformers in the preparatory phase of the Chinese democratic revolution!

Commemorate the magnificent contributions he made in leading the people to overthrow the monarchy and to found the republic in the 1911 revolution!

Commemorate his great contribution to the development of the old Three Principles of the People into the new Three

Principles of the People in the period of the first Kuomintang-Communist co-operation!

He left to us a great deal of political thought that has been beneficial to us.

Apart from a handful of reactionaries, all modern Chinese are successors to Mr. Sun's revolution.

Having completed Mr. Sun's unfinished democratic revolution, we proceed to develop it into the socialist revolution which is being accomplished by us.

Things are always developing. Since the 1911 revolution, in merely forty-five years, the appearance of China has completely changed. In another forty-five years when [we] enter the twenty-first century in 2001 [*sic*], the appearance of China will again change. She will become a big and strong socialist industrial country. She should be so, for she is a country of 9,600,000 square kilometres in area and 600,000,000 people. She should make great contributions to mankind. That such contributions have, for a long time in the past, been meagre makes us feel ashamed.

But [we] must be modest, now, in forty-five years, and for ever. In international dealings, the Chinese should resolutely, thoroughly, and completely eliminate their big nation chauvinism.

Mr. Sun was a humble man; I listened to his speeches on several occasions and felt that he had a powerful personality. From his painstaking study of Chinese history and present-day social conditions and from his careful study of the conditions in other countries including the Soviet Union, I know that he was a humble man.

He devoted all his life wholeheartedly to the reconstruction of China, truly in the spirit of 'doing [my] utmost till I die'.[1]

Like all great historical figures who have channelled the trend of events of their times, Mr. Sun had his shortcomings. These shortcomings should be explained in terms of history so that they can be understood. [We] must not judge our forerunner too harshly.

[1] Quoted from the first memorial to the throne on the eve of his military expedition by Chu-ko Liang of the State of Shu (221–63) in the Three Kingdoms period.

Talks and Conversations

TALK AT THE CONFERENCE ON INTELLECTUALS CALLED BY THE
CENTRE   20.1.1956
SHWS (Excerpts)

The target plans of all the departments should be practicable.
What can be and should be done but has not yet been done, is
[due to] rightist conservatism; what is ill-founded and completely unworkable and yet is being done, is [due to] a blindness
or 'leftist' adventurism. In my view, this [the leftist adven-
turism] is not the general orientation of the whole party,
although it is detectable. Some comrades are a bit woolly and
dare not say that they are being realistic because of the ugly
label of rightist conservatism and opportunism. If they examine
and study [things carefully], [they will be able to] say or insist
on saying what cannot be done. What cannot be done should
be deleted from our plans so that they may rest on a solid,
reliable basis.

ON EDUCATION—Conversation with the Nepalese Delegation of
Educationists   1964
SHWS

Our education is fraught with problems, the most prominent
of which is dogmatism. We are in the process of reforming our
educational system. The school years are too long, courses too
many, and various methods of teaching unsatisfactory. The
children learn textbooks and concepts which remain [merely]
textbooks and concepts; they know nothing else. [They] do not
use their four limbs; nor do [they] recognize the five kinds of
grain.[1] Many children do not even know what cows, horses,

---

[1] A quotation from *the Analects* by Confucius.

chickens, dogs, and pigs are; nor can they tell the differences between rice, canary seeds, maize, wheat, millet, and sorghum.[1] When a student graduates from his university, he is already over twenty. The school years are too long, courses too many, and the method of teaching is by injection instead of through the imagination. The method of examination is to treat candidates as enemies and ambush them. (laughter) Therefore I advise you not to entertain any blind faith in the Chinese educational system. Do not regard it as a good system. Any drastic change is difficult, [as] many people would oppose it. At present a few may agree to the adoption of new methods, but many would disagree. I may be pouring cold water on you. You expect to see something good, but I only tell you what is bad. (laughter)

However, I am not saying that there is nothing good at all. Take industry and geology for instance. The old society left to us only 200 geologists and technicians; now we have more than 200,000.

Generally speaking, the intellectuals specializing in engineering are better, because they are in touch with reality. Scientists, pure scientists, are worse, but they are still better than those who specialize in art subjects. [Liberal] art subjects are completely detached from reality. Students of history, philosophy, and economics have no concern with studying reality; they are the most ignorant of things of this world.

As I have said before, we have nothing marvellous, only things we have learnt from ordinary people. Of course, we have learnt a little Marxism-Leninism, but Marxism-Leninism alone won't do. [We] must study Chinese problems, starting from the characteristics and facts of China. We Chinese, myself included, did not know much about China. We knew that we ought to fight against imperialism and its lackeys, but we did not know how to do it. So we had to study the conditions of China, just as you study the conditions of your country. We spent a long time, fully twenty-eight years from the foundation of the CCP to the liberation of the whole country, in forging step by step a set of policies suitable to Chinese conditions.

The source of [our] strength is the masses. If a thing does not represent the people's wish, it is no good. [We] must learn from

[1] A quotation from the children's classic, *the San Tzu Ching* ('The Three-character Classic').

the masses, formulate our policies, and then educate the masses. Therefore if we want to be teachers, we have to be pupils to begin with. No teacher begins [his career] as a teacher. Having become a teacher, he should continue to learn from the masses in order to understand how he himself learns. That is why there are courses on psychology and education in teachers' training. What [one] learns becomes useless if [one] does not understand the reality.

There is a factory attached to the science and engineering faculties at Tsinghua University,[1] because students must learn from [both] books and work. But [we] cannot set up factories for arts faculties such as a literature factory, a history factory, an economics factory, or a novel factory; these faculties should regard the whole of society as their factory. Their teachers and students should make contact with the peasants and urban workers as well as with agriculture and industries. How else can their graduates be of any use? Take students of law, for example. If they do not understand crimes in a society, they cannot be good students of law. It is out of the question to set up a law factory; so society is their factory.

Comparatively speaking, our arts faculties are the most backward owing to a lack of contact with reality. Students and teachers do only class work. Philosophy is book philosophy. What is the use of philosophy if it is not learnt from society, from the masses, and from nature? It can be composed only of vague ideas. Logic is the same. [One] does not understand much of it if one merely reads through the textbook once. But one understands it gradually through application. I did not understand much when I read logic. The understanding came to me when I used it.

I have been talking about logic. There is also grammar which one does not quite understand simply by reading it. But one grasps the use of sentence structure when one is actually writing. We write and speak according to the customary usages and it is not really necessary to study grammar. As to rhetoric, it is an optional subject. Great writers are not always rhetoricians. I studied rhetoric myself, but did not understand it at all. Do you study it before you write?

[1] On the western outskirts of Peking.

Chairman: 'Nieh Yüan-tzu's[1] big-character poster of 25 May is
the declaration of the Chinese Paris Commune of the sixties
of the twentieth century; its significance far surpasses that of
the Paris Commune. It is beyond our ability to write this
kind of big-character poster.'

(Some members of the Young Pioneers stuck up big-character posters about their fathers, saying that their fathers had
forgotten the past and neglected to explain Mao Tse-tung's
thought to them. The fathers only asked about their marks at
school and gave prizes to good marks.)

Chairman Mao asked Comrade Ch'en Po-ta[2] to tell these
youngsters: 'You have done well to put up those big-character posters.'

'I tell you that the young people are the main force of the
great Cultural Revolution! We must fully mobilize them.'

'On my return to Peking, I feel sorry that things are so
quiet. Some schools are shut; some even suppress student
movements. Who [in the past] suppressed student movements? Only the northern warlords. It is anti-Marxist for the
communist party to be afraid of student movements. Some
people talk about the mass line, talk about serving the
people every day, but they actually follow a capitalist line and
serve the bourgeoisie.'

'The centre of the League [the Young Communist League]
ought to be on the side of the student movement and yet it is
actually on the side of its suppressors.'

'Who are against the great Cultural Revolution? American
imperialism, Russian revisionism, Japanese revisionism, and
the reactionaries.'

'The pretext of "inside and outside [the party] being
different" shows a fear of the revolution. To cover up what
has been stuck [on the walls] cannot be allowed. [To do so]

---

[1] A woman instructor at Peking University who was the first to write a big-
character poster, inaugurating the Cultural Revolution in 1966. See below, p. 113,
instruction no. 33.
[2] See below, p. 27, n. 1.

shows a mistake in our line and we must switch around quickly and smash all the restrictions (lit. "frames").'

'We trust the masses and must be their pupils before becoming their teachers. The great Cultural Revolution is a world-shaking event which [tries us out to see] whether we can or cannot, dare or dare not pass the test. This is the final test which will eliminate class distinction and reduce the three great differences.'

'Oppose, especially oppose the bourgeois "authoritative" thought; that is destruction (*p'o*), Without this destruction, there cannot be the construction (*li*) of socialism. We must first struggle, then criticize, and finally reform.'

'It will not do to listen to reports in one's office; we must depend on the masses, trust the masses, and fight to the end. We must be prepared for the revolution to hit at us. The leadership of both the party and government must be so prepared and the responsible members of the party must also be so prepared. Now, the revolution must be carried right through to the end and in the process we must train and remould ourselves. Only in this way can we [members of the party] catch up. Otherwise [the revolution] can depend only on those who are outside [the party].'

'Some comrades struggle fiercely against others, but not against themselves. They will never pass the test.'

'You will have to direct the revolution (lit. "fire") towards yourselves, ignite it, and fan it up. Will you do that? It will burn you!'

Comrades reply in this way: 'We shall prepare ourselves. If that will not do, we shall resign. We live as communists and shall die as communists. Easy chairs and electric fans do not suit our style of life.'

'It will not do to impose restrictions on the masses. Seeing the students rise up, Peking University imposes a restriction on them, euphemistically calling it "to direct them to the right way". In fact, it was directing them to the wrong way.'

Some schools label students as counter-revolutionaries. (Chang Yen, a liaison man, went out and was labelled a counter-revolutionary twenty-nine times!)

Chairman: 'In that way, we set the masses against us. We must not be afraid of bad people. After all, how many bad people are there? Most of the students are good.'

(Someone mentioned riots and asked what should be done if the archives were destroyed.)
Chairman: 'Who is afraid of anyone? If a bad man comes, prove that he is bad. Why should you be scared of good people? The word "fear" must be replaced by "dare" and ultimately one should prove that one can pass the socialist test.'

'Anyone who suppresses student movements will end badly.'

TALK AT THE RECEPTION OF SECRETARIES OF BIG REGIONS AND MEMBERS OF THE CENTRAL CULTURAL REVOLUTION TEAM—Notes for Circulation   22.7.1966
SHWS

The secretaries of all big regions and members of the Central Cultural Revolution Team are here today. The purpose of this conference is to put our records straight, principally to reform the method of despatching work teams. The great Cultural Revolution must be led by the cultural revolution teams of schools as organized by revolutionary teachers, students, and neutrals who are the only people in the schools who know anything at all. The work teams know nothing. Some work teams have even created trouble. The great Cultural Revolution in the schools is no more than 'struggle and repudiation'. Work teams only hinder the movement. Can we struggle and reform? Take Chien Po-tsan[1] for example. He has written so many books. Since you have not even read them, how can you struggle against and reform him? Affairs at schools are [as a proverb says]: 'Big gods in a small temple and many tortoises in a shallow pond.' They have to be dealt with by the forces in the schools themselves, not by work teams, you, me, or the provincial [party] committees. They have to depend on the schools themselves not on work teams. Can work teams be changed into liaison teams? To transform them into advisory teams may give them too much

[1] (1897–   ) born in T'aoyuan in Hunan of Uigur descent. A well-known historian, Chien announced that he was a member of the CCP in Hong Kong, 1948. Since 1952 he was the head of the Department of History at Peking University before his removal under severe criticism at the beginning of the Cultural Revolution.

power. Perhaps [we] can call them 'observers'. [Some] work teams are a nuisance to the revolution; others are not. A nuisance to the revolution will sooner or later become counter-revolution. The University of Communications in Sian did not allow people [the revolutionaries] to make telephone calls or to send someone to the Centre. Why are they afraid of sending people to the Centre? Let them come and besiege the State Council. But it must be written in documents: 'Telephone call approved,' or 'Despatch of people approved'. How can it be all right to get scared like that? So, the newspaper offices in Sian and Nanking were besieged for three days and [everybody] was scared stiff. Frightened like that? Oh, you, you do not want a revolution; but now the revolution has come to you. At some places it is forbidden to surround newspaper offices, to go to the provincial [party] committee, or to send people to the State Council. Why are you so scared? When [the revolutionaries] got to the State Council, they were received by some small fry who could not explain a thing. Why was it done that way? If you do not want to step out [and see them], I will. However you argue, it is just a matter of fear, fear of counter-revolution, fear of use of arms. How can there be so many counter-revolutionaries? Lately K'ang Sheng, Ch'en Po-ta, and Chiang Ch'ing[1] have

---

[1] K'ang Sheng (1903–   ) was born in Chuch'eng, Shantung, under the name Chang Shao-ch'ing (his other aliases including Chang Wen and Chao Yung). While studying at the middle school of Shanghai University, he joined the Communist Youth League (1920) and later the CCP when he became a student at the university. He took part in the three uprisings in Shanghai just before the capture of the city by the National Revolutionary Army in 1927. Thereafter, it is reported, he and Ku Shun-chang created the special service branch of the CCP. He was the head of the Organization Department of the party before his departure for Moscow in 1932, whence he went to Germany. In 1937 he went back to China with Wang Ming to become a member of the Politburo and helped Mao in the latter's Rectification Campaign of 1942–4. After 1949, he worked in Shantung and his political career seems to have received a setback in 1956 when he was demoted to an alternate member of the Politburo. He visited Romania in 1960, Moscow in 1962 and 1964, and Albania in 1966. He is now on the Standing Committee of the Politburo and one of the most important lieutenants of Mao.

Ch'en Po-ta (1903–   ) born in Huian in Fukien, studied at a teachers' training college in Amoy before he went to Shanghai to study at the Labour University where he joined the CCP. In 1927 he was a student at the Sun Yat-sen University, Moscow, and in 1935 he helped Liu Shao-ch'i organizing the December 9th Student Demonstration against Chiang Kai-shek's appeasement of Japan. He has worked in Yenan since 1937 and became an alternate member of the Central Committee of the CCP in 1947. After 1949 he was a deputy head of the party's Propaganda Department and since 1955 the deputy head of the Academy of Sciences. Ch'en

gone to the lower levels, to read 'big-character posters' at schools. How can anyone do anything without having had a feeling for the reality? Nobody wants to go to the lower levels; everybody is preoccupied with daily routine. Go down to the levels below, stop your routine work, and get some real feeling for things. Nanking has done better; no one there has prevented students from coming to the Centre. (K'ang Sheng interrupts: 'There were three debates in Nanking—the first on the lack of revolutionary spirit of the *New China Daily*, the second on that of the Kiangsu provincial [party] committee with the conclusion that the committee was after all revolutionary, and the third on dunce-capping and parading K'uang Ya-ming.') In the schools, the majority is revolutionary; only a minority lacks revolutionary spirit. Whether K'uang Ya-ming should wear a dunce-cap and be paraded in the street can be decided only by a discussion.

Comrades at this conference should go to Peking University and the School of Broadcasting to read their big-character posters and to take a look at the places stricken with problems. But perhaps not today, because we are dealing with documents. When you go there to read the posters, say that you are there to learn, to help the revolution, and to ignite [the revolution] in support of revolutionary teachers and students. You are not there to listen to rightists' gibberish. For two months now, there has not been an ounce of real understanding, only bureaucratism. Students will surround you. Let them. You will be surrounded as soon as you begin to talk to them. More than a hundred people have been beaten up at the School of Broadcasting. This is the beauty of our age—the left beaten up by the right and thus disciplined. Nothing will be achieved in six months or in a year only by sending work teams. You have to depend on the people on the spot. First, struggle and then reform. To struggle is to reform and to reform is to construct. Teaching material cannot be improved in six months. First of all, [we] must simplify it by throwing parts of it away. The bad

became an alternate member of the Politburo in 1956 and the editor of the party organ, *Red Flag*, in 1959. Since the Cultural Revolution, his political importance has been greatly enhanced, being the leader of the Cultural Revolution Team, a full member of the Politburo, and a loyal supporter of Mao. He is widely believed to have been Mao's secretary for many years.

Chiang Ch'ing, Mao's wife, now a member of the Politburo.

and repetitive stuff ought to be cut by one third or a half. (Wang Jen-chung[1] interrupts: 'Cut two-thirds and study *Chairman Mao's Quotations.*') Political material, directives of the Centre, and newspaper editorials are all guidance for the masses which are not to be regarded as dogmas. It will not do to omit the question of beating people up in our communiqués. This is a matter of orientation, of guidance. [We] must decide on our orientation quickly and try to alter things. [We] must rely on revolutionary teachers and students and the left. It does not matter if the right takes part in the revolutionary committees at schools. Useful rightists can be regarded as our 'negative' teachers, but do not help to unite them. The municipal [party] committee of Peking need not have too big a staff. If it is too big, the staff only make telephone calls and issue orders. Cut down the number of secretaries. When I was on the Front Committee,[2] I had a secretary called Hsiang Pei. But I had no secretary at all during the retreat [the Long March]. It is enough to have one person to deal with outgoing and incoming correspondence. (K'ang Sheng interrupts: 'Chairman has talked about four things—the reorganization of the municipal [party] committee of Peking which is done, the reorganization of the Central Department of Propaganda which is done, the abolition of the Team of Five of the Cultural Revolution[3] which is also done, and finally the transformation of some Ministries into sections which is not done yet.') Yes, Ministries! The Ministers who actually work can stay. Never mind whether they are Ministers, heads of departments, chiefs of bureaux, and heads of sections. Change them if they do not do any work. Change to Metallurgical Section, Coal Section, and so on. (Someone interrupts: 'Peking University has had four debates on whether the June the 18th Incident[4] was counter-revolutionary. Some say that it was because hooligans were involved in it and others say that it was

[1] (1906–). A man of Hopei, he took part in the Long March and entered the North Shensi Public School as a student. After 1949 he worked in Hupei, to become the first secretary of the Wuhan branch of the CCP in 1954 and the first secretary of the Hupei branch of the party two years later. Before his downfall in 1966 he was the first secretary of the Central-south Bureau of the CCP.

[2] See the chronology in J. Ch'en, *Mao*, 1969, p. 69.

[3] This was set up at the beginning of the Cultural Revolution which drafted the February Outline. P'eng Chen was the leader of this Team. See SCMP, no. 3952 (5 June 1967) and instruction no. 32 below.

[4] See below, instruction no. 39.

not, because it was only a mistake on the part of the work team. More than forty people in the school affiliated to the University proposed the removal of Chang Ch'eng-hsien from the head of the work team.') Many work teams actually hinder the movement and Chang Ch'eng-hsien's is one of them. But do not arrest people at will. Do not arrest those who have posted reactionary slogans. Set them up as the opposition, struggle against them, and then decide what to do about them.

ANOTHER VERSION OF THE SAME TALK   21.7.1966
NT

We have met for two days now, discussing the work of the great Cultural Revolution, chiefly on the abolition of work teams and a change in the policy towards them. The day before yesterday, we examined the incompetence of the work teams. The old municipal [party] committee was rotten; the Central Department of Propaganda was rotten; the Ministry of Culture was rotten; and the Ministry of Higher Education, too, was rotten. The *People's Daily* was no good. On 1 June when the decision to publicize big-character posters[1] was taken, [our view] was that this was the only way and the great Cultural Revolution must depend on them. What else could we rely on? You left without any understanding of the situation. You have not understood it in two months; you will not understand it in six months or a year. Take Chien Po-tsan for example. He has written so many books. Can you read them all? Can you criticize them? They [the revolutionaries] are the only ones who understand the situation. Even I cannot do much to help. We must depend on the revolutionary teachers and students.

Now, the first thing is fear, fear of making trouble. Well, schools have stopped teaching, but their canteens continue to provide meals. Meals give them [the students] energy and energy leads to trouble-making. What should they do, if it is not to make trouble? [We] can depend only on them to carry on. But [if they are] to carry on in the present way, [as] quietly [as] in the past two months, how many more months and years will it take? Yesterday we said that you must change your work team

[1] See below, instruction no. 33.

policy. What are the work teams doing? 1. Being a nuisance, and 2. being incompetent in struggle and in reform. I cannot help it. Now, there is no recourse but revolution—to struggle against bad people and to reorient [our] ideology. The great Cultural Revolution is the repudiation of capitalist ideological 'authorities'. How much struggle is needed against Lu P'ing?[1] How much against Li Ta?[2] Chien Po-tsan has written a lot of books. Can you struggle him down? But the masses unite together and call him 'A gust of evil wind in a small temple and a lot of tortoises in a shallow pond.' [They] have got him. Can you do it? Not me; not the provinces. As to the reform of teaching and learning, I know nothing about it. The only way is to rely on the masses and then centralize.[3]

To transform work teams into either liaison teams or advisory teams. You say that advisory teams would be too powerful. Well, call them liaison teams then. In a month or so they have hampered the revolution; in fact they have helped the counter-revolution. Some of them just sit there and watch 'the tigers fight', students fight students. The University of Communications in Sian controls telephone calls, telegrams, and the despatch of people to Peking. It must be written in the documents: 'Telephone call approved,' 'telegram approved,' or 'sending so-and-so to the Centre approved'. These things have been said in the party constitution already. The offices of the Nanking *New China Daily* are besieged. I do not think any harm will be done if they are besieged for three days and there are three days without that paper. If you do not revolt, the revolution will come to your doorsteps! Why is it impermissible to surround the offices of provincial or municipal [party] committees, of newspapers, and of the State Council? When good people come, you refuse to see them. All right, [in that case] I will see them. You send

[1] He was the head of the party branch at Peking University.

[2] (1890–), studied metallurgy at the Imperial University, Tokyo. On his return, he joined Ch'en Tu-hsiu as an editor of the *New Youth* magazine. In 1921 he was a founder of the CCP, although shortly afterwards he resigned from the party. Before 1949 he had taught economics and in 1952 he was appointed the chancellor of Wuhan University. He was one of the victims in the early stages of the Cultural Revolution.

[3] 'To rely on the masses' is what Mao understands as 'democracy'; 'to centralize' is what he often speaks of as the other aspect of the contradiction between democracy and centralism.

small fry to see them instead of yourselves. But I will see them. In one word, scared. Scared of revolution, of use of arms. Nobody is willing to go to the lower levels, to go to the trouble spots, to use his own eyes. Li Hsüeh-feng and Wu Teh,[1] you will not go and see; you are preoccupied everyday by routine business. You have no real understanding. How can you guide anything? I think the three debates at the University of Nanking are good. All those who are here at this conference should go to the trouble spots. Some people are afraid of opening their mouths. When you are asked to speak, say something like this: 'We come to learn, to support your revolution.' Go at once when you are asked to go [to the trouble spots], and go again.

What you call revolutionary teachers and students are really perfect. In one or two months of work you have not acquired an ounce of real understanding. When you go, you will be surrounded. Take the question of beating people up at the Peking College of Education and the School of Broadcasting. Some people are afraid of being man-handled and so they call in work teams to protect them. (Chairman asks: 'Does anyone get killed?') Beating up the left is a discipline for the left. In short, the work teams can neither struggle nor reform, not in six months or a year. The only people who can are those in the organizations in question. Struggle is destruction and reform is construction. [New] textbooks can be compiled in six months. I think they should be simplified and mistakes in them should be eliminated. There may not be time to add [new material], except the editorials and directives issued by the Centre. (Someone suggests that the Chairman's works should be added.) But they are the sign-posts to the [correct] direction, not dogmas. For instance, what book tells you how to handle the question of beating people up at the School of Broadcasting? Which general

[1] Li Hsüeh-feng (1907–   ), born in Yungchi, Shansi, became a member of the CCP when he studied at the National Teachers' Training College, Taiyuan. During the Anti-Japanese war he was active in the T'aihang region and in 1952 became the first deputy secretary of the Central-south Bureau of the party. After his visit to Moscow in 1959, he was appointed the first secretary of the North China Bureau in 1963; after his visit to Indonesia in 1965, he became the first secretary of the Peking branch of the party in 1966.

Wu was appointed the deputy secretary of the Peking branch at the same time as Li's appointment. He was born in 1909, a man of Tangshan, Hopei. He studied at China University, Peking, where he joined the CCP. Since 1955 he worked in Kirin to become a secretary of the Northeast Bureau.

reads and conducts a war at the same time? At this stage [we] must switch round the general orientation.

The cultural revolution committees should have the left, the neutrals, and the right. Yes, there must be a few rightists. For example, Chien Po-tsan can be made use of by the right or by the left. He is a walking dictionary. Do not help to unite [the right]. Follow the example of the Chung-hua Book Company by setting up training classes. Walking dictionaries, if not intensely hated by the masses, [should be included in the cultural revolution committees.] Conferences of representatives and revolutionary committees must have an opposition. This, however, does not apply to the Standing Committee [of the Politburo].

Apart from you, Li Hsüeh-feng, the municipal [party] committee must not have too many people on it. If there are too many, they will 'revolt', make telephone calls, and issue reports and charts. I have only one person, quite enough. Nowadays each Minister has a secretary (or secretaries). Get rid of them. I did not have any when I was in Yenan. The municipal [party] committee may have a man in charge of outgoing and incoming correspondence; there is no need of a secretary. Go down and do some manual work. Some of the Ministries of the State Council may be reduced to sections. [We] have never had excessively big organizations.

People do not seem to think. First, classes are stopped; second, canteens continue to serve meals; and third, troubles start. Trouble-making is revolution. After work teams appeared on the scene, some people wanted a restoration [of the *status quo ante*]. What does that matter? Are some of our Ministers really reliable? Who are in control of some of our Ministries and newspapers? Four days after my arrival in Peking, I was still inclined to preserve the existing order of things. Some work teams are a nuisance to the movement, e.g. those at Tsinghua and Peking Universities. It must be written in the documents: Counter-revolutionaries are those who raise fires and instil poison. Do not arrest those who stick up big-character posters or reactionary slogans. Some of them write: 'Support the party Centre; down with Mao-Tse-tung!' Why arrest such people? They still support the party Centre! History counter-revolution [*sic*] should be kept for future use. Struggle against those whose manifestations are bad but do not beat them up! Let them 'bloom and contend'! Do not be afraid of a few big-character posters or reactionary slogans.

CLOSING SPEECH AT THE ELEVENTH PLENUM OF THE CENTRAL COMMITTEE 8.8.1966
SHWS

As to the convocation of the Ninth Congress,[1] I am afraid that a year's preparation is necessary. We must prepare for it and decide when it should be called. It has been some time; it will be ten years in two years' time, since the second session of the Eighth Congress.[2] Now there is the need for another national congress which might be convened some time next year. We must prepare for it. May I propose that the preparation be done by the Politburo and its Standing Committee?

Whether the decisions taken at this plenum are right or wrong only the future can tell. It seems that our decisions will be welcomed by the masses. For instance, one of the important decisions of the Centre concerns the great Cultural Revolution which is supported by the broad masses of the students and revolutionary teachers. They have resisted the line taken in the past, and our decision is based on their resistance [to the line of the past]. However, the workability of our decision depends on all grades of leaders, including those who are here and those who are not. Take our reliance on the masses for instance. One of the mistakes was the refusal to follow the mass line. We must not take it for granted that all that is written in our resolutions will be carried out by our comrades. Some of them are unwilling to do so. But the situation may be better than in the past, as in the past no such openly discussed resolutions were taken. Furthermore, these resolutions are guaranteed by the organization [of the party].

This time there have been some changes in the organization. The adjustments in the full and alternate membership of the Politburo, the secretaries in the Secretariat, and the membership of the Standing Committee should guarantee the realization of the resolutions and the communiqué of the Centre.

[1] The Ninth Congress was actually convened in April 1969.
[2] This was held in 1958.

We must always show a way to the comrades who have committed mistakes, giving them a chance to reform themselves. Please do not deny other people a chance to correct their mistakes. Our policy is 'to punish those who have committed mistakes so that others will not follow them and to cure the disease in order to save the patient'. We 'first watch and then help' and 'unite-criticize-and-unite'. Do we have a party outside our party? I think we have a party outside it and factions inside it. When the Kuomintang said that 'there should not be a party outside this party and factions inside it', we criticized it by saying: 'No party outside this party means autocracy; no factions inside it is in fact an optical illusion.' We are exactly the same. You say that there are no factions in our party, but factions do exist. On the question of the masses, for instance, we have two factions. The question is really which of the two is the majority faction. If we had not held this meeting, and instead had waited for a few more months, things would be far worse. So we have had a good meeting and achieved good results.

TALK AT THE WORK CONFERENCE OF THE CENTRE   23.8.1966
SHWS

The main question is what policy to adopt towards the so-called chaos at various places. In my opinion, we should let the chaos go on for a few months and just firmly believe that the majority is good and only the minority bad. It does not matter if there are no provincial [party] committees. There are still district and county [party] committees! The *People's Daily* has published an editorial, calling on the workers, peasants, and soldiers to stop interfering with students' activities, and advocating non-violent, not violent, struggles.

In my view, Peking is not all that chaotic. The students held a meeting of 100,000 and then captured the murderers. This caused some panic. Peking is too gentle. Appeals have been issued, [but after all] there are very few hooligans. Stop interfering for the time being. It is still too early to say anything definite about the reorganization of the centre of the [Youth] League; let us wait four months. Decisions taken hurriedly can do only harm. Work teams were despatched in a hurry; the left was struggled against in a hurry; meetings of 100,000 were called in a hurry; appeals were issued in a hurry; opposition to the new municipal [party] committee of Peking was said, in a hurry, to be tantamount to an opposition to the [party] Centre. Why is it impermissible to oppose it? I have issued a big-character poster myself, 'Bombard the Headquarters!' Some problems have to be settled soon. For instance, the workers, peasants, and soldiers should not interfere with the students' great Cultural Revolution. Let the students go into the street. What is wrong with their writing big-character posters or going into the street? Let foreigners take pictures. They take shots to show aspects of our backward tendencies. But it does not matter. Let the imperialists make a scandal about us.

TALK AT THE ENLARGED WORK CONFERENCE OF THE CENTRE

1966

SHWS (Incomplete Text)

Freedom means recognition of the inevitable and reform of the objective world. Only on the basis of recognition of the inevitable can people act freely. This is the dialectical law of freedom and inevitability. Before this recognition our action is, to some extent, unconsciously blind. We are just a bunch of fools at that stage. In recent years didn't we do a lot of stupid things?

Things are like that. In the democratic revolution, we passed through victory, defeat, victory again, defeat again, and then final victory, before we understood the objective laws of reality of China.

We must be prepared for the defeats and set-backs due to the blindness of our action, draw lessons from them, and win the final victory. From this point of view, it is advantageous if we take a long-term view. To take a short-term view would be harmful. . . .

It seems that there are still a lot of problems. To put demo-cratic centralism honestly and truly into practice requires inten-sive education, setting up experimental points, and popularizing

36

their results. The process should be repeated again and again before democratic centralism can be fully realized. Any other way would reduce it to empty words as far as the majority of our comrades are concerned.

Comrades, I am going to discuss a few points, all together six, centring on the system of democratic centralism. I shall touch on other problems as well. . . .

Secondly, concerning the question of democratic centralism, . . . some comrades are afraid of the masses, their criticism, and what they say. Are there any grounds on which a Marxist-Leninist can justify this fear? If he does not talk about his own mistakes or allow others to talk about them, the fear will grow. I do not think a fear of this kind is necessary. What is there to be afraid of? Our attitude is to hold fast to truth and correct our mistakes. The questions of right or wrong, correct or mistaken, belong to the category of the internal contradictions of the people which can be resolved only by the method of reasoning, discussing, criticism and self-criticism. In short, by democratic methods, by allowing the masses to speak up.

What I am saying is that in all the historical period of human history there have been instances of solving problems in this way. In a class society there are many such instances; even in a socialist society they are not entirely avoidable. . . . To curse [them] only ends in one's own downfall, being disqualified from doing this kind of work, being demoted to work at a lower level or transferred to another type of work. But what is wrong with that? . . . I think demotions or transfers of this sort, whether done rightly or wrongly, are a good thing, [because] they can steel one's revolutionary spirit, lead to the investigation and study of new situations, and add to one's useful knowledge. I have had this sort of experience myself and have drawn benefit from it.

Without democracy it is impossible to have the right sort of centralism. This is because centralism cannot be established on the basis of a confusion of views, in the absence of a unified [common] understanding. What do [we] mean by centralism? First of all, centralization of correct views. On the basis of that, [we] proceed to a unified understanding, unified policy, unified plan, unified command, and unified action—i.e. centralist unification. If problems are not yet properly understood, views [on them] are not yet expressed, and tempers are not yet calmed down, how is it possible to have centralism? When there is a lack of democracy, when a situation is only vaguely appreciated, when different views are not gathered together to facilitate communication between those who are above and those who are below, and when the decisions of leading organizations are taken on the basis of partial or unreliable information, subjectivism is unavoidable and true centralism unattainable.

Some of our comrades are allergic to opposition views and criticism. This is quite wrong. . . . (When the secretary comes, everyone at the provincial [party] committee becomes as quiet as a mouse.) [They are] irresponsible, afraid of responsibility; [they] intimidate others into silence or appear frightful like the backside of a tiger which cannot be touched. Ten out of ten people who adopt this attitude will fail. People *will* talk. Is the backside of a tiger really untouchable? [We] *will* touch it!

Without democratic centralism it is impossible to consolidate the proletarian dictatorship. . . .

Thirdly, we must know which classes to ally with and which classes to treat as enemies. This is the basic problem of [our] standpoint. . . . To begin with we must ally with the peasants. . . . As to the intellectuals, do we unite only with the revolutionary ones? No, we should unite with all those intellectuals who are patriotic and let them do their good work. . . .

Fourthly, there is the question of understanding the objective world. The leap from the realm of the inevitable to the realm of freedom is a process of understanding objective [reality]. I say that our party toiled during the period of democratic revolution. The whole object of this kind (?) of historical situation[1] is to lead [our] comrades [to] understand this: there has to be a process of understanding socialist construction which begins with practice, which moves from inexperience to experience, from understanding socialism—i.e. from the comprehended realm of inevitability—to the gradual elimination of blindness [ignorance and vagueness]—from understanding objective laws to the attainment of freedom, enabling, thereby, a leap to occur in our understanding which lands [us] in the realm of freedom.

In the reign of Ch'ien-lung (1736–95), capitalist productive

---

[1] Misprints in the Chinese text, as the sentence up to this point does not really make much sense.

relations began to appear in China, but [Chinese] society remained feudal. . . .

Fifthly, with regard to the international communist movement. . . . At all times during our life-time and the life-time of our sons and grandsons, we must learn from the Soviet Union—learn from its [positive] experience, not its mistakes. Some people may ask: 'As the Soviet Union is dominated by revisionists, do we still have to learn from it?' [Yes,] we learn from its good people and good things, learn the good experiences of the Soviet party, and the good experiences of Soviet workers, peasants, other labouring peoples, and intellectuals. As to the bad people, bad things, and revisionists of the Soviet Union, we can regard them as our 'negative' teachers and draw lessons from them.

Sixthly, [we] must unite the whole party and the people of the whole country. . . .

4. Do not label people in an irresponsible manner. Some of our comrades make a habit of repressing people by sticking labels on them. Whenever they open their mouths, labels come tumbling out to frighten people into silence. . . .

5. Take a friendly and helpful attitude towards people who have made mistakes and towards those who do not allow others to speak up. Do not create the kind of atmosphere in which no mistake is permitted, in which a mistake is a great crime, or in which a mistake means eternal damnation.

6. Develop democracy by encouraging and listening to criticism. We must be able to sustain criticism and must take the initiative by criticizing ourselves first. Whatever there is to be inspected, let it be inspected. . . . In one hour, or at most two, one should be able to make a clean breast of things. That is all. If others are not satisfied, ask them to criticize. If what they say is correct, accept it. . . .

In short, letting other people speak will not lead to the sky falling down on us nor to one's own downfall. What will happen if we do not allow others to speak? In that case one day we ourselves will inevitably fall.

TALK AT THE GENERAL REPORT CONFERENCE OF THE CENTRE'S
POLITICAL WORK   24.10.1966
NT

Teng Hsiao-p'ing[1] is deaf. Whenever we are at a meeting together, he sits far away from me. For six years, since 1959, he has not made a general report of work to me. He always gets P'eng Chen[2] to do the work of the Secretariat [of the party] for him. Do you say that he is able? Nieh Jung-chen[3] says: 'That bloke is lazy.'

[1] (1903–   ) born in Chiangan, Szechwan. He was a work-study student in France and later was admitted into the Sun Yat-sen University, Moscow, where he joined the CCP in 1924. Returning to China in 1926, he worked in Kwangsi where he and his comrades were forced to abandon their soviet in 1930 and flee to the soviet of Mao and Chu Teh. In 1932 he was the party secretary of Juichin, the red capital and the editor of the three-daily, *Red Star*. He was criticized when the so-called 'Lo Ming Line' was under attack in 1933. During the Long March he was the head of propaganda of the 1st Army Corps under Lin Piao. In 1937 he became the political commissar of the 192nd Division commanded by Liu Po-ch'eng which was the mainstay of the Chin-Chi-Lu-Yü border region. In 1947 he was appointed the political commissar of the Central China Field Army of the PLA. After the revolution, he became a deputy Premier in 1952 and the secretary-general of CCP in 1954. In that capacity and as a full member of the Politburo (1955), he was responsible for the revision of the party constitution in 1956. In 1956 and 1957 he visited Moscow twice and once again in 1960. He has been in disgrace since the Cultural Revolution.

[2] (1902–   ) born in Ch'üwo, Shansi. At twenty he finished his primary education and went to a teachers' training college. Later he taught at a primary school and joined the CCP. He was one of the attendants at the Sixth Congress of the CCP in Moscow. In 1930 he was arrested and imprisoned till 1935. He helped to organize the December 9th Student Demonstration in Peking, 1935, and in 1941 he went to Yenan, having worked in the Chin-Char-Chi border region, to become the deputy head of the party school, in which capacity he partook in the Rectification of 1942–4. In 1945 he headed the party's Northeast Bureau and three years later became the deputy head of the Organization Department of the CCP. In 1956 he was made the first secretary of the party's Peking branch and a member of the Politburo, and visited Eastern Europe. At the Romanian party congress in 1960 he joined Khrushchev in an open polemic. In 1966 he was the first important leader of the party to fall into disgrace.

[3] (1899–   ) a man of Chiangchin, Szechwan, who studied at a middle school in Chungking before going to France as a work-study student. In 1922 he joined the communist group organized by Chou En-lai and went to work in Belgium. In the next year he returned to Paris to become a communist party member, whence to Moscow to study in a military school. In 1927 he took part in the famous Nanch'ang Uprising on 1 August and the Canton Commune in December. He did not go to the Kiangsi soviet till 1931 and soon was appointed the political commissar of the 1st Army Corps. His co-operation with Lin Piao, commander of the Army Corps, was resumed in 1937 when he became the political commissar of the 115th Division of the 8th Route Army, in which capacity he was chiefly responsible for the creation

My view of the situation is that it is big in the middle and small at both ends. Only Honan puts the word 'dare' ahead of all others; most people put the word 'fear' in first place; only a very few people firmly place the word 'revolt' in front of other words. Anti-party and anti-socialist people include Po I-po, Ho Ch'ang-kung, Wang Feng, and also Li Fan-wu.[1]

Real 'four-kind' cadres (the rightists)[2] make up only one, two, or three per cent. (The Premier, [Chou En-lai] says: 'More than that now.') Never mind how many more. We shall suppress them (*p'ing-fan*). Some will not be kept where they are; they should be transferred to other places.

In Honan one [party] secretary does productive work while five others receive [the revolutionaries]. In the whole country there is only Liu Chien-hsün[3] who has written a big-character poster to give support to the minority [the reactionaries]. That is a good thing.

What about Nieh Yüan-tzu?[4] (K'ang Sheng[5] says: 'She must be protected.' Li Hsien-nien[6] says: 'All those who wrote the first big-character posters should be protected.') Good!

of the Chin-Char-Chi border region. In 1945 he became a member of the Central Committee of the CCP, and ten years later a marshal of the PLA.

[1] Po I-po (1907–) joined the CCP when he was a student at the Taiyuan Teachers' Training College in 1926. Later he studied at Peking University and led the Sacrifice League in Shansi during the Anti-Japanese war. He was elected to the Central Committee, CCP, in 1945 and made the political commissar of Chin-Chi-Lu-Yü border region. In 1959 he became one of the deputy Premiers in charge of industrial development.

Ho Ch'ang-kung (1898–) studied in France and Belgium and joined the CCP in 1921. In 1929 he was under P'eng Teh-huai and in the following year the C.O. of the 8th Red Army. He supported Chang Kuo-t'ao in 1935 and served as the head of the Organization Department of Chang's 'Centre'. In 1952 he was the deputy Minister of the 2nd Ministry of Heavy Industries and two years later, the deputy Minister of the Ministry of Geology.

Wang Feng (1906–) was born in Shensi and studied at Peking University. Since 1949 he had been working in Northwest China and held the post of the first secretary of the CCP Kansu branch.

Li Fan-wu (1908–), a deputy Minister of the Ministry of Forestry in 1952 and the secretary of the CCP Heilungkiang branch.

[2] The wealthy, rightist, reactionary, and bad.

[3] See above, p. 6, n. 1.

[4] See above, p. 24, n. 1.

[5] See above, p. 27, n. 2.

[6] (1906–), born in Huangan, Hupei, and worked as a carpenter. He joined the CCP in 1927. In 1954 he was made a deputy Premier in special charge of finance. At the 8th Congress, 1956, he was elected to the Politburo and the Secretariat of the CCP.

(On the question of the great 'get-together' (*ta ch'uan-lien*),[1] the Premier says: 'It should be done with proper preparation.') What preparation? Where cannot one find a bowl of rice?[2]

There are different views on the [present] situation. In Tientsin half a million people went to Wan Hsiao-t'ang's funeral and they thought the situation was excellent. In fact, that was a demonstration against the party, an attempt to repress the living by using the dead.

Li Fu-ch'un[3] has been asked to rest for a year. Even I do not know who is in charge of the Planning Commission. [Li] Fu-ch'un respects the [party] discipline. He told some things to the Secretariat which were not reported to me. Teng Hsiao-p'ing respects me but keeps me at arm's length.

TALK AT THE WORK CONFERENCE OF THE CENTRE ON 25.10.1966
SHWS (The first part of this talk is translated and published in Jerome Ch'en, *Mao*, N.J.: Prentice-Hall, 1969, pp. 96–7.)

(cont'd)

Second, the great Cultural Revolution raised havoc—I mean [my] comment on Neih Yüan-tzu's big-character poster, [my] letter to the Tsinghua Middle School, and my own big-character poster.[4] It was done in a short period of time—June, July, August, September, and October—less than five months. It is not surprising that many comrades have not yet grasped its meaning. It covered a short space of time but it had tremendous momentum—in both exceeding my expectations. Once the Peking University big-character poster was broadcast,[5] the whole nation rose up. Before the letter to them was made public,[6] the Red Guards of the whole country began to move. The

---

[1] This literally means to go out and get people together.

[2] This proverb means that life is much easier than one imagines.

[3] (1900–) born in Ch'angsha, Hunan, studied in France as a work-study student, where he joined the communist party. He took part in the Nanch'ang Uprising of 1927. In 1945 he was a member of the Politburo and in 1950 the Minister of the Ministry of Heavy Industries. He has been in charge of the National Planning for economic construction.

[4] See below, instruction no. 47.

[5] See below, instruction no. 33.

[6] See below, instruction no. 44.

tidal waves strike you with all their might. Since I am responsible for this havoc, I can hardly blame you if you grumble. At our last meeting, I lacked confidence. I had said that it [the Cultural Revolution] might not be carried out. So, many comrades still did not understand [it]. After two months, as we acquired some experience, things got better. This conference had gone through two stages—in the first stage the discussion had a touch of abnormality, but it got better later. It has been only five months. The campaign may last two more five-month periods or longer.

The democratic revolution went on for twenty-eight years, from 1921 to 1924 [*sic.* 1949?]. At the beginning, no one knew how to go about it. The path was found by path-finders who in the twenty-eight years had [periodically] summed up [their] experience. It was impossible to ask comrades to understand [what they were doing]. Last year, many comrades did not bother to read or did not pay any attention to the articles criticizing Wu Han.[1] Previously, the criticism of *Wu Hsün Chuan*[2] and of *Hung Lou Meng*[3] were piecemeal efforts which were just [attempts to] kill a pain in the head or in the foot, and that method did not do the trick. In January, February, March, April, and May, the first five months of this great Cultural Revolution, there were many articles and directives from the Centre which failed to attract much attention. But big-character posters and the Red Guards attacked and they succeeded in attracting attention. It is impossible to ignore them. The revolution has come to your doorstep and you must quickly sum up your experience, [only] two months after [the previous one]? It is important to sum up our experience and do our political ideological work. When you go back, you will have a great deal of political ideological work to do. The central bureaux, provincial [party] committees, district [party] committees, and county [party] committees ought to call meetings and explain

[1] Wu Han (1909–) born Iwu, Chekiang, took his first degree at Tsinghwa University, Peking. His scholarship attracted the attention of Dr. Hu Shih and from 1937 to 1946 he was on the staff of the Southwest Associated University, Kunming. He became the vice-mayor of Peking while continuing his work on the history of the Ming dynasty. Yao Wen-yüan's article attacking Wu's opera and writings on Hai Jui and other personalities of the Ming history was published in the *Liberation Daily*, Shanghai, 10 November 1965.

[2] See below, instruction no. 2.

[3] See below, instruction no. 4.

43

the problems. Do not have illusions that you can explain every-thing. Some people say: 'A thorough grasp of the principles does not guarantee the correct handling of concrete problems.' At first I did not quite understand this. How was it possible to have a thorough grasp of principles and yet be incompetent in handling concrete problems? Now I see that there is something in that statement. [The reason,] I am afraid, lies in insufficient political ideological work. After [our] last conference and before meetings were convened properly at some places, seven or eight secretaries [of the party] out of ten began to receive [the Red Guards]. They were thrown into a panic by the Red Guards. They did not realize that the Red Guards were annoyed by them. They lost the initiative when they were taken aback by some of the questions. But the lost initiative can be recovered. That is why my confidence in this conference has increased. What do you think? But if you follow the old regulations, pre-serve the *status quo*, and let one faction of the Red Guards support you and another oppose you, I do not think the situa-tion will change or improve. Of course, [we] must not ask too much; [we must not demand] the multitude of cadres in the central bureaux, provinces, districts, and counties to understand everything over night. [We] cannot be sure of that. Some of them will never understand and a small minority will oppose [us]. However, I believe that most of them will understand.

Let me speak about two things.

The first is history. In seventeen years the first and second lines have led to disunity.[1] The responsibility belongs to others and myself.

The second is that I ignited the great Cultural Revolution of the past five months. [But] it is only five months, a short time, compared with the twenty-eight years of the democratic revolu-tion and seventeen years of the socialist revolution. It is under-standable that there should still be ignorance and inconsistencies after less than six months. In the past, you worked on industries, agriculture, and communications, but not on a great cultural revolution. Similar situations existed in the Ministry of Foreign Affairs and the Military Commission. What you did not expect has now come. Let it come, I think it is a good thing to have this tidal wave. Brains which have not thought for many years may

[1] J. Ch'en, *Mao*, 1969, p. 96.

think again under its impact. At the worst, it is just a mistake. Whatever line, if it is a mistake, should be corrected. And that is all. Who wants to knock you down? I do not. I do not believe that the Red Guards want to do that either. Two Red Guards told Li Hsüeh-feng:[1] 'Isn't it strange that our elder is afraid of us?' There is also Wu Hsiu-ch'üan[2] whose four children are divided into four factions. Their school-mates, scores of them, went to their home in batches. I think there are advantages in making contact with small groups. Large-scale contacts with one or half a million people, lasting a few hours, are another method. Each has its usefulness.

At this conference there are only a few brief reports and I have read all of them. I would feel sorry if you could not pass this test. I am just as anxious as you are. It has not been a very long time yet and I do not blame you, Comrades. Some comrades say: 'The mistakes are not deliberate ones; they are made because of muddle-headedness. They are therefore forgivable.' [We] cannot shift all the blame to Comrade [Liu] Shao-ch'i and [Teng] Hsiao-p'ing. They are to be blamed; so is the Centre [as a whole]. The Centre has not done its job. Because of a lack of time and energy, [I] have not prepared [the answers] to new problems. Political ideological work which has not been done properly will be improved after these seventeen days of conference.

Any other business? That is all for today. Let us adjourn.

TALK AT THE MEETING OF THE CENTRAL CULTURAL REVOLUTION TEAM on 9.1.1967
NT

Now, the left has taken over the *Wen-hui Pao*; the revolt occurred on the 4th and on the 6th there was a revolt in the *Liberation Daily*. The general trend is good. I have read the issues

---

[1] See above, p. 37, n. 1.

[2] (1903–), born in Wuch'ang, Hupei, studied at Wuhan Middle School and was introduced into the CCP by Tung Pi-wu. In 1927 he studied infantry in Moscow and upon return taught at a university in Shanghai. He acted as Li Teh's (Otto Braun) interpreter in 1933. In 1950 he was in Russia again with Mao and in the same year he appeared at the UN Security Council to defend China's participation in the Korean war. He was her ambassador to Yugoslavia in 1955 and attended the Bulgarian party congress in 1962. He has worked as a diplomat since 1949.

of the *Wen-hui Pao* since the take-over. They have published a selection of Red Guard posters. Some good articles ought to be published [elsewhere] selectively. The *Wen-hui Pao* message to the people of Shanghai on the 5th may be reproduced in the *People's Daily* or may be broadcast. It is a good thing to have internal revolts. [I] shall make a general report in a few days. This is a matter of one class toppling another, a great revolution. In my view, many newspapers ought to be suspended. But there must be newspapers. The question is: who will run them? The reform of the *Wen-hui Pao* and *Liberation Daily* is excellent. These two papers will have their influence on east China; they will even influence all the provinces and cities of the whole country. To revolt, one must first of all create a public opinion. On 1 June, the *People's Daily* was taken over when the Centre sent a work team [to the paper]. The editorial, 'Sweep away All the Freaks and Demons', appeared. I do not think that the *People's Daily* should be replaced by a new paper, but I insist on its take-over. [When] xxx replaced Wu Leng-hsi,[1] the masses were suspicious at first because the *People's Daily* had lied in the past and there was no announcement of any kind. The power struggle in the two newspapers [*Wen-hui* and *Liberation*] is a national matter and therefore the revolts need our support. Our papers ought to publish Red Guard articles, which are well-written, unlike [the papers' usual] dull stuff.

The Central Department of Propaganda can be done away with, but let the staff continue to have their meals there. The Department and the Ministry of Culture cannot cope with a lot of things. I cannot even cope with you (referring to Comrade [Ch'en] Po-ta).[2] But as soon as the Red Guards came, everything was all right.

The rise of Shanghai revolutionary forces gives hope to the entire country; it cannot fail to influence the whole of east China and all the other provinces and cities of the country. 'The Message to the People of Shanghai' is rare, excellent. The Shanghai problems discussed in it are [in fact] also national problems.

---

[1] (1909–   ), born in Kiangsi, studied at Wuhan University. In 1949 he was the deputy director of the New China News Agency and in 1954 attended the Geneva Conference. He became the chief editor of the *JMJP* in 1958.

[2] See above, p. 27, n. 1.

In the revolutionary work today some people [are so grasping that they] demand this and that. Since 1920 we have been doing revolutionary work, beginning from the Youth League and then the CCP. We had no money, no publishing houses, no bicycles. When we edited newspapers, we got on intimate terms with printing workers. We chatted with them and edited articles at the same time.

We must have contacts with all sorts of people—the left, the neutrals, and the right. I have never agreed that an organization ought to be perfectly 'pure'. (Someone remarks: 'Wu Leng-hsi is really comfortable; he has put on weight.'[1]) [Yes], Wu Leng-hsi is allowed to be too comfortable. But I do not think people like him ought to be dismissed. ('Keep them where they are and put them under the supervision of the masses.')

When we began our revolution, we had contact not with Marxism-Leninism, but with opportunism. When [I was] young, I had not even read the *Communist Manifesto*.

We must get down to revolution and encourage production; we must not revolt and forget all about production. The conservatives do not encourage production. This is a class struggle.

Don't believe that 'Once the butcher is dead, [we] will have to eat pork with bristles on.' Don't believe that we cannot do anything without him.

TALK AT THE ENLARGED MEETING OF THE MILITARY COMMISSION
(Transmitted by Premier Chou)   27.1.1967
NT

1. The armed forces' attitude towards the great Cultural Revolution. At first they chose non-involvement, but they were in fact involved in such ways as documents being sent to them for safe keeping and some cadres going [to work] among the units. In the present situation, when the struggle between the two lines has become extremely acute, they cannot stay aloof and their participation must mean their support of the left.

2. Most of the old comrades have so far failed to come to

---

[1] 'To put on weight' is regarded by the Chinese as a healthy sign.

grips with the great Cultural Revolution. They have lived on their 'capital', depended on their past records. They should discipline and reform themselves in this movement and set up new records and **make** new contributions. (At this juncture, Chairman quotes from Ch'u Che's audience with the Queen of Chao in the *Chan Kuo Ts'e.*[1]) They must resolutely stand on the side of the left; they must not try to muddle through; they must firmly support the left. Then they must do their work well under the control and supervision of the left.

3. With regard to the power struggle in the newspapers, it is a struggle for power against the capitalist 'roaders' and the faction in authority and against the die-hards of the bourgeois reactionary line. How else can [we] struggle for power? Now it seems that [we] should carefully divide . . .[2] [and] take over power before other things can be done. [We] must not be metaphysical [superficial?] about it. Otherwise [we] shall be constrained. After the struggle for power [we] should examine the true nature of the faction in authority and then pass judgement on it and we should report it to the State Council for approval.

4. The old cadres before the power struggle and the [new] cadres after it should co-operate in working together and preserve the secret of the state.

CONVERSATION WITH PREMIER CHOU ON POWER STRUGGLE 1967
NT

Chairman: 'How's the power struggle? The Public Security Bureau is an instrument of the dictatorship.'
Premier: 'It was taken over only about a day ago.'
Chairman: '[We] ought to choose the typical cases.'
Premier: 'The municipal [party] committee of the Bureau held a meeting and decided on several kinds of power struggle. Cadres belong to the faction in authority [who are]: 1. the "black gang" soaked through [with erroneous ideology] and therefore "black"; 2. the capitalist "roaders" in power; 3. those adamantly upholding the capitalist reactionary line;

---

[1] See J. I. Crump Jr., *Intrigues*, Ann Arbor: University of Michigan Press, 1964, pp. 77–9.
[2] Words missing.

4. those admitting some mistakes but leaving the rest intact; and 5. [among them] individual cases of the general mistake (the majority of the cases).'

Chairman: 'Make the first two categories smaller and isolate and attack the smallest minority. Take-over is in itself a revolution, a creation of something new. According to different circumstances, there are five different ways. 1. Complete reorganization (as Chang Ch'un-ch'iao and Yao Wen-yüan [have done in Shanghai]¹). 2. After take-over, adopt different methods in dealing with the faction in authority. Criticize them while keeping them at work under supervision (according to the work assigned to them). 3. Suspend their posts but keep them at their work. 4. Dismiss them but keep them at their work. Or 5. cashier and punish them.'

Premier: 'That is a good way—dismiss them, keep them at their work, but struggle against them. There will then be an opposition to help [us] to enlarge and strengthen our own ranks. To take on too much work [themselves] (referring to the revolutionary rebels) can only make them "passive" [slaves of work]. Keep them [the faction in authority] at their work and struggle against them. In the Academy of Sciences, the left have grown strong. Their work of "Get Down to Revolution and Encourage Production" is done very well. [But] they let the faction in authority sweep the street and after that [the reactionaries] just go to sleep. It is really cushy. [We] must not let ourselves be bogged down by routine business. ([We] must pay attention to this problem.) To take-over is a big thing which will touch off a chain of changes. It is a revolution. [We] must be clear about the aim of the take-over, about the problems involved in it, and about how to do it. [We] must know how to tackle [those] questions and must have concrete policies (e.g. how to deal with the staff of the bureaux, Ministries, departments, and sections.). [We] have seized power, but it may be snatched away [from us] again. In some organizations this tug-of-war may be a discipline in

¹ Chang Ch'un-ch'iao was the head of the Shanghai *Liberation Daily* 1953 and in the following year he went to study the press in the USSR. In 1965 he was the secretary of the CCP Shanghai branch.

Yao Wen-yüan, son of Yao P'eng-tzu, a left-wing writer of the 1930s, became famous as a literary critic in 1957 when the Hundred Flowers Campaign turned into an anti-rightist movement. He is believed to be Mao's son-in-law.

itself. [But we] must keep the power. This depends chiefly on the strength of the left. When the strength of the left is small, power may be snatched away from it again. [Therefore] the left must be strong. I support the power struggle. After it, [we] must get down to revolution and encourage production.

Written Statements

COMMENT ON THE SECOND GROUP OF MATERIAL ON THE HU FENG[1]
ANTI-PARTY CLIQUE   1955
NT (Excerpts)

What Hu Feng calls 'uniformity of public opinion' refers to the prohibition of counter-revolutionaries to voice their counter-revolutionary views. It is true that under our system counter-revolutionaries have no freedom of speech. Freedom of speech is the exclusive right of the people, among whom there can be a spectrum of views—i.e. freedom of criticism, freedom to express divergent views, freedom to publicize theism or atheism (materialism). In any society at any point of time there are advanced and backward people whose views are contradictory to and contending with each other. Advanced views always prevail over backward ones. It is therefore impossible and undesirable to have 'uniformity of public opinion'. The only way to make progress is to promote what is advanced so that it can prevail over what is backward. But at a time when there still exist classes and a class struggle both at home and abroad, the proletariat and popular masses who have seized state power must suppress all attempts of the counter-revolutionary classes, cliques, and individuals to oppose the revolution and restore their own power. They must forbid all counter-revolutionaries to use freedom of speech for their counter-revolutionary purposes. Thus counter-revolutionaries like Hu Feng feel the inconvenience of the 'uniformity of public opinion'. Their inconvenience is our convenience, and this is precisely

---

[1] His given name is Chang Kuang-jen, and he was born in Itu, Hupei. Having studied in Japan, he became a literary critic and organizer of writers and attracted the attention of Lu Hsün. During the Anti-Japanese war he edited the fortnightly, *July*, in Chungking.

what we aim at. Our public opinions are both uniform and divergent. Among the people, the advanced and the backward are allowed to use our newspapers, periodicals, and platforms freely to compete with each other, in the hope that the advanced will be able to educate the backward and reform their thinking and their systems by means of democratic persuasion. When one contradiction has been conquered, another emerges. The same process of competition repeats itself. In this way, society forges ahead continuously. The existence of contradictions means divergence, the resolution of contradictions means a temporary uniformity before the emergence shortly afterwards of new contradictions which create divergence and require another resolution. In the case of the contradiction between the people and the counter-revolutionaries, there must be the people's dictatorship under the leadership of the working class and the communist party, over the counter-revolutionaries. Here, instead of democracy, dictatorial and totalitarian methods are applied. They [the counter-revolutionaries] have to observe the rules; they must not be allowed to say or do anything they like. Here not only public opinion but also the laws are uniform.[1] On this question, Hu Feng and other counter-revolutionaries seem to have a lot to say. Some muddle-headed people even feel incoherent *vis-à-vis* their arguments. Is it not unpleasant to talk about 'uniformity of public opinion', 'suppression of public opinion', or 'restriction of freedom'? Such people [who feel the unpleasantness because they] cannot distinguish the twin concepts of 'internal among the people' and 'external to the people'. Internally [among the people], it is criminal to restrict freedoms, to stifle people's criticisms of the mistakes and weaknesses of the party and government, and to suppress free academic discussions; this is our system. But it is legitimate to do so in a capitalist society. Externally [to the people], it is criminal to allow counter-revolutionaries to say or do whatever they like and it is legitimate to practise dictatorship; this is our system. The opposite is the case in a capitalist country. There the capitalist dictatorship does not allow the people to say or do what they like,[2] it only permits them to observe rules and regulations.

---

[1] '*Erh ch'ieh fa-lü yeh i-lü*'. I do not quite understand what this means. Perhaps Mao thought law should be discriminately applied to different categories of people.

[2] Literally 'to behave in a disorderly manner'.

At any place and any time, exploiters and counter-revolutionaries are the minority and the exploited and revolutionaries the majority. Therefore, the dictatorship of the former is never justified whereas that of the latter always is. Hu Feng also says: 'The overwhelming majority of readers belongs to one organization or another in which the atmosphere is oppressive.' Internally among the people we are opposed to compulsory or commandeering methods and insist on democratic persuasive methods. There the atmosphere should be free; the 'oppressiveness' is a mistake. It is a good thing that 'the overwhelming majority of the readers belongs to one organization or another'. There has not been such a good thing for thousands of years. The possibility for the people to transform themselves from the state of a mass of loose sand easily exploited by the reactionaries to a state of unity came only after a long and bitter struggle waged by the people under the leadership of the communist party. It became a reality in the years after the victory of the revolution. What Hu Feng means by 'oppressive' refers to those who suppress the counter-revolution. They [the counter-revolutionaries] are indeed frightened and feel that they are 'like young daughters-in-law living under the fear of being thrashed'. 'Even a cough is recorded on tape.' In our opinion, this, too, is a good thing which has not occurred for thousands of years. These 'bad eggs' feel hardships only after a protracted and arduous struggle by the people under the leadership of the communist party. In short, when the popular masses are happy, the counter-revolutionaries are going through an ordeal. This is the first thing we celebrate each year on the National Day. Hu Feng also says: 'In fact the most economical solution to literary and artistic problems is a mechanistic theory.' The 'mechanistic theory' is an antithesis of dialectical materialism and 'most economical' is just Hu Feng's nonsense. The most economical theory in the world is idealism or metaphysics because it enables people to say whatever they wish, regardless of objective reality, with no need for corroboration with facts. Materialism and dialectics require hard work, as they have to rest on objective reality and be corroborated with facts. To save labour is to slip into idealism and metaphysics. In his letter Hu Feng raised three problems of principles, all of which in our view should be repudiated in detail. He also says in the same letter: 'At the present there is hostility everywhere and demands for something more.' He wrote this in 1950 when Chiang Kaishek's main forces had just been crushed on the mainland but there were still many bandits and armed counter-revolutionaries to be liquidated, large-scale campaigns for land reform and against counter-revolutionaries had not yet begun, nor had the rectifications in the fields of culture and education. What Hu Feng said did reflect the situation as it existed then. But he did not tell the whole story. He should have put it this way: 'At present there is everywhere counter-revolutionary hostility towards revolution and counter-revolutionary demands to the revolutionaries for something more disruptive.'

JMJP, 24 May 1955 (But this cannot be found in the *JMJP* of that date.)

COMMENT ON THE THIRD GROUP OF MATERIAL ON THE HU FENG ANTI-PARTY CLIQUE[1]   1955
NT (Excerpts)

Representatives of all the exploiting classes, when they are in an unfavourable situation, often adopt the tactics of an offensive for their own defence, in an attempt to survive and wait for another day. They may spread utterly unfounded rumours; they may seize upon some superficial phenomenon of a matter [in order to] attack its true substance; they may do one thing but with an eye on something else so as to drive a wedge somewhere to embarrass us. In short, they are always designing ways and means to deal with us. They are always on the look-out for opportunities for a victory. They may even feign death while waiting for a chance to mount a counter-attack. They have rich experience in class struggles of all shapes and forms—legal and illegal forms. We, members of the revolutionary party, must know all these tricks, study them, and defeat them. We must not be book-wormish about them or oversimplify what are in fact complicated class struggles.

JMJP, 10 June 1955

[1] The *JMJP* published three groups of material on Hu Feng in 1955—the first on 13 May, the second on 24 May, and the third on 10 June. In neither of the first two was there a comment introduced by the word *an* (note or comment), but in the third there are 22 comments so introduced. The above quoted is one of them, the fourth.

THE BOURGEOIS ORIENTATION OF THE *WEN-HUI PAO* FOR A PERIOD
OF TIME   1957
JMJP, 14.6.1957, signed by the *JMJP* Editorial Board

The article reproduced below appeared in the *Wen-hui Pao* on
10 June, entitled 'For Reference'.[1] Although for a period of
time in the past the *Wen-hui Pao* in Shanghai and the *Kwang-
ming Jih-pao* in Peking published a large number of good reports
and good feature articles, their basic political orientation was
that of a capitalist newspaper. In a period of time these two
papers, making use of the slogan, 'A Hundred Schools Contend',
and the CCP's rectification campaign, carried many seditious
reports showing the bourgeois point of view which [the papers]
were not prepared to criticize. These issues of the papers are
there for anyone to consult. Some people on the staff of the
papers seriously misconstrued the functions of newspapers. They
confused the principles of the press of a capitalist country with
those of the press of a socialist country. Similar confusion can be
found among the editors and reporters of other newspapers and
among the staff of some departments of journalism at the universities. It is not confined to the *Wen-hui Pao* and *Kwang-ming
Jih-pao* alone, though it is more prominent with these papers.
Mistaken views can be studied, examined, criticized, and then
reformed. [This is what] we expect from these papers. In the
last few days their policy seems to have changed somewhat. Of
course, non-party newspapers should not be exactly the same as
party organs; they should have their individualities. None the
less, their general orientation should be the same as other papers,
because in a socialist country the press reflects through its reports the planned socialist economy based on public ownership.
This is different from the press of a capitalist country which
reflects through its reports the anarchy and group competition of
the capitalist economy. As long as class distinction exists in the
world, newspapers are instruments of class struggle. We hope a
discussion on this issue will be developed in order to arrive at a
common understanding. Some journalists who are members of
the CCP or the Communist Youth League also have a bourgeois view on journalism; they, too, should study, examine,

[1] This was by Yao Wen-yüan.

criticize, and then reform their view. Doctrinaire views on journalism and the style of the 'eight-legged essay' should also be
criticized. These nauseating mistakes are shared by party organs
as well, including this paper. They should be criticized in the
discussions. In that case, a struggle on the two fronts against
both the 'left' and the right in the field of journalism should be
waged. Yao Wen-yüan's article points out, albeit reservedly, the
bourgeois tendencies of the *Wen-hui Pao* and sees clearly the
harmful tendencies of some people on it to wage a struggle from
the standpoint of the bourgeoisie against the proletariat. It is a
good article and therefore it is reproduced here. We take this
opportunity to clarify our views to our professional friends on the
Wen-hui Pao and *Kwang-ming Jih-pao* for their consideration.

THE SITUATION IN THE SUMMER OF 1957   1957
NT

Our aim is to create a political situation which is centralist
and yet democratic, disciplined and yet free, ideologically united
and yet individually content, and dynamic and lively. It will
help the socialist revolution and construction to overcome
difficulties more easily, to build up modern industries and agriculture more quickly, and to make the party and state stronger
and better able to sustain dangers and risks. . . . Members of the
CCP must have the spirit of dawn, firm revolutionary will, and
determination to overcome difficulties with no fear of setbacks;
they must overcome their individualism, particularism, absolute
egalitarianism, and liberalism.[1] Otherwise, they are communist
in name only. . . . Members of the party must be good at discussing and handling affairs with the masses; they must not at
any time detach themselves from the masses. The relationship
between the party and masses is comparable to that between
fish and water. Unless this relationship is properly forged, the
socialist system can neither be established nor consolidated.

---

[1] For Mao's definition of 'liberalism', see 'Combat liberalism' in *SW*.

SIXTY POINTS ON WORKING METHODS—A Draft Resolution from the Office of the Centre of the CCP   19.2.1958
NT

The people of our country, under the leadership of the CP, having won basic victories in the socialist ownership system in 1956, achieved further basic victories on the ideological and political front in the rectification campaign of 1957. In that year, [they] also overfulfilled the first Five-year Construction Plan. In this way, more than 600 million people of our country, led by the CP, clearly see their own future and duties and have exorcized the evil anti-party, anti-people, and anti-socialist wind fanned up by bourgeois rightists. At the same time they have rectified, and are still rectifying, the mistakes and weaknesses rooted in the subjectivism which the party and people have inherited from the old society. The party has become more united, the morale of the people further heightened, and the party-masses relationship greatly improved. We are now witnessing greater activity and creativity of the popular masses on the production front than we have ever witnessed before. A new high tide of production has risen, and is still rising, as the people of the whole country are inspired by the slogan—'Overtake Britain in Iron and Steel and Other Major Industrial Production in Fifteen or More Years'. To meet this new situation, certain methods of work of the party Centre and local committees have to be modified. Not all the points listed below are new. Some are; others come from years [of experience]. They are the conclusions reached at the Hangchow and Nanning conferences of the comrades in the Centre and regions in January 1958. These points, largely indebted to the inspiration of what was said at the conferences, are thought over and written down by me. Some are simply notes of what other comrades have said; the important points (on rules and regulations) are drafted by Comrade Liu Shao-ch'i after consultations with comrades working in the regions; only a few are put forward by me. Not all the points concern working methods—some are on actual work-tasks and some on theory and practice, but mostly on working methods. Our main purpose is to improve our working methods so as to meet the changed political conditions and needs. The points are suggestions for [your] comments. Their number can be increased or reduced, as it is by no means definite. Comrades, you are hereby invited to study them and make known your views on them. These points will be revised in the light of your comments before being submitted to the Politburo for approval, in the hope that they may become a document for internal circulation.

Mao Tse-tung

31 January 1958

1. Party committees above the county level must get down to the work of construction and there are fourteen items: *a.* industries; *b.* handicrafts; *c.* agriculture; *d.* village subsidiary production; *e.* forestry; *f.* fishery; *g.* animal husbandry; *h.* transport and communications; *i.* commerce; *j.* public and other finance; *k.* labour, wages, and population; *l.* sciences; *m.* culture and education; *n.* public health.

2. Party committees above the county level must get down to socialist industrial work and here there are also fourteen items: *a.* targets of output; *b.* quality of products; *c.* experiment in new products; *d.* new techniques; *e.* advanced targets; *f.* raw material economy and discovery and use of substitutes; *g.* labour organization, labour insurance, wages, and welfare; *h.* costs; *i.* sinking fund and variable capital for production; *j.* division of labour and co-ordination between enterprises; *k.* equilibrium of supply, manufacture, and sales; *l.* geological exploration; *m.* uses of resources; *n.* design and manufacture. These are preliminary items. Later [we] must step by step develop a forty-point programme for industrial development.

3. Party committee at all levels must get down to socialist agricultural work. Again fourteen items: *a.* targets of output; *b.* irrigation; *c.* fertilizers; *d.* soil; *e.* seeds; *f.* changes in the system of farming, such as enlarging the areas of a second crop, changes from late to early crops, from dry [rice] to paddy, etc.; *g.* diseases and pests; *h.* mechanization (modern tools, two-wheel and two-blade ploughs, pumps, tractors designed to suit different local conditions in China, motorized transport vehicles, etc.); *i.* intensified farming; *j.* animal husbandry; *k.* subsidiary products; *l.* afforestation; *m.* elimination of the 'four pests'[1]; *n.* medical and health services. These are fourteen

---

[1] Such as rats, sparrows, and so on.

items in the forty-point programme of agrarian development, which should be put into practice as a whole. The purpose of singling out these fourteen items is to show where the emphasis of the programme lies. Once they are grasped, the programme as a whole will consequently be materialized.

4. The three important methods are: over-all planning, regular inspection, and annual reviews and comparisons. By them, both the over-all situation and the details will receive appropriate attention, experiences can be summed up and outstanding achievements can be made known in time; morale can be heightened in order to make a concerted progress.

5. The method of timing is: the previous winter determines what can be done in this year, this year determines what can be done in the next two years, and the first three years determine what can be done in a quinquennium. [We] should have greater confidence [in our work] with emphasis on different periods of time.

6. There must be at least four inspections per annum—once each season at the Centre and the provincial level whereas [the number of inspections] at a lower level is to be decided according to [local] conditions. Monthly inspection is necessary before an important task gets into a smooth running order. This is a method of timing over the period of a year.

7. How to review and compare? Province with province, city with city, county with county, commune with commune, factory with factory, mine with mine, and work site with work site. Agreed rules of comparison are not absolutely necessary. It is easier to review and compare agricultural [than industrial achievements]. In industries, [we] just compare what is comparable in a given line of production.

8. When to submit plans? Province, autonomous regions, cities, special regions, and counties should formulate their plans according to Points 1, 2, and 3, which must have foci of attention. They must not try to do everything at the same time. The plans of districts, villages, and communes must essentially be based on Point 3, but the items may be increased or reduced in the light of local conditions. They should draw up a five-year plan first, which may be in an outline form, to be submitted before 1 July 1958. The plans should be examined level after level. To facilitate comparison, a provincial committee should select the

best and worst from county, district, village, and commune plans and submit them to the Centre for consideration, but all provincial and special region plans should be sent up to the Centre.

9. There are three production plans: two are central plans—one must be fulfilled and this is the one to be published and the other is expected to be fulfilled but not to be published. Two are local plans—the first local plan is the second central plan which from the point of view of a locality must be fulfilled, and the other is expected to be fulfilled. The second central plan is the basis of comparison.

10. From this year onward, the party committees of provinces, cities, and autonomous regions must really get down to manufacturing industries, public and business finance, and commerce. Each year, they should review these problems four times, especially in July (or August), November, and the first ten days in January. If we refuse to come to grips with them, the slogan of 'Overtaking Britain in Fifteen Years' will be like a burst bubble. Cadres shouldering important responsibilities in industrial, financial, and commercial departments should go to local meeting places—those at the Central level should go to the regions; those at the provincial, city, and autonomous region levels should go to special regions, suburbs, and counties. This is also what the comrades at the Centre and in the regions want to do.

11. The [total] value of industrial output at a place (including those of the factories and mines taken over from the Centre and of the publicly owned industries and handicrafts which have always been managed by local authorities, but excluding those of the factories directly managed by the Centre) must within five, seven, or ten years overtake the [total] value of agricultural output of that place. All the provinces and cities must at once get down to drawing up their plans before 1 July. This is in the main to make industries serve agriculture. All of us should do some industrial work so that we know what it is all about.

12. The forty-point programme for agrarian development should be fulfilled in five, six, seven, or eight years and it should be discussed by all the provincial, city, and autonomous region party committees. In the country as a whole, it may not be possible to fulfil all the forty points in five years, but it may

be generally possible in six or seven years or more likely in eight years.

13. [We] must strive to make a basic change in the appearance of most areas in three years and the [next] three years will determine [the achievement] of the [next] decade. In the rest of the country [we] may fix a longer period [for the task]. Our slogan: Bitter struggle for three years. Our method: Arouse the masses in an entirely uninhibited manner and everything must be tried out first.

14. Oppose wastefulness. During the rectification, each unit must devote a few days to a bloom-contend-rectify-reform campaign directed against wastefulness. Every co-operative, every shop, every office, every school, and every military unit must seriously conduct its own anti-wastefulness campaign and will continue to do so once every year.

15. In our national economy, the question of an optimum ratio between [capital] accumulation and consumption is one of cardinal importance to our economic development, which should be studied by all of us.

16. What should also be studied is the question of the ratio between accumulation and consumption in the agricultural co-operatives. The views of comrades in Hupei are as follows. On the basis of the production and distribution of 1957, future increases in production should be divided 40/60 (i.e. 40 per cent to members of co-operatives and 60 per cent for co-operative accumulation), 50/50, or 60/40 (i.e. 60 per cent to members of co-operatives and 40 per cent for co-operative accumulation). At places where production and income have reached the level of wealthy middle peasants, after bloom-contend debates and after agreement has been reached among the masses, the increase in production may be either divided 30/70 (i.e. 30 per cent to the members of co-operatives and 70 per cent for co-operative accumulation) or not divided at all in one or two years in order to enlarge the accumulation in preparation for a great leap forward. All the regions are requested to discuss the adequacy of this suggestion.

17. The contradiction between collective and individual economies must be resolved by fixing an adequate ratio between them. The present situation is like this. In the income of some rural households at some places, the ratio between individual

and collective economies is 60/40 or 70/30 (i.e. income from domestic subsidiary production and the private plot makes up 60 or 70 per cent of the total income of a household). This situation inevitably affects the peasants' enthusiasm for socialist collective economy and must be altered. The provinces can find a way to control it through bloom-contend debates, and make suitable readjustment of the economic relations. On the basis of encouraging the peasants' enthusiasm in production and a comprehensive development in production, [we] must in a few years gradually change the ratio of individual and collective economies to 30/70 or 20/80 (i.e. the peasants get 70 or 80 per cent of their income from co-operatives).

18. Popularize experimental fields. This is a very important method of leadership. In this way the style of our party's leadership in the field of economy will rapidly change. In the country, the experimental fields are important; in the cities it is the advanced factories, mines, machine-tool shops, work sites, or work sections. A break-through at one point may induce the rest [of the entire system] to move.

19. Seize both ends and drag the middle along with them. This is an excellent method of leadership. Every situation has two ends—the advanced and backward extremes. Once you seize them, the middle can be dragged along with them. This is a dialectical method, too, [because] to seize the two ends, the advanced and backward extremes, is to seize a pair of opposites.

20. Two other good methods of leadership are to organize tours for cadres and the masses to see and learn from advanced experience and to organize exhibitions of good quality products and their techniques of production. These methods can raise the technological level, popularize advanced experience, and encourage competition. Many problems can be solved by an on-the-spot inspection. Communes, villages, provinces, and counties may organize tours to visit each other, while the Centre, provinces, cities, special regions, and counties may organize exhibitions of manufactures.

21. Uninterrupted revolution. Our revolutions come one after another. Starting from the seizure of power in the whole country in 1949, there followed in quick succession the anti-feudal land reform, the agricultural co-operativization, and the socialist reconstruction of private industries, commerce, and

handicrafts. The three great socialist reforms—i.e. the socialist revolution in the ownership of means of production—were basically completed in 1956 and there came the socialist revolution on the ideological and political front last year. This revolution may draw to the end of one stage by 1 July this year, but the problems [involved] are not yet solved. For a considerable period of time to come they will continue to be solved by annual bloom-contend-rectify-reform campaigns. [But] now we must start a technological revolution so that we may overtake Britain in fifteen or more years. Chinese economy is backward and China is materially weak. This is why we have been unable to take much initiative; we are spiritually restricted. We are not yet liberated in this sense. We must make a spurt [forward in production]. We may have more initiative in five years, and more still in ten. After fifteen years, when our foodstuffs and iron and steel become plentiful, we shall take a much greater initiative. Our revolutions are like battles. After a victory, we must at once put forward a new task. In this way, cadres and the masses will forever be filled with revolutionary fervour, instead of conceit. Indeed, they will have no time for conceit, even if they like to feel conceited. With new tasks on their shoulders, they are totally preoccupied with the problems for their fulfilment. The technological revolution is designed to make everyone learn technology and science. The rightists say that we are small intellectuals incapable of leading big intellectuals. Some even suggest that we 'buy' old cadres—pensioning them off, because they do not understand science and technology although they know how to fight and how to conduct land reform. We must summon up our energy to learn technology so as to accomplish the great technological revolution history has left to us [to accomplish]. This question must be discussed at a conference of cadres, to find out what other talents we have. In the past we had talents in fighting and land reform. These talents are not enough now and we must learn new things such as a real understanding of business matters, science, and technology. If we do not, we shall not be able to lead. In 'On the People's Democratic Dictatorship', which I wrote in 1949, I have said: 'The serious task of economic reconstruction lies before us. We shall soon put aside some of the things we know well. This means difficulties. . . . We must overcome difficulties. We must learn what we do not know.' Eight years have passed [since this was written]. In the eight years, one revolution followed another. They preoccupied our thoughts, thus leaving little time for us to learn science and technology. From this year onward, simultaneously with the accomplishment of the continued socialist revolution on the ideological and political front, [we] must shift the foci of attention of the whole party. Members of party committees at all levels may prepare the ground for this by explaining it to the cadres, but for the time being there is not yet the need to publicize it in the newspapers. We shall say a great deal about it after 1 July when the basic level rectification will have been more or less completed and when the party's focus of attention can be transferred to a technological revolution. With the focus on technology, [we are] apt to neglect politics. Therefore [we] must carefully combine technology with politics.

22. Red and expert, politics and business—the relationship between them is the unification of contradictions. We must criticize the apolitical attitude. [We] must oppose empty-headed 'politicoes' on the one hand and disoriented 'practicoes' on the other.

It is beyond any doubt that politics and economy, politics and technology must be unified. This must be so and will for ever be so. This is the meaning of 'red and expert'. The term, 'politics', will continue to exist, but in a different sense. To ignore ideology and politics, to be always preoccupied with business matters—the result will be a disoriented economist or technologist and that is dreadful. Ideological and political work is the guarantee for the completion of economic technological work and it serves the economic base. Ideology and politics are, moreover, the commanders, the 'soul'. A slight relaxation in our ideological and political work will lead our economic and technological work astray.

At present there is on the one hand the grave class struggle between the socialist and imperialist worlds; on the other there still exist classes and class struggle within our country. [We] must give these two aspects [of class struggles] our full consideration. In the past politics meant basically struggles against [our] class enemies. But once the people have seized political power, the relationship between the people and the government is essentially an internal relationship among the people. The method [of political struggle] to be employed is [therefore] persuasion not suppression. This is a new political relationship. This government uses various degrees of suppression only temporarily on the criminals who break the law and order of society, and used them to supplement persuasion. In the transition from capitalism to socialism, there are still anti-socialist elements hiding among the people, e.g. the bourgeois rightists. With regard to the problems of these people, our solutions are essentially the bloom-contend type of mass debate. Suppression applies only to serious counter-revolutionary saboteurs. When the transition is over and classes are eliminated, the politics of a country become purely a matter of internal relationship among the people. Even then, ideological and political struggles between men and revolutions will continue to occur; they will never cease. The laws of unification of contradictions, of quantitative to qualitative changes, and of affirmation and negation will hold good universally and eternally. However, the nature of struggles and revolutions will be different. They will not be class struggles, but struggles between advanced and backward techniques. The struggle during the transition from socialism to communism will also be a revolution. In the communist era there will be many, many phases of development. The development from one phase to another must necessarily be a relationship between quantitative and qualitative changes. All mutations, all leaps forward are revolutions which must pass through struggles. The theory of cessation of struggles is sheer metaphysics.

Political workers must have some knowledge of business matters. It may be difficult to know a lot [about them]; but it will not do to know only a little. They must know something. [Those who] have no practical knowledge are pseudo-red, empty-headed politicoes. [We] must unite politics and technology. In agriculture [this means] experimental fields and in industries it means picking out the advanced types and trying out new techniques and new products. The method to be used is comparison. Compare the advanced with the backward under identical conditions and encourage the backward to catch up with the advanced. They are the two extremes of a contradiction and comparison is the unification of them. Disequilibria exist between enterprises, machine shops, teams, and individuals. Disequilibrium is a general, objective rule. The cycle, which is endless, evolves from disequilibrium to equilibrium and then to disequilibrium again. Each cycle, however, brings us to a higher level of development. Disequilibrium is normal and absolute whereas equilibrium is temporary and relative. The changes into equilibrium or disequilibrium in our national economy consist of the process of an over-all quantitative change and many qualitative changes. After a certain number of years, China will complete a leap by transforming herself from an agrarian to an industrial country. Then she will pick up the process of her quantitative changes again.

Comparison applies not only to production and technology, but also to politics, i.e. to the art of leadership in an endeavour to find out who are better leaders.

23. The superstructure must meet the needs of the development of the economic base and productive force. A part of the superstructure is the rules and regulations formulated by government departments. Many of them, drawn up during the past eight years, are still applicable, but a considerable number of them have become obstacles to heightening the activism of the masses and the development of the productive force. The latter kind should be revised or abolished. Recently, the masses had acquired many advanced experiences, e.g. the improved workers' welfare scheme at the Shihchingshan Power Station, the improved workers' dormitory system at the Hsiangchiang Machine Manufacturing Factory, the improved bonus system at the Ch'iyeh Power Station in Kiangsu, and the amalgamation of several first-grade commercial enterprises in Kwangsi thereby reducing their employees from 2,400 to 350 (i.e. a cut of six-sevenths). In revising or abolishing irrational rules and regulations, [we] must establish a general principle—under the premiss of developing socialist enterprises according to the principles of 'more, faster, better, and more economical', of planning, and of [keeping things] to the right proportions, on the basis of raising [the standard] of understanding of the masses, [we] permit and encourage the masses to break those rules and regulations which restrict the development of the productive force.

All the departments of the Centre and the party committees of all the provinces, cities, and autonomous regions should send responsible comrades to the basic level units of all localities to sum up advanced experiences of the masses. They should develop innovations of this kind [attained] at the basic level and by the masses which are beneficial to socialist construction, recommend them to the authorities concerned for approval, stop the operation of some articles in the existing rules and regulations in these basic level units, and spread their advanced experiences to other units.

All departments of the Centre and the party committees of all the provinces, cities, and autonomous regions should in this respect systematically sum up exemplifying and mature advanced experiences. The more important and nationally significant kinds should have the approval of the Centre and the State Council; the locally significant kinds need only have the approval of the local party committees or local governments; the technically significant kinds have to have the approval of the departments concerned. Then they are popularized among similar units throughout the country or province. After a period of time, if it is necessary, old rules and regulations will be revised or new ones introduced in the light of new experiences. This is the mass-line method of formulating and revising rules and regulations.

24. The rectification must be carried through to the end. The party as a whole should summon up its energy to get rid of bureaucratism, to come to grips with reality, and to unite with the people. It must do its best to rectify the mistakes and weaknesses in its work, style, and institutions.

25. Members of the party committees of the Centre, provinces, cities, and autonomous regions, apart from the old and sick, should leave their offices for four months every year, to investigate and study at a lower level and to attend meetings at various places. They ought to adopt the methods of 'flower viewing on horse back' and 'flower viewing at a lower level'.[1] It is of some use even if [one] pays a flying visit to a place for only three or four hours. [One] must contact workers and peasants and enhance one's real understanding. Some of the conferences of the Centre may be held away from Peking; some

---

[1] 'Flower viewing on horse back' is to scan, to have a general impression of things; 'flower viewing at a lower level' is a paraphrase of this, to mean 'to have a general impression of what is going on below'.

of those of a provincial [party] committee may be held away from the capital of the province.

26. [We] must adopt an attitude of genuine equality towards cadres and the masses and make people feel that relationships among men are truly equal. [We] must make others feel that there is full and open-hearted communication. [We] must learn from Lu Hsün,[1] who communicated with his readers and evoked responses from them. People do different work and hold different jobs. No matter how high one's position is, one must appear among people as an ordinary worker. One must not assume airs; one must get rid of bureaucratism. One must patiently listen to the end [of what others say] and consider the divergent views expressed by the lower grades. One must not lose one's temper as soon as one hears an opinion different [from one's own] and take it as a personal insult. This is one way of treating people as one's equal.

27. Members of party committees at all levels, especially those responsible ones who resolutely follow the correct line of the Centre, must be prepared for criticism. If the criticism is correct, we must accept it and reform ourselves; if it is not, especially if it is foul, we must toughen the skin of our head[2] and take [whatever is showered upon us]. Then we investigate [the charges] before acting on the criticism. Under such circumstances, [we] must not bend ourselves to whichever way the wind is blowing; [we] must fearlessly stand up against the wind. We have already passed the test in 1957.

28. The party's leadership principles must be discussed at the cadre meetings of the provincial, district, and county, and perhaps also the village levels, in an attempt to make sure whether the principles are correct.

'Concentrate important powers in one hand;
Diffuse less important ones.

Decisions are to be taken by party committees
And to be carried out by all concerned.

[1] See above, pp. xx and 12–14.
[2] To receive a setback in one's career is, in a Chinese metaphor, 'to knock one's head against a nail'. Therefore one needs to toughen the skin of one's head so as to be able to sustain setbacks.

Implementation implies decision-making,
But this must not deviate from the principles.

As to inspecting work
Party committees have that responsibility.'

In these few lines, the responsibility of party committees is shown
to consist of decision-making on matters of importance and inspecting the implementation of the decisions. 'Concentrate
important powers in one hand' is an old saying which normally
means personal dictatorship. We use it to mean that essential
powers should be concentrated collectively in the hands of the
party committees of the Centre and regions, so as to combat the
diffusion of powers. How can important powers be diffused?
These eight lines were coined in 1953 with the diffusion of
powers at that time in mind. 'And to be carried out by all concerned' does not mean implementation of decisions by members
of the party alone. It means that members of the party should
get in touch and discuss and consult with others in government
organizations, in co-operatives, in independent bodies, and in
cultural and educational institutions, modify what is inadequate,
and obtain a general agreement before carrying out the decisions. The word 'principles' in the third couplet refers to the
party representing the highest form of proletarian organization,
democratic centralism, the unification of collective leadership,
and the role of the individual (i.e. the unification [of the contra-
diction] between a party committee and its first secretary), and
decision-taking at the Centre or a high level.

29. Is it necessary to consult the first secretary on everything?
No, only on important matters. There must be the second and
third in command who can take over when the first secretary is
absent.

30. Party committees must handle military affairs, placing
armed units under their supervision. Basically this remains the
situation today and this has been a good tradition of our armed
forces. Comrades engaged in military work want central and
local party committees to handle these matters. In recent years,
[however], we handled less because of our preoccupation with
social reform and economic construction. This tendency must be
averted by dealing with military matters periodically every year.

31. Meetings of large, medium, and small sizes are necessary

and should be arranged well by the departments or at various places. Small size meetings of a few or one or two dozen are better for discovering and discussing problems. Large ones of over a thousand can adopt only the method of discussion following reports and they should not be too frequent, perhaps twice a year. But there must be at least four small and medium size meetings which are better held at a low level. [For instance] a provincial [party] committee may call a meeting of the county party secretaries of a district or of several districts; members of the Centre or of the State Council may go to districts separately to call meetings there. An economic co-operative district may call a meeting whenever there are problems to discuss, at least four times a year.

32. The method of meeting must be the unification of [factual] material and views. It is a very bad method if it fails to link up material with views, to review material without any view, or to expound views without material [to substantiate them]. The worst is to present a great pile of material without either a favourable or an unfavourable view. [We] must learn to use material to explain our views. [We] must have material but [we must] also have a clear and definite view [on how] to control it. There must not be too much material, just enough to make clear our views. [We] need anatomize only one or two sparrows, not too many [so to speak]. Although [we] must have a great deal of material at our disposal, [we] present only the representative pieces. [We] must understand that to hold a meeting is not to write a *magnum opus*.

33. Generally speaking, [we] must not impose a huge pile of material and views in a matter of a few hours on those who are not familiar with them. There must be several meetings a year to make people familiar with them. There must be several meetings a year to familiarize people with business matters. [We] must give them the kind of primary and processed source materials they need. [We] must not present to them only the finished products, the conclusions, suddenly in a morning [so to speak]. [They] need a trickle not a deluge of several hundred centimetres. The system of 'compulsory instruction' must be abolished. 'Rubber stamping' must be reduced to the minimum. Perfect communication comes from sharing the necessary information in the first place.

34. The question of ten fingers. A man has ten fingers and a cadre must learn to see the differences between nine fingers and one, or the difference between a majority and minority of fingers. Nine fingers are not the same as one finger. This seems an elementary matter, but not many people understand it. Therefore we must publicize this point of view—the differences between the larger and smaller situations, general and specific [situations], and main and subsidiary trends [of development]. We must seize upon the main trend unless we want to tumble down. This is a question of understanding, of logic. It is more vivid and more suitable to our work to put it in the form of nine fingers and one finger. Unless there is a mistake in its basic line, our work depends mainly on its achievements. This view, however, does not apply to some people, e.g. the rightists. All the fingers of many extreme rightists are diseased. The majority of the ordinary rightists among students have more than one bad finger, but not all their fingers are bad. That is why they may remain at school.[1]

35. 'Attack one or a few points, exaggerate them, and ignore the rest.' This is an unpractical, metaphysical method. In 1957 the bourgeois rightists virulently attacked socialism in precisely this way. Our party had been harmed grievously by this method in its [past] history, i.e. when it was dominated by dogmatism. The [Li] Li-san line, revisionism, or rightist opportunism, the Ch'en Tu-hsiu line and Wang Ming line during the anti-Japanese war period, [all] employed this method. In 1943 [sic] Chang Kuo-t'ao used it, and in 1953 the Kao Kang–Jao Shu-shih anti-party alliance used it too. We must sum up our experience in the past and criticize this method from the point of the theory of knowledge and methodology in an attempt to awaken our cadres so that they may not be harmed by it any more. Even good people when they are wrong may unconsciously adopt this method; therefore it is necessary for them to study methodology.

36. The processes of conceptualization, judgement, and reasoning, are the processes of investigation, and study, and thinking. The human brain can reflect the objective world, although it is not easy to do so correctly. Correct reflection or the reflection which is closest to reality can be arrived at only after

[1] To undergo further training. If all the fingers of a person are bad (thoroughly evil), such a person is beyond salvation, hence useless for further training.

thinking and rethinking. Having arrived at the correct point of view and correct thought, [we] must design an adequate way of expressing them [to make them intelligible] to others. The processes of conceptualization, judgement, and reasoning are the processes 'from the people'; those of communicating one's own points of view and thoughts to others are the processes 'to the people'. This simple truth is perhaps not yet grasped by many of our cadres. However great a man may be, his thoughts, views, plans, and methods are a mere reflection of the objective world, and the raw materials and half-digested facts [for this conceptualization] come from the practice of the masses or his own scientific experiments. His mind is only a processing plant in which finished products are manufactured. Otherwise it is utterly useless. The usefulness and correctness of such finished products are tested by the popular masses. Unless our comrades understand this, they will bang their heads on a nail.[1]

37. Essays and documents must be written precisely, clearly, and in a lively [manner]. Precision is a matter of logic, of concepts, judgements, and reasoning. Clarity and liveliness are matters of both logic and rhetoric. Most essays nowadays suffer from *a*. vague conceptualization, *b*. inadequate judgement, *c*. a lack of logic in the process of using concepts and judgement in reasoning, *d*. a lack of literary merit. [As a result] reading an essay becomes an ordeal, a gigantic waste of energy for very little reward. This bad tendency must be averted. Comrades engaged in economics work must pay attention not only to precision but also to clarity and liveliness when they are drafting [something]. [They] must not think [clarity and liveliness] are [only] for language and literature teachers, not for gentlemen like themselves. Important documents must be written, not by the second or third, but by [the first in command] himself or jointly [with the others].

38. [We] must not depend on secretaries or 'back-benchers' [underlings?] entirely. [We] must do things ourselves, accepting only other people's help. The secretary system should not be allowed to become an epidemic. Wherever a secretary is unnecessary, there should not be one. To depend entirely on secretaries for everything is a symptom of the decline of revolutionary spirit.

[1] See p. 68, n. 2.

39. Learn some natural and applied sciences.

40. Learn some philosophy and political economy.

41. Learn some history and jurisprudence.

42. Learn some literature.

43. Learn some grammar and logic.

44. [I] propose that responsible comrades in the Centre, provinces, and cities voluntarily learn a foreign language, aiming at the middle school standard in five or ten years.

45. Those who are shouldering heavy responsibility at the Centre and the provincial level may each have an apprentice secretary.

46. A cadre from another place should learn the dialect of the place [where he works]; all cadres should learn the *p'u-t'ung-hua* [the standard Han-Chinese]. [We] must draw up a five-year plan, aiming at a certain [linguistic] standard. Han cadres who work in a minority area must learn the language of that minority. Likewise cadres of a minority must learn Han-Chinese.

47. All the departments of the Centre, provinces, special regions, and counties should foster *'hsiu-ts'ai'* [young people of intellectual potential]. It will not do to be without an intelligentsia. [But] the proletariat must have its own intelligentsia which knows more about Marxism and has achieved a certain cultural standard, scientific knowledge, and literary facility.

48. All secondary technical schools and schools for technicians should, if possible, experiment in setting up workshops and farms to attain complete or partial self-sufficiency by engaging in production. Students should do part-time study and part-time work. Under favourable conditions, these schools can take on more students but should not at the same time cost the country more money.

All the industrial colleges should try to set up laboratories and workshops for teaching and research and also for production. In addition, their students and teachers may sign contracts with local factories to take part in their work.

49. All agricultural schools, apart from productive work on their own farms, may sign work contracts with local agricultural co-operatives. Their teachers should be sent to the co-operatives enabling them to unite their theory with practice. Local co-operatives should recommend qualified students to study at these schools.

The middle and primary schools of a village should sign contracts with local co-operatives to take part in agricultural and subsidiary production. Rural students should make use of their summer vacation, other holidays, and leisure time to work in their own village.

50. Under favourable conditions, universities and urban middle schools may jointly set up factories or workshops and they may sign work contracts with factories, work sites, or service industries.

All universities and middle and primary schools which have land should run their own farms. Those which do not have land of their own may participate in the production work of the agricultural co-operatives on the outskirts of a city.

51. Develop a patriotic public health campaign centring on the elimination of the 'four pests', and have monthly inspections this year, so that the groundwork of [this campaign] may be laid. Other pests may be added to the list according to local conditions.

52. The Centre, provinces, and special regions may set up chemical fertilizer plants. The chemical industrial departments of the Centre ought to help the regions in designing medium or small-scale plants of this kind and the engineering departments of the Centre ought to help equip them.

53. The provinces, autonomous regions, and cities should set up farming-tool research institutes specially responsible for the improvement of tools and medium to small sized machines. They should have a close association with farming-tool factories so that once an improved tool is designed it can be given to a factory to produce.

54. In the Lien-meng commune of Hsiaokan, Hupei, some land produces 2,130 catties per *mou* in one crop a year; in the Ch'ien-chin commune of Jenshou, Szechwan, the land produces 1,680 catties per *mou* in one crop a year; in the Ch'ing-ho commune of Ichün, Shensi, some of its hilly land produces 1,650 catties per *mou*; in the Na-p'o commune of Paise, Kwangsi, some land produces 1,600 catties per *mou* in one crop a year. The experience gained by these examples of high yields in one crop should be studied and emulated by other places.

55. The problem of adequate proportions of different kinds of seeds (i.e. the sowing of several types of seed of the same crop in a given area) should be studied at various places.

56. Root-crops are extremely useful things—for human and pig consumption, for distilleries, for making sugar, and for making noodles, which may be manufactured at various places. The planting of root-crops should be popularized in conjunction with adequate planning.

57. Afforestation. Trees that can be planted at any time of the year should be planted every season; those that can be planted only in two or three seasons of the year should be planted in those seasons.

58. In the special region, Shanglo, in Shensi, every household grows a pint of walnuts. This experience is well worth studying. It may be extended to other cash crops such as fruit, mulberry, oak, tea, cashew, and oil, if the masses agree to it after a bloom-contend type of discussion.

59. Forests should be measured in terms of covered areas. The covered areas and their ratios [to the un-covered areas] in all the provinces, special regions, and counties should be measured and then the target for covered areas [at each place] can be determined.

60. Before September this year the question of my retirement from the Chairmanship of the Republic should be raised at the bloom-contend type of meetings, first among cadres of all grades and then in factories, in an attempt to sound out the views of both the cadres and the masses and to arrive at a majority agreement to it. My retirement from the Chairmanship of the Republic and concentration on [the duties] of the chairman of the party Centre will enable me to save a great deal of time in order to meet the demands of the party. This is also the way most suitable to my condition. If during discussions the masses are opposed to this proposal, it must be explained to them. Whenever the nation is urgently in need [of my services] and if the party decides [to recall me], I will shoulder this leadership task once again. Now the country is at peace, it is better for me to be relieved of the Chairmanship. This request has been agreed to and regarded as a good move by the Politburo of the Centre and by many comrades in the Centre and other places. Please explain all this clearly to cadres and the masses so as to avoid misconstruction.

*　　*　　*

The method of communication [of the results] of these conferences: These views should be explained clearly and gradually to cadres. Do not adopt the method of a 'sudden deluge'.

The views recorded here are all suggestions. Our comrades should take them back [to their respective regions] to sound out the cadres. They can be refuted or developed. They are to be drawn up as a formal document after a few months.

PART II

MAO'S INSTRUCTIONS (CHIH-SHIH)

January 1944–April 1969

EDITOR'S NOTES:

1. Most of the instructions are translated from the Chinese by the editor himself.
2. The instructions are arranged chronologically with precise dates, wherever possible, given at the beginning of each item. The dates usually agree with the dates of publication in the *JMJP* or other periodicals. They are therefore not repeated unless the dates of publication differ from the dates of issue.
3. The titles are given by the editor.
4. The square brackets in the texts indicate the editor's insertions whereas the round brackets are in the Chinese texts.

Before 1955

1. 9.1.1944 Letter to the Yenan Peking Opera Theatre after Seeing 'Driven to Join the Liangshan Mountain Rebels'[1]

Having seen your performance, I wish to express my thanks to you for the excellent work you have done. Please convey my thanks to the comrades of the cast! History is made by the people, yet the old opera (and all the old literature and art,

[1] The Peking opera 'Driven to Join the Liangshan Mountain Rebels' is an episode from *Shui Hu Chuan* ('Heroes of the Marshes', 'Water Margin', or 'All Men Are Brothers'), the fourteenth-century classical novel. It tells how Lin Ch'ung, spurred on by the strength shown by the people, resolved to join their rebellion against the reactionary rulers.

which are divorced from the people) presents the people as though they were dirt, and the stage is dominated by lords and ladies and their pampered sons and daughters. Now you have reversed this reversal of history and restored historical truth, and thus a new life is opening up for the old opera. That is why this merits congratulations. The initiative you have taken marks an epoch-making beginning in the revolutionization of the old opera. I am very happy at the thought of this. I hope you will write more plays and give more performances, and so help make this practice a common one which will prevail throughout the country.

Five Documents on Literature and Art
(Peking, FLP, 1967), pp. 1–2.

2.   20.5.1951   Give Serious Attention to the Discussion on the Film *The Life of Wu Hsün*[1]

The questions raised by the *The Life of Wu Hsün* are fundamental in character. Living in the era of the Chinese people's great struggle against foreign aggressors and the domestic reactionary feudal rulers towards the end of the Ch'ing dynasty, people like Wu Hsün did not lift a finger to disturb the tiniest fragment of the feudal economic base or its superstructure. On the contrary, they worked fanatically to spread feudal culture and, moreover, sedulously fawned upon the reactionary feudal rulers in order to acquire the status they themselves lacked for spreading feudal culture. Ought we to praise such vile conduct? Can we ever tolerate such vile conduct being praised to the masses, especially when such praise flaunts the revolutionary flag of 'serving the people' and is underlined by exploiting the failure of the revolutionary peasant struggle? To approve or tolerate such praise means to approve or tolerate reactionary

---

[1] This is an extract from an editorial written by Mao for the *JMJP*. The film was produced by Sun Yü in 1950, based on the life of Wu Hsün (1838–1896), a beggar in T'angyi, Shantung, who invested his savings from begging in free schools for poor boys. This instruction and the *JMJP* editorial were based on a personal report to Mao by his wife, Chiang Ch'ing. See Ting Wang, 'Chiang Ch'ing yü hsi-ch'ü kai-ke yun-tung,' (Chiang Ch'ing and opera reform), part 2. *Ming Pao Monthly*, Hong Kong, no. 20, pp. 61–2.

propaganda vilifying the revolutionary struggle of the peasants, the history of China, and the Chinese nation, and to regard such propaganda as justified.

The appearance of the film *The Life of Wu Hsün*, and particularly the praise lavished on Wu Hsün and the film, show the degree of ideological confusion reached in our country's cultural circles!

In the view of many writers, history has developed not by the replacement of the old by the new, but by the straining of every effort to preserve the old from extinction, not by class struggle to overthrow the reactionary feudal rulers who had to be overthrown, but by the negation of the class struggle of the oppressed and their submission to these rulers, in the manner of Wu Hsün. Our writers have not studied history to ascertain who were the enemies oppressing the Chinese people, and whether there is anything praiseworthy in those who submitted to these enemies and served them. Moreover, they have not tried to find out what new forms of social economy, new class forces, new personalities, and ideas have appeared in China and struggled against the old forms of social economy and their superstructure (politics, culture, etc.) in the century and more since the Opium War of 1840, and they have accordingly failed to determine what is to be commended and praised, what is not to be commended nor praised, and what is to be condemned.

Certain Communists who have reputedly grasped Marxism warrant particular attention. They have learnt the history of social development—historical materialism—but when they come across specific historical events, specific historical figures (like Wu Hsün) and specific ideas contrary to history (as in the film *The Life of Wu Hsün* and the writings about Wu Hsün), they lose their critical faculties, and some have even capitulated to these reactionary ideas. Is it not a fact that reactionary bourgeois ideas have found their way into the militant Communist Party? Where on earth is the Marxism which certain Communists claim to have grasped?

For the above reasons, there should be discussion on the film *The Life of Wu Hsün* and on books and essays relating to Wu Hsün so as thoroughly to straighten out the confused thinking on this question.

ibid., pp. 3–6.

3. 30.6.1953 At the Reception of the Presidium of the Second National Congress of the Youth League

I shall say a few words to [our] young people: first, I wish them well; second, I wish their study well; and third, I wish their work well.

Under the leadership of the party, the Youth League has mobilized millions of its members and united the youths of the whole country. Co-ordinating with the essential work of the party, it has made great achievements.

Young workers, peasants, students, and soldiers are brave and active, and well disciplined. Without them neither the revolution nor construction can be accomplished.

Now, since the completion of our social and democratic reform, a new epoch of construction has begun. Apart from its continued co-operation with the work assigned by the party Centre, the Youth League ought to develop its own work which is particularly suitable to the young people. New China should think on behalf of her youths, and look after her younger generation. The young people need study and work. But youth is also the time for physical development. Because of this, full attention must be given to the study and work of the young, and also their recreation, physical training, and rest.

Hsin-hua yüeh-pao, 1953, no. 8, p. 33
and *SHWS*, p. 14.

4. 16.10.1954 On the Study of 'The Red Chamber Dream'[1]

Enclosed are two articles refuting Yü P'ing-po. Please look them over. They are the first serious attack in over thirty years on the erroneous views of a so-called authoritative writer in the field of study of 'The Red Chamber Dream'. The authors are two Youth League members. First they wrote to the *Wen-yi Pao* ('Literary Gazette')[2] to ask whether it was all right to criticize

[1] 'The Red Chamber Dream' is an eighteenth-century novel by Ts'ao Hsüeh-ch'in and this instruction, in the form of a letter, was addressed to the Politburo.

[2] A theoretical journal on literature and art published by the Union of Chinese Writers.

Yü P'ing-po, but were ignored. Having no other alternative, they wrote to their teachers at their alma mater—Shantung University—and got support. Their article refuting 'A Brief Comment on "the Red Chamber Dream" ' was published in the university journal *Wen Shih Che* ('Literature, History, and Philosophy'). Then the problem came up again in Peking. Some people asked to have this article reprinted in the *JMJP* in order to arouse discussion and criticism. This was not done because certain persons opposed it for various reasons (the main one being that it was 'an article written by nobodies' and that 'the party paper is not a platform for free debate'). As a result a compromise was reached, and the article was allowed to be reprinted in the *Wen-yi Pao*. Later, the 'Literary Legacy' page of the *Kuang-ming Jih-pao* carried another article by the two young men refuting Yü P'ing-po's book, 'Studies of "the Red Chamber Dream" '. It seems likely that the struggle is about to start against the Hu Shih school of bourgeois idealism which has been poisoning young people in the field of classical literature for more than thirty years. The whole thing has been set going by two 'nobodies', while the 'big shots' usually ignore or even obstruct it, and they form a united front with bourgeois writers on the basis of idealism and become willing captives of the bourgeoisie. It was almost the same when the films *Inside Story of the Ch'ing Court* and *The Life of Wu Hsün* were shown. The film *Inside Story of the Ch'ing Court*, which has been described by certain people as patriotic but is in fact a film of national betrayal, has not been criticized and repudiated at any time since it was shown all over the country. Although *The Life of Wu Hsün* has been criticized, up to now no lessons have been drawn; what is more, we have the strange situation in which Yü P'ing-po's idealism is tolerated and lively critical essays by 'nobodies' are obstructed. This deserves our attenton.

Towards such bourgeois intellectuals as Yü P'ing-po, our attitude should naturally be one of uniting with them, but we should criticize and repudiate their erroneous ideas which poison the minds of young people and should not surrender to them.

Five Documents on Literature and Art, pp. 7–9.

1957

5. 25.5.1957 At the Reception of the Delegates to the Third
National Congress of the Youth League

You have been having a good congress. I hope you will unite
to serve as the nucleus leading the youths of our country. The
CCP is the nucleus of the country as a whole. Without it, the
socialist cause cannot prevail.

Your congress is one of unity which will have a tremendous
impact on the young people of our country. I wish you success.

Comrades, unite and fight resolutely and bravely for the
great socialist cause. All words and deeds that deviate from
socialism are utterly wrong.

Hsin-hua pan-yüeh-k'an, 1957, no. 12,
p. 57 and *SHWS*, p. 15.

1958

6. 31.1.1958 Red and Expert

Red and expert, politics and business are the unifications of
two pairs of opposites. [We] must criticize the a-political attitude. [We] must on the one hand oppose empty-headed poli-
ticos and on the other confound practical men.

There is no doubt that politics and economy, and politics and
technology should be united. It has been so in the past and will
be so for ever. This is what red and expert mean. In future, the
term 'politics' will continue to exist but in a different sense. To
pay no attention to politics and to be fully occupied with business matters is to become a perplexed economist or technician.
And that is dangerous. Ideological and political work is the
guarantee for the accomplishment of our economic and technological work; it serves the economic basis. Ideology and
politics are the commanders, the soul. A slight relaxation in our
ideological and political work will lead our economic and technological work astray.

Political workers must have some knowledge of business. It
may be difficult for them to have a lot, but it may not do for
them to have only a little. They must have some. To have no
practical knowledge is to be pseudo-red, empty-headedly poli-

tical. Politics and technology must be combined together. In agriculture, this means carrying out experiments; in industries, understanding advanced models, trying out new techniques, and producing new goods.

See above pp. 64 ff. *SHWS*, p. 17.

7. February 1958   Part-time Work and Part-time Study

If possible, all technical middle schools and technical colleges should set up workshops and farms for production so as to become self-sufficient or partly self-sufficient. Their students are to become part-time workers and part-time students. When circumstances permit, these schools may admit more students, but they must not incur additional expenses on the government.

All agricultural schools, apart from their productive work on their own farms, may sign contracts with the rural co-operatives in their locality so as to participate in the work of the co-operatives. Their teachers should be sent to the co-operatives so that theory and practice can be linked up. The co-operatives should recommend their qualified members to study at agricultural schools.

Middle and primary schools in the villages ought to arrange contracts with local agricultural co-operatives and take part in their work. School-children from rural areas should go back to their villages to work in the holidays or when they have spare time.

If conditions allow, universities and urban middle schools may set up their workshops or factories jointly or sign contracts with factories, work sites, or service trades to participate in their work.

All universities, middle, and primary schools which have land should organize their own farms; those schools without land but near rural areas may take part in the productive work of nearby agricultural co-operatives.

SHWS, p. 17.

8. March 1958   National Minorities

The Mongols and Han should co-operate closely and have faith in Marxism. All our minority nations should trust each other, no matter what nationalities they are. They must see on which side truth lies. Marx himself was a Jew; Stalin belonged to a minority nation; and Chiang Kai-shek is a Han, a bad one, whom we strongly oppose. We must not insist that only people of a given province take charge of the administration of that province. The place of origin of a man is irrelevant—northerner or southerner, this national minority or that minority, [they are all the same]. The questions are whether they have communism and how much. This point should be explained clearly to our national minorities.

To begin with, the Han was not a big race, but a mixture of a great number of races. The Han people have conquered many minority nations in history and driven them to the highlands. [We] must take a historical view of our nationality question and find out that we either depend on minority nationalism or on communism. Of course we depend on communism. We need our regions but not regionalism.

SHWS, p. 18.

9. June 1958 Atom Bombs

Let us work on atom bombs and nuclear bombs. Ten years, I think, should be quite enough.

JMJP, 18.6.1967, p. 1.

10. 13.8.1958 At the University of Tientsin

In future, schools should have factories and factories schools.

Teachers should do manual work. It will not do to move only their lips and not their hands.

Colleges should grasp three things: party committee leadership, mass line, and the co-ordination of education and production.

SHWS, p. 18.

11. 12.9.1958 At the University of Wuhan

It is a good thing that the students themselves spontaneously ask for part-time study and part-time work; this is a logical result of the campaign to build workshops at schools. More permissions should be given to this kind of request and also active encouragement and support. In school reform, notice must be paid to the development of the activism of the broad teaching staff and students and to the gathering together of the wisdom of the masses.

SHWS, p. 18.

12.   September 1958   At the Hupei Iron and Steel Works

Large-scale enterprises like the Wuhan Iron and Steel Works should be gradually built up as industrial complexes. In addition to a wide range of iron and steel products, machinery, chemical products, and building materials may be attempted. . . . In such a large-scale industrial complex, there must also be some affiliated agriculture, commerce, education, and military service.

SHWS, p. 18.

1962

13.   1962   The People and Revisionism

The peoples of all countries who form ninety per cent of their total populations will eventually want revolution, will eventually support Marxism-Leninism. They will not support revisionism. Although some of them are supporting it for the time being, they will abandon it. They will gradually wake up, fight against imperialism and the reactionaries of all countries, and oppose revisionism.

JMJP, 6.6.1968, commentator, p. 1.

1963

14.   9.1963   Operas (At a work conference of the Centre)

Operas should develop what is new from what is old, rather than what is old from what is old. They must not sing only of emperors, kings, generals, ministers, talented young gentlemen, pretty ladies, and their maids and escorts.

SHWS, p. 26.

15.   12.12.1963   Comments on Comrade K'o Ch'ing-shih's
Report[1]

This ought to be [widely] read.

Problems abound in all forms of art such as the opera, ballads, music and fine arts, the dance, the cinema, poetry, and literature, and the people involved are numerous; in many departments very little has been achieved so far in socialist transformation. The 'dead' still dominate in many departments. What has been achieved in the cinema, new poetry, folk songs, the fine arts, and the novel should not be underestimated, but there, too, quite a few problems exist. As for such departments as the opera, the problems are even more serious. The social and economic base has changed, but the arts as part of the super-structure, which serve this base, still remain a serious problem. Hence we should proceed with investigation and study and attend to this matter in earnest.

Isn't it absurd that many communists are enthusiastic about promoting feudal and capitalist art, but not socialist art?

SHWS, p. 25.

16.   13.12.1963   The Centre's Instruction on Learning from
Each Other and Overcoming Complacency
and Conceit

To be complacent and conceited; to refuse to apply Marxist dialectical, analytical method, i.e. the method of splitting one into two (both achievements and shortcomings); to work in one's own field, studying only the achievement but not the short-comings and mistakes; to like flattering but dislike critical words; to have no interest in organizing competent high and middle cadres to learn and investigate the work of other pro-vinces, cities, regions, or departments so as to link the result with one's own circumstances and improve the work of one's own province, city, region, or department; to be blindly con-ceited, i.e. to limit oneself to one's own district, the small world of one's department, the inability to widen one's scope, and the

---

[1] K'o's report is entitled, *Ta-hsieh shih-san nien* (Write prolifically on the thirteen years), 1 January 1963. Mao's comments are translated into English and pub-lished by the FLP, Peking, under the title 'Instruction on 12 December 1963' in *Five Documents on Literature and Art*, 1967, pp. 10–11.

ignorance of other spheres of work; to show and talk to foreigners, visitors from other places, and people sent by the Centre only about the achievements, not the weaknesses, in one's own area of work; to talk only superficially and perfunctorily [—these are the faults common to all our comrades]. The Centre has more than once raised this problem to our comrades: a communist must have at his disposal the Marxist dialectical method of 'splitting one into two': achievements and shortcomings, truth and mistakes. All matters (economic, political, ideological, cultural, military, party, and etc.) are always in a process of development; this is common sense to a Marxist. However, many of our comrades in the Centre and regions do not use this method of thinking and working. There is a formal logic deeply planted in their minds which they cannot uproot. Formal logic denies the unification of the opposites of things, the contradiction of opposites ('splitting one into two'), and under given conditions the transformation of one pair of opposites into another. Therefore, these comrades become complacent, conceited, observant of achievements only, blind to weaknesses, capable of hearing only favourable words but not criticisms, unwilling to criticize themselves (i.e. splitting into two), and afraid of other people's criticism. The old saying, 'Conceit courts harm while modesty is beneficial' still holds good from the point of view of the proletariat and the interest of the people.

1. Conceit grows under all circumstances and in all forms. Generally, it is likely to grow with success and victory. This is because under adverse conditions one can easily see one's own weaknesses and is comparatively more cautious. Under the pressure of difficulties, modesty and caution are the only attitudes to adopt. But with success comes the gratitude of other people. Even one-time enemies may turn round and pay tribute [to one's prowess]. One can therefore easily lose one's head in favourable circumstances following success and feel light enough to fly. 'From now on the empire will be at peace,' one believes. We are fully aware that the party is more vulnerable to attack by the virus of conceit at a time of victory and success.

2. Conceit grows under conditions of victory—i.e. the conceit of swollen-headedness and an inflated ego. This is one kind of conceit. Another kind grows under normal conditions with neither spectacular victory nor ignominious defeat, when

people intoxicate themselves with such thoughts as 'Not as good as the better but better than the worse' and 'To have served as a daughter-in-law for twenty years automatically makes one a mother-in-law.'[1]

There is a third kind which flourishes in backward conditions. Some people take pride in being backward, because they think: 'Our work is not all that good, but it is better than in the past,' or 'So and so are even x x[2] worse than us.' Whenever they want to show off their history, they make a quick switch from any other subject, their faces light up, and they begin thus: 'Once upon a time.'

3. We become conceited as soon as we overlook the strength of the masses; as soon as our subjective understanding lags behind the development of the objective reality; as soon as we overrate our own achievement.

4. Essentially, conceit is derived from individualism and nurses the growth of individualism. It is individualistic.

5. Speaking from a class analytical point of view, conceit comes first from the ideology of the exploiting class and then from that of small producers.

6. As workers, small producers have many good qualities. They are industrious, thrifty, not afraid of hardships, cautious, and realistic. But as small owners, they are individualistic and, what is more important, limited by their working conditions and methods and their use of out-dated means of production, they are scattered, narrow-minded, and ill-informed. They are often blind to the strength of the collective; they see only that of the individual. Furthermore, they are easily satisfied. A small achievement may induce them to think: 'That's not bad at all,' 'This is super,' 'Ah, let's enjoy a bit,' and 'Not as good as the better but better than the worse'.

7. Conceit is based on the bourgeois, idealist world view. It can lead people to x x,[3] to a way of dealing with reality which is against the laws of the development of reality [sic], and eventually to failure. The materialist historical view provides that the history of social development is not the history of big men,

---

[1] In the Chinese family before 1920, daughters-in-law lived under the same roof with their mothers-in-law and had to take orders from them.

[2] Crosses in original, perhaps in place of a swear word.

[3] See n. 2.

but of the labouring masses. None the less, conceited people always exaggerated the role of the individual, take [undue] credit, and become proud of themselves. They underestimate or completely overlook the strength of the masses.

8. Hence, conceit is against Marxism-Leninism, against the dialectical and historical materialist world view of our party.

9. Conceited people cannot forget their merits. They hide their own shortcomings and disregard other people's strong points. They often compare their own merits with other people's demerits, thereby drawing satisfaction. When they see the strong points of others, they say: 'Not much,' or 'Nothing to make a song and dance about.'

10. In fact, the more one overrates oneself, the worse the result is likely to be. Leo Tolstoy, the great Russian writer, put it humorously: 'A man is like a mathematical fraction, whose actual talent can be compared to a numerator and his own estimate of it to a denominator. The bigger the denominator, the smaller the fraction.'

11. Modesty is a necessary virtue for every revolutionary. It benefits the people's cause whereas conceit leads the people's cause to defeat. Therefore modesty is an expression of one's responsibility to the people's cause.

12. A revolutionary in name and practice must be able to:

First, respect the creativeness of the masses, listen to their views, and regard himself as one of the masses. He must not have a single grain of selfishness or exaggerate his own role and must work honestly for the masses. This is the spirit which Lu Hsün describes as 'Hanging my head low, I willingly serve as the young people's ox'.[1] This is modesty.

13. Second, he must have an indefatigable progressive spirit and must be forever alert and clear-minded. He must be observant of new things and consider them well. He must therefore have modesty so that he does not accredit himself with undeserved merits; nor be satisfied with his own achievements. This is a realistic attitude, the noble virtue of modesty.

14. If a man can learn seriously from work, life, and actual struggles, if he can regularly sum up his thought and action in an effort to find out his deficiencies, shortcomings, and errors, if he can ruthlessly and resolutely fight against his conceit and

[1] A line from the introductory poem to Lu Hsün's *Hua-kai Chi*.

self-satisfaction and unreservedly overcome them, it is absolutely within his power to train himself to be a man of humility.

15. A truly modest man is also a man who enthusiastically, unconditionally, loyally, and actively works for the cause of the party, the people, and the collective. He works not to show off or for awards and fame, not for any selfish desire, but whole-heartedly for the happiness and interests of the people. There-fore, he is always buried in hard work for the benefit of the party and the people, never giving a thought to his own distinction, status, reputation, or salary. He does not brag about his achieve-ments to other people; he does not even entertain such thoughts in his mind. He considers nothing more than how to serve the people better.

16. Why must a true collectivist demand humility from himself?

First, because he understands that although he plays a part in the achievement of knowledge or other results, the part the masses play is far greater. Without the help and support of the masses, he would not be able to have knowledge; nor would his work be successful. As a collectivist, he must not discount the merits of the masses, or 'rob other people of their merits'. He knows that it is shameful to be conceited.

Second, he understands that what he has learnt and done forms only a tiny drop in the ocean of revolutionary knowledge and work: it is infinitesimal. Moreover, revolutionary know-ledge and work are incessantly developing. As a collectivist, he must do his utmost to acquire the knowledge which is useful to the people and to devote his ability to the revolution. There-fore, he must feel that there is no room for complacency, for becoming stagnant.

Third, he knows that work is constructed like a huge machine with its wheels, screws, steel frames, and other parts of different sizes and shapes, each being indispensable. As a collectivist, he should respect each man's work and each man's achievement. For the perfection of the revolutionary work, he must co-ordi-nate his own work with that of others. He must feel that he cannot bear to be left out of the collective, and that he passion-ately loves his colleagues. Because of this, he must treat people with modesty, never with pride or conceit.

Fourth, he understands that the scope of an individual view

is narrow and limited, whereas the scope of revolutionary work and knowledge is broad and their contents extremely rich and complex. Thus he understands that it is inevitable for an individual to have faults and be likely to commit mistakes. These faults and mistakes often escape his full attention. Since he is a collectivist, he would demand of himself a deeper and wider vision to detect his own faults and mistakes in time and to correct them quickly, so that he can do revolutionary work well and be responsible to the people. Because of this, he is modest, humbly learns from others, and sincerely welcomes other people's criticism.

From these points [we] may see a true collectivist possesses humility, a fact that reflects his progressive spirit and realistic attitude.

17. Another method of overcoming one's conceit and nurturing one's humility is to heighten one's communist consciousness. This requires more intensive study of Marxism-Leninism. Why?

18. Because the theories of Marxism-Leninism can help us to understand scientifically the world and the relationships between individuals and the masses, individuals and collectives, individuals and organization, and individuals and the party.

[They also help us to] understand correctly the roles of the masses and individuals in revolutionary struggles. Marxism-Leninism tells us that the working people are the creators of social wealth and the mainstay in a revolutionary struggle. In order to build socialism and communism in China, we must depend on the creative power of the working class and the millions of labouring people under the leadership of their vanguard. As for an individual, he is no more than a small screw in the revolutionary works. Marxism-Leninism tells us: all achievement is the result of the strength of the collective, no individual can detach himself from a collective, and an individual, without the party to lead him or an organization and the masses to support him, cannot accomplish anything. If we do not [sic] really understand the part played by the masses and the individual in history and their mutual relationship, we automatically become modest.

Because [sic] Marxism-Leninism can raise our understanding of the future and the destination we are going to, can widen our scope, and can free our thought from parochialism. When people see only what is under their feet, not what lies above the mountains and beyond the seas, they are likely to be as boastful as 'the frog at the bottom of a well'. But when they raise their heads to see the immensity of the world, the kaleidoscope of man's affairs, the splendour and magnificence of the cause of humanity, the richness of man's talents, and the breadth of knowledge, they become modest. What we are dedicated to is a world-shaking task. We must focus not just on the work and happiness in front of our eyes, but also on the work and happiness of all of us in the distant future. Marxism-Leninism helps us to overcome the self-satisfaction of a small producer due to a small success or a small achievement. It arouses our desire for ceaseless progress. At the same time, it helps us to eliminate our idealistic subjective way of thinking.

19. Modesty and self-abasement are not synonymous. Modesty does not mean belittling oneself; it is an expression of a realistic attitude and the progressive spirit which enables one to see facts objectively, whereas self-abasement is an expression of unrealism, a lack of self-confidence, and a fear of difficulty.

Self-abasement and self-advertisement or a feeling of superiority are based on subjectivism and are wrong. They represent two extreme and erroneous subjective estimates of oneself. The boastful person detaches himself from reality and overestimates himself, exaggerates his actual ability and role. He feels superior, out of the ordinary, and therefore stops making progress or learning new things. Inevitably, he must make mistakes. The self-abasing person is apparently the opposite of the boastful, but he is just as unrealistic. He underestimates himself, forgets that he can be improved and disciplined in his work, and belittles the part he has played and will play in the revolution. Consequently, he loses his courage and confidence in making progress and relaxes his fighting spirit.

In short, both self-abasement and conceit are wrong, because both represent an erroneous assessment of one's part in the revolution, and an unrealistic and unscientific attitude. Both can do harm to the revolution. That is why we must resolutely oppose conceit and boastfulness, and also strictly distinguish modesty from self-abasement. In this way we may avoid drifting from one extreme to another.

NT, pp. 4–7.

1964

17.   13.2.1964   Spring Festival Day on Education

Chairman: 'Today I would like to discuss education with you. Since industries have made progress, I think, education should be reformed [accordingly]. It is still not good enough.'

Chairman: '[School years] may be shortened.'

Chairman: 'There may be girls' militia and women's contingents. Girls of sixteen or seventeen can spend six months or a year on military training. They can join up when they reach seventeen.'

Chairman: 'There are too many classes, doing untold harm to the students. Primary and middle school children and university students live under tremendous tension every day. The equipment and lighting are bad, and as a result there are more and more near-sighted children.'

Chairman: 'Half of the classes ought to be cut. Confucious taught only six subjects—propriety, music, archery, riding, poetry, and history (*shu*); yet he had trained such wise disciples as Yen [Hui], Tseng [Seng], Tzu [Ssu], and Meng [Mencius]. It will not do for children to have no cultural recreation, swimming, and physical exercise.'

Chairman: 'There has never been a *chuang-yüan*[1] who was a distinguished scholar. Li Pai and Tu Fu[2] were neither *chin-shih* nor *han-lin*;[3] Han Yü and Liu Tsung-yüan[4] were merely *chin-shih* of the second class; Wang Shih-fu, Kuan Han-ch'ing, Lo Kuan-chung, P'u Sung-ling, and Ts'ao Hsüeh-ch'in[5] were not *chin-shih* or *han-lin*. All *han-lin* and *chin-shih* were no good.

In the Ming dynasty, there were only two good emperors—

---

[1] The highest honour given to a successful candidate of a palace examination initiated in the T'ang dynasty.

[2] Li Pai or Li Po (705?–62) and Tu Fu (712–70) were both great poets.

[3] Successful candidates at a metropolitan examination were awarded the degree of *chin-shih*—a system initiated in the Sui dynasty (589–618). The *han-lin*, also a T'ang creation, was initially a court official, not necessarily a scholar. The *Han-lin* Academy with its staff selected from the successful candidates of metropolitan examinations was not introduced until the Ming dynasty (1368–1643) to take charge of the secretarial duties of the imperial court.

[4] Han Yü (768–824) and Liu Tsung-yüan (773–819) were celebrated essayists.

[5] Ts'ao Hsüeh-ch'in, an eighteenth-century novelist, author of 'The Red Chamber Dream'. The others were famous novelists or dramatists.

T'ai-tsu and Ch'eng-tsu,[1] one of whom was illiterate and the other semi-literate. Later, in the Chia-ching reign (1522–66), intellectuals took power and the country became misgoverned. Too much book learning does not produce good emperors; it is just harmful. Liu Hsiu was a student at the state college and Liu Pang uneducated.'[2]

Chairman: 'The present examination system is more suited for enemies, than for the people; it is like an ambush, because the questions are remote, strange, and still in the old tradition of the eight-legged essays.[3] I am against it. My suggestion is to publish the questions first, let the students study them and answer them with the help of their books. For instance, [we] set twenty questions on the 'Red Chamber Dream'.[4] If a student can answer ten of them really well with original ideas, [we] give him a hundred marks. Of course he may answer all twenty; but if his answers are ordinary without any originality, [we] give him only fifty or sixty marks.[5] At an examination, the candidates are quite free to discuss with each other and A is allowed to write B's script. If A's answer is good, B should be allowed to copy it. Discussions and impersonations at an examination used to be done covertly; now let them be done overtly. If I do not know how to answer [a question], you do it and let me copy it from you. This should work. Let us try it.

Students should be permitted to doze off when a lecturer is teaching. Instead of listening to nonsense, they do much better taking a nap to freshen themselves up. Why listen to gibberish anyway?'

Chairman: 'The present system strangles talents, destroys young people. I am not in favour of it. Too much reading. The examination system fights [the students] like enemies. It is murderous and must be stopped.'

(Then someone says: 'Students are burdened with work.

---

[1] T'ai-tsu (r. 1368–1399) and Ch'eng-tsu (r. 1403–1424).

[2] Liu Hsiu (r. 25–7), founder of the Later Han dynasty; Liu Pang (r. 206–193 B.C.), founder of the Former Han dynasty.

[3] The set style for government examinations introduced in the Ming dynasty. This stereotyped writing became an object of ridicule towards the end of the Ch'ing dynasty in the closing years of the nineteenth century.

[4] See p. 93, n. 5.

[5] 60 is the pass mark.

1
From left to right:
Mao Tse-t'an (1905–35);
Mao Tse-min (1896–1943);
Mao's mother; Mao

2 *From left to right*: Mao Tse-t'an; Mao's father; Mao's uncle; Mao

4 Mao's eldest son, An-ying (1922–50), who died in action in Korea

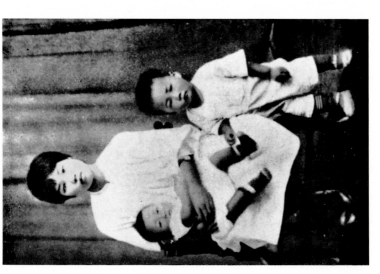

3 Mao's first wife, Yang K'ai-hui (1902–30), killed in Ch'angsha and her sons—

There is homework for every subject. [We] have three systems—Confucian, Dewey, and Russian.')

Chairman: 'Confucius did not use this system. He gave only six courses. Li Tung-yang[1] was not a *chin-shih* but he became the prime minister.'

(Then someone says: 'Last year there was a flood in Hopei during which school buildings collapsed. This made the Department of Education work intensively. Temporary schools were put up, with the result that the number of primary and middle school children increased.')

Chairman: 'The flood washed away dogmatism. Let us do away with both foreign and native dogmatisms.'

Chairman: 'Let us drive opera singers, poets, playwrights, and men of letters out of the cities, and drive all of them to the countryside. Send them down to villages and factories in groups and at different times. Do not let them stay in offices all the time; they cannot write anything there. If you do not go down, no meals will be served to you; once you go down, there will be meals.'

Chairman: 'Li Shih-chen[2] of the Ming dynasty often went to the countryside to look for herbs, Tsu Ch'ung-chih[3] had never been to any middle school or university. Confucius came from a poor family, a shepherd boy who had not been to any university. He was also a trumpeter who blew the instrument at funerals. He had been a book-keeper and knew how to play the lute, shoot arrows, ride a chariot. He came from the masses when he was young and therefore knew their sufferings. Later he became an official in the state of Lu, a big intellectual and thus cut off from the masses, probably because of Tzu-lu, his bodyguard, who kept the masses away from him. Confucius offered only six courses; *shu* might be history. [We] must not throw away the tradition of Confucius. Our orientation is correct; only our method is wrong. The

---

[1] Li Tung-yang of the Ming dynasty was in fact a *chin-shih* of the T'ien-shun reign (1457–64) who became a Grand Secretary in the Hung-chih reign (1488–1505).

[2] Li Shih-chen of the Ming dynasty was the compiler of a catalogue on medicinal herbs, the *Pen-ts'ao kang-mu*.

[3] Tsu Ch'ung-chih, a man of the Southern Ch'i dynasty who flourished at the beginning of the Sung (960–1126) and excelled in mechanical knowledge and mathematics.

present school years, syllabus, methods of teaching, and the examination system should be changed; they are all harmful.'

Chairman: 'Gorky was at school only for two years; he taught himself. Franklin of America was a newspaper boy. Watt, the discoverer of steam power, was a working man.'

(When somebody suggests: 'Before entering a university, one should do a period of work in a factory or village')—

Chairman: 'Or in the armed forces.'

Chairman: 'Now, there are too many courses and too many books; the load is too heavy. Some courses need not be examined, such as logic and grammar which can be learnt in a middle school but need not be examined. Real understanding comes gradually from actual work. It is enough just to *know* some logic and some grammar.'

(Someone says: 'There are two schools of educational thought—one insists on explaining everything thoroughly and the other on explaining the general outlines with emphasis on understanding, on how to use knowledge, but not on the amount taught. Many schools adopt the theory of explaining everything thoroughly.')

Chairman: 'That is scholasticism which is doomed to perish. Take the study of the classics for instance. So many commentaries, but they have all vanished. I think students trained in this method, be they Chinese, Americans, or Russians, will perish, will negate themselves. There were many Buddhist sutras. The result of Hsüan-tsang's textual studies was one sutra of just over 1,000 words. There were also those sutras by Chiu-mo-lo-shih[1]—very wordy. They have disappeared, however. The *Five Classics* and the *Thirteen Classics* cannot find readers any more.

One must not read too much. Books by Marx should be read, but not too many of them. A few dozen volumes will do. Too much reading will lead you to the opposite of what you expect to be, a bookworm, a dogmatist, a revisionist.

Confucius's scholarship does not include industry and

---

[1] An Indian Buddhist scholar who came to Ch'angan, the capital of the later Ch'in state, in 401 to be treated with respect and favour by the Tibetan royal court. Under its auspices, Chiu-mo-lo-shih translated many Buddhist classics into Chinese.

agriculture, hence "the four limbs are not laboured and the five kinds of cereals unrecognized."[1] This must be remedied.'

SHWS, pp. 26–8.

18. 10.3.1964 Courses and Examinations

There are too many courses offered at schools [and universities] which place a heavy burden on students. They are not often properly taught. The examination system treats students like enemies; it pounces on them suddenly. These are detrimental to the development, in a lively and spontaneous manner, of the moral, intellectual, and physical capabilities of the young people.

SHWS, p. 28.

19. 27.6.1964 Literature and Art

In the last fifteen years these associations,[2] most of their publications (it is said that a few are good), and *by and large* the people in them (that is, not everybody) have not carried out the policies of the party. They have acted as high and mighty bureaucrats, have not gone to the workers, peasants, and soldiers, and have not reflected the socialist revolution and socialist construction. *In recent years*, they slid right down to the brink of revisionism. Unless they remould themselves in real earnest, at some future date they are bound to become groups like the Hungarian Petöfi Club.

JMJP, 28.5.1967
and *Five Documents on Literature and Art*, p. 11.

20. August 1964 Comments on the Report of the Public Showing and Criticism of the Films— 'South China in the North' (*Pei-kuo Chiang-*

---

[1] In the last chapter of Confucius's *Analects*, there are many stories of the master being questioned, criticized, and embarrassed, one of which is the criticism referred to here by Mao. The authenticity of this chapter is open to doubt and meticulous scholars do not normally take it seriously. It is a forgery of a later date.

[2] These are mass organizations in the field of literature and art.

nan) and 'Early Spring in the Second
Month' (*Tsao-ch'un Erh-yüeh*)—by the Department of Propaganda of the Centre.

There may not be only these two films [of this kind]. Others
should be criticized also, so that revisionist material is made
known to the public.

SHWS, p. 26.

21.   Date uncertain, 1964   Notes on the Directive of Strengthening Political Work by Learning
from the PLA

Now the whole country is learning from the PLA and the
Tach'ing [Oilfield] and schools too should learn from the PLA.
What the PLA excels in is the field of political ideology. It is
also necessary to learn from the advanced units in the cities,
agriculture, industries, commerce, and education, throughout
the country.

There are people who suggest that the industrial departments
at all levels (from the Departments to the factories and communes) throughout the country should learn from the PLA by
setting up political departments and political bureaux and
appointing political commissars, and by adopting the 'four
firsts'[1] and the 'three-eight style'.[2] It seems that this is the only
way to arouse the revolutionary spirit of millions of cadres and
workers in the industrial (as well as agricultural and commercial) departments.

SHWS, p. 30.

1965

22.   January 1965   Talk at the National Work Conference of
the Politburo

During the transitional period, there exist class struggle, the
conflict between the proletariat and bourgeoisie, and the con-

[1] The 'four firsts' are: in man's relationship with his weapons, man comes first;
in all activities, political activities come first; in political work, ideological work
comes first; in ideological work, creative study comes first.

[2] The 'three-eight style' of the PLA: three phrases, correct political orientation;
plain, hard-working style; flexible strategy and tactics. Eight characters: unity,
alertness, earnestness, and liveliness.

flict between the socialist and capitalist roads. If we forget this fundamental theory and practice of our party, we may go astray.

JMJP, 3.10.1966, p. 1
and *RF* editorial, 1966, no. 13.

23. January 1965   Comment on the Article—'How to Play
Table Tennis' by Comrade Hsü Yin-sheng

Comrade Hsü Yin-sheng's talk and Comrade Ho Lung's comment should be printed and circulated among the comrades in the Centre, who, I hope, will have more of this kind of thing printed and distributed when they go back to their regions. Comrades, this is the young 'generals' challenge to us, the old ones! Should we refuse to learn anything from them? The talk is full of dialectical materialism and is throughout opposed to idealism and metaphysics. [I] have not read anything so good for years. What he [Hsü] talks about is a ball game; what we can learn from it are theory, politics, economy, culture, and military affairs. If we do not learn from the young 'generals', we shall be doomed.

SHWS, p. 31.

24. 29.1.1965   Notes on Comrade Ch'en Cheng-jen's Report
on his 'Squatting Point'[1]

Management is a form of socialist education. If the managerial staff do not go to the lathe shop to work on the 'three sames'[2] and to look for teachers from whom they may learn one or two crafts, then they will live in a state of class conflict with the workers. In the end they will be knocked down like capitalists by the workers. They cannot manage well, if they do not learn and remain ignorant of any productive skill. It is impossible to make other people understand, if they themselves are confused.

[1] Ch'en is an old comrade of Mao, who worked with him in the land reform, Kiangsi, 1930–1 and his 'squatting point' sounds like a factory where he stayed and worked. He was 'sent down' (*hsia-fang*), but not as a form of punishment.
[2] Same food, same accommodation, and same work.

The bureaucrats and the workers and the middle-poor peasants are acutely antagonistic classes.

Such people [the bureaucrats] are already or are becoming capitalist vampires to the workers. How can they have sufficient understanding? They are the objects of struggle and revolution; socialist education cannot depend on them. We can only rely on those cadres who are not hostile to the workers and are imbued with revolutionary spirit.

SHWS, p. 31.

25. June 1965 Public Health

Tell the Department of Public Health that it serves only fifty per cent of the population of the country. These fifty per cent consist of gentlemen; the broad peasant masses have no medical care—neither doctors nor medicine. The Department of Public Health does not belong to the people; it should be re-named the Department of Urban Public Health, Gentlemen's Public Health, or City Gentlemen's Public Health. Medical education should be reformed, because there is no need to read so many books. How many years had Hua T'o[1] studied? How many had Li Shih-chen of the Ming dynasty studied? Medical schools do not have to admit only senior middle-school graduates; it is quite proper to take in third-year children from junior schools. The main point is to raise their standard during practice. The physicians trained this way may not be very competent, but far better than fake doctors and witch doctors. Furthermore, villages can afford them. More study only makes them stupid. The methods of check-up and treatment used in our hospitals now are quite unsuitable for the countryside; they are mainly for the cities. But China has more than 500 million peasants!

To allocate a great deal of manpower and resources to the study of difficult illnesses and to carry out penetrating research is to aim at the peaks, to detach [medical work] from the masses. The result is to ignore or to assign only small amounts of manpower and resources to the prevention or cure of common, frequent, widespread diseases. 'Peaks' are not being

[1] A famous surgeon who flourished in the first half of the third century.

abandoned, but they are going to receive less manpower and resources. The lion's share of manpower and equipment should be allocated to tackling the problems most urgently demanded by the masses.

There is another curious thing. When a doctor examines a patient, he always covers his mouth with a gauze mask, whatever the patient's illness. Is he afraid of passing germs to his patient? I think he is more likely to be afraid of his patient passing germs to him. He must make a difference here [between the patients with infectious diseases and those without]. To wear a mask under all circumstances is to build a barrier between him and his patients.

City hospitals should keep [also] some doctors who have graduated after one or two years and are not very good. The others should all work in the villages. The 'four purifies' ended in 19xx,[1] basically completed. Their completion does not mean the completion of public health and medical work in the villages. Indeed the focus of medical and public health work should be transferred to the villages.

NT, p. 9.

26.   3.7.1965   Notes on the Report of the Investigation of the Peking Teachers' Training College

Students are heavily loaded [with work] and their health suffers. Their study therefore becomes useless. [I] suggest a cut of one third of their total activities [work]. Please ask representatives of staff and students to discuss this problem a few times, take decisions, and carry them out. Please consider whether this is feasible.

The next few decades will be precious and important for the future of our country and the destiny of mankind. The twenty-year-olds [of today] will be forty or fifty in twenty or thirty years' time. This generation of young people will take part in building our 'poor and bare' country into a great strong socialist

---

[1] Purify politics, organization, ideology, and economy. This campaign was basically completed in 1964.

power and will fight and bury imperialism with their own hands. The task is arduous and the road long. Chinese young people of lofty ambitions must dedicate their lives to the accomplishment of our great historic mission! And for this, people of our generation must determine to fight hard for the rest of their lives!

Politics must follow the mass line. It will not do to rely on leaders alone. How can the leaders do so much? The leaders can cope with only a fraction of everything, good and bad. Consequently, everybody must be mobilized to share the responsibility, to speak up, to encourage other people, and to criticize other people. Everyone has a pair of eyes and a mouth and he must be allowed to see and speak up. Democracy means allowing the masses to manage their own affairs. Here are two ways: one is to depend on a few individuals and the other is to mobilize the masses to manage affairs. Our politics is mass politics. Democratic rule is the rule of all, not the rule of a few. Everyone must be urged to open his mouth. He has a mouth, therefore he has two responsibilities—to eat and to speak. He must speak up wherever he sees bad things or bad styles of work. He must follow his duty to fight.

Nothing can be done well, if it depends entirely on the leader not on the leadership of the party. [We] must rely on the party and [our] comrades to deal with matters, not on a solitary leader. An active leader followed by inactive masses will not do; it must be established as a practice that the masses use both their hands and their mouths. The only way to have things done well is to depend on the leadership of the party from above and [the support of] the masses from below.

SHWS, p. 30.

27. September 1965 Talk at a Work Conference of the Centre

If revisionism appears in the Centre, what are you going to do? It is probable that [revisionism] will appear [in the Centre] and this is a great danger.

RF, 1967, no. 13, p. 16.

28. 9.12.1965 Broadcasting

Use the broadcasting service well, for the peoples of China and the world.

JMJP, p. 1.

1966

29. 11.2.1966 The Intelligence of the People

It is to the advantage of despots to keep people ignorant; it is to our advantage to make them intelligent. We must lead all of them gradually away from ignorance.

RF, 1966, no. 2, p. 18.

30. end of March, 1966 Down with the Demon King

Down with the Demon King; liberate little devils.

JMJP, 13.8.1967, p. 2.

31. 7.5.1966 The May the Seventh Instruction (or Notes on the Report of Further Improving the Army's Agricultural Work by the Rear Service Department of the Military Commission)

Dear Comrade Lin Piao,

I have received the report from the Rear Service Department which you sent me on 6 May. I think it is an excellent plan. Is it possible to send this report to all the military districts and ask them to hold discussions of it among the cadres at the army and division levels? Their views should be reported to the Military Commission and through it to the Centre for approval. After that, suitable directives should be issued to them. Please consider this [suggestion].

In the absence of a world war, our army should be a big school. Even under conditions of the third world war, it can still serve as a big school. In addition to fighting the war, it must

103

do other work. In the eight years of the second world war, did we not do just that in the anti-Japanese base areas? In this big school, the army should learn politics, military affairs, and culture, and engage in agricultural production. It can build up its own middle- and small-size work-shops to produce goods for its own use and the exchange of other goods of equal value. It can take part in mass work, factory work, and rural socialist education. After socialist education, there are always other kinds of mass work for it to do, to unite the army and people as one. The army should also participate in the revolutionary struggle against capitalist culture. In this way, it carries out military-educational, military-agricultural, military-industrial, and military-civilian work. Naturally, [these kinds of work] should be properly co-ordinated and a distinction should be made between major and subsidiary work. A unit can select one or two from the agricultural, industrial, and civilian combination, but not all three. In this way, the tremendous power of several million soldiers will be felt.

Likewise, workers should, in addition to their main industrial work, learn military affairs, politics, and culture, and take part in the socialist educational movement and in criticizing the capitalist class. Under adequate conditions, they should also engage in agricultural production, following the example of the Tach'ing Oilfield.

The communes do their main agricultural work (including forestry, fishing, animal husbandry, and subsidiary trades), but they must also learn military affairs, politics, and culture. When circumstances allow, they should collectively set up small-scale factories and take part in criticizing the capitalist class.

The students are in a similar position. Their studies are their chief work; they must also learn other things. In other words, they ought to learn industrial, agricultural, and military work in addition to class work. The school years should be shortened, education should be revolutionized, and the domination of our schools by bourgeois intellectuals should by no means be allowed to continue.

Under favourable conditions, people in commerce, service trades, and party and government offices should do likewise.

What has been said above is neither new nor original. Many people have been doing this for some time, but it has not yet become a widespread [phenomenon]. Our army has been working in this way for decades. Now it is on the threshold of new developments.

SHWS, pp. 34–5;
fragments of it reported in *JMJP* editorials,
1 and 2.8.1966 and 27.10.1967 and 19.11.1967.
See also BBC 1, FE/2627/B10.

32.   16.5.1966   Circular of Central Committee of CCP

To all regional bureaux of the Central Committee, all provincial, municipal and autonomous regional party committees, all departments and commissions under the Central Committee, all leading party members' groups and party committees in government departments and people's organizations, and the General Political Department of the PLA:

The Central Committee has decided to revoke the 'Outline Report on the Current Academic Discussion made by the Group of Five in Charge of the Cultural Revolution' which was approved for distribution on 12 February 1966, to dissolve the 'Group of Five in Charge of the Cultural Revolution' and its offices, and to set up a new Cultural Revolution group directly under the Standing Committee of the Political Bureau. The outline report by the so-called 'Group of Five' is fundamentally wrong. It runs counter to the line of the socialist cultural revolution set forth by the Central Committee and Comrade Mao Tse-tung and to the guiding principles formulated at the Tenth Plenary Session of the Eighth Central Committee of the party in 1962 on the question of classes and class struggle in socialist society. While feigning compliance, the outline actually opposes and stubbornly resists the great Cultural Revolution initiated and led personally by Comrade Mao Tse-tung, as well as the instructions, regarding the criticism of Wu Han, which he gave at the work conference of the Central Committee held in September and October 1965 (that is, at the session of the Standing Committee attended also by the leading comrades of all the regional bureaux of the Central Committee).

The outline report by the so-called 'Group of Five' is actually an outline report by P'eng Chen alone. He concocted it according to his own ideas behind the backs of Comrade K'ang Sheng, a member of the 'Group of Five', and other comrades. In handling such a document regarding important questions which affect the over-all situation in the socialist revolution, P'eng Chen had no discussions or exchange of views at all within the 'Group of Five'. He did not ask any local party committee for its opinion; nor, when submitting the outline report, did he make it clear that it was being sent to the Central Committee for examination as its official document, and still less did he get the approval of Comrade Mao Tse-tung, Chairman of the Central Committee. Employing the most improper methods, he acted arbitrarily, abused his powers, and, usurping the name of the Central Committee, hurriedly issued the outline report to the whole party.

The main errors of the outline report are as follows:

1. Proceeding from a bourgeois stand and the bourgeois world outlook in its appraisal of the situation and the nature of the current academic criticism, the outline completely reverses the relation between the enemy and ourselves, putting the one into the position of the other. Our country is now in an upsurge of the great proletarian Cultural Revolution which is pounding at all the decadent ideological and cultural positions still held by the bourgeoisie and the remnants of feudalism. Instead of encouraging the entire party boldly to arouse the broad masses of workers, peasants, and soldiers, and the fighters for proletarian culture so that they can continue to charge ahead, the outline does its best to turn the movement to the right. Using muddled, self-contradictory, and hypocritical language, it obscures the sharp class struggle that is taking place on the cultural and ideological front. In particular, it obscures the aim of this great struggle, which is to criticize and repudiate Wu Han and the considerable number of other anti-party and anti-socialist representatives of the bourgeoisie (there are a number of these in the Central Committee and in the party, government, and other departments at the central as well as at the provincial, municipal, and autonomous region level). By avoiding any mention of the fact repeatedly pointed out by Chairman Mao, namely, that the key point in Wu Han's drama *Hai Jui Dismissed from Office* is the question of dismissal from office, the outline covers up the serious political nature of the struggle.

2. The outline violates the basic Marxist thesis that all class struggles are political struggles. When the press began to touch on the political issues involved in Wu Han's *Hai Jui Dismissed from Office*, the authors of the outline went so far as to say: 'The discussion in the press should not be confined to political questions, but should go fully into the various academic and theoretical questions involved.' Regarding the criticism of Wu Han, they declared on various occasions that it was impermissible to deal with the heart of the matter, namely, the dismissal of the right opportunists at the Lushan plenum in 1959 and the opposition of Wu Han and others to the party and socialism. Comrade Mao Tse-tung has often told us that the ideological struggle against the bourgeoisie is a protracted class struggle which cannot be resolved by drawing hasty political conclusions. However, P'eng Chen deliberately spread rumours, telling many people that Chairman Mao believed political conclusions on the criticism of Wu Han could be drawn after two months. P'eng Chen also said that the political issues could be discussed two months later. His purpose was to channel the political struggle in the cultural sphere into the so-called pure academic discussion so frequently advocated by the bourgeois politics and opposing giving prominence to proletarian politics.

3. The outline lays special emphasis on what it calls 'opening wide'. But, playing a sly trick it grossly distorts the policy of 'opening wide' expounded by Comrade Mao Tse-tung at the party's National Conference on Propaganda Work in March 1957 and negates the class content of 'opening wide'. It was in dealing with this question that Comrade Mao Tse-tung pointed out: 'We still have to wage a protracted struggle against bourgeois and petty-bourgeois ideology. It is wrong not to understand this and to give up ideological struggle. All erroneous ideas, all poisonous weeds, all ghosts and monsters, must be subjected to criticism; in no circumstance should they be allowed to spread unchecked.' Comrade Mao Tse-tung also said, 'To "open wide" means to let all people express their opinions freely, so that they dare to speak, dare to criticize, and dare to debate.' This outline, however, poses 'opening wide' against exposure by the proletariat of the bourgeoisie's reactionary stand. What it means by 'opening wide' is bourgeois liberalization, which would allow only the bourgeoisie to 'open wide', but

would not allow the proletariat to 'open wide' and hit back; in other words, it is a shield for such reactionary bourgeois representatives as Wu Han. The 'opening wide' in this outline is against Mao Tse-tung's thought and caters for the needs of the bourgeoisie.

4. Just when we began the counter-offensive against the wild attacks of the bourgeoisie, the authors of the outline raised the slogan: 'everyone is equal before the truth'. This is a bourgeois slogan. Completely negating the class nature of truth, they use this slogan to protect the bourgeoisie and oppose the proletariat, oppose Marxism-Leninism, and oppose Mao Tse-tung's thought. In the struggle between the proletariat and the bourgeoisie, between the truth of Marxism and the fallacies of the bourgeoisie and all other exploiting classes, either the East wind prevails over the West wind or the West wind prevails over the East wind, and there is absolutely no such thing as equality. Can any equality be permitted on such basic questions as the struggle of the proletariat against the bourgeoisie, the dictatorship of the proletariat over the bourgeoisie, the dictatorship of the proletariat in the superstructure, including all the various spheres of culture, and the continued efforts of the proletariat to weed out those representatives of the bourgeoisie who have sneaked into the communist party and who wave 'red flags' to oppose the red flag? For decades the old-line Social Democrats, and for over ten years the modern revisionists, have never allowed the proletariat equality with the bourgeoisie. They completely deny that the several thousand years of human history is a history of class struggle. They completely deny the class struggle of the proletariat against the bourgeoisie, the proletarian revolution against the bourgeoisie, and the dictatorship of the proletariat over the bourgeoisie. On the contrary, they are faithful lackeys of the bourgeoisie and imperialism. Together with the bourgeoisie and imperialism, they cling to the bourgeois ideology of oppression and exploitation of the proletariat and to the capitalist system, and they oppose Marxist-Leninist ideology and the socialist system. They are a bunch of counter-revolutionaries opposing the communist party and the people. Their struggle against us is one of life and death, and there is no question of equality. Therefore, our struggle against them, too, can be nothing but a life-and-death struggle, and our

relation with them can in no way be one of equality. On the contrary, it is a relation of one class oppressing another, that is, the dictatorship of the proletariat over the bourgeoisie. There can be no other type of relation, such as a so-called relation of equality, or of peaceful coexistence between exploiting and exploited classes, or of kindness or magnanimity.

5. The outline states: 'It is necessary not only to beat the other side politically, but also, by academic and professional standards, truly surpass and beat it by a wide margin.' This concept which makes no class distinction on academic matters is also very wrong. The truth on academic questions, the truth of Marxism-Leninism, of Mao Tse-tung's thought—which the proletariat has grasped—has already far surpassed and beaten the bourgeoisie. The formulation in the outline shows that its authors laud the so-called academic authorities of the bourgeoisie and try to boost their prestige, and that they hate and repress the militant new-born forces representative of the proletariat in academic circles.

6. Chairman Mao often says that there is no construction without destruction. Destruction means criticism and repudiation; it means revolution. It involves reasoning things out, which is construction. Put destruction first, and in the process you have construction. Marxism-Leninism, Mao Tse-tung's thought, was founded and has constantly developed in the course of the struggle to destroy bourgeois ideology. This outline, however, emphasizes that 'without construction, there can be no real and thorough destruction'. This amounts to prohibiting the destruction of bourgeois ideology and prohibiting the construction of proletarian ideology. It is diametrically opposed to Chairman Mao's thought. It runs counter to the revolutionary struggle we have been waging on the cultural front for the vigorous destruction of bourgeois ideology. And it amounts to prohibiting the proletariat from making any revolution.

7. The outline states that 'we must not behave like scholar-tyrants who are always acting arbitrarily and trying to overwhelm people with their power' and that 'we should guard against any tendency for academic workers of the left to take the road of bourgeois experts and scholar-tyrants'. What is really meant by 'scholar-tyrants'? Who are the 'scholar-tyrants'?

Should the proletariat not exercise dictatorship and overwhelm the bourgeoisie? Should the academic work of the proletariat not overwhelm and eradicate that of the bourgeoisie? And if proletarian academic work overwhelms and eradicates bourgeois academic work, can this be regarded as an act of 'scholar-tyrants'? The outline directs its spearhead against the proletarian left. Obviously, its aim is to label the Marxist-Leninists 'scholar-tyrants' and thus to support the real, bourgeois scholar-tyrants and prop up their tottering monopoly position in academic circles. As a matter of fact, those party people in authority taking the capitalist road who support the bourgeois scholar-tyrants, and those bourgeois representatives who have sneaked into the party and protect the bourgeois scholar-tyrants, are indeed big party tyrants who have usurped the name of the party, have no contact with the masses, have no learning at all, and rely solely on 'acting arbitrarily and trying to overwhelm people with their power'.

8. For their own ulterior purposes, the authors of the outline demand a 'rectification campaign' against the staunch left in a deliberate effort to create confusion, blur class alignments and divert people from the target of struggle. Their main purpose in dishing up the outline in such a hurry was to attack the proletarian left. They have gone out of their way to build up dossiers about the left, tried to find all sorts of pretexts for attacking them, and intended to launch further attacks on them by means of a 'rectification campaign,' in the vain hope of disintegrating their ranks. They openly resist the policy explicitly put forward by Chairman Mao of protecting and supporting the left and giving serious attention to building up and expanding their ranks. On the other hand, they have conferred on those bourgeois representatives, revisionists, and renegades who have sneaked into the party the title of 'staunch left', and are shielding them. In these ways, they are trying to inflate the arrogance of the bourgeois rightists and to dampen the spirits of the proletarian left. They are filled with hatred for the proletariat and love for the bourgeoisie. Such is the bourgeois concept of brotherhood held by the authors of the outline.

9. At a time when the new and fierce struggle of the proletariat against the representatives of the bourgeoisie on the ideological front has only just begun, and in many spheres and

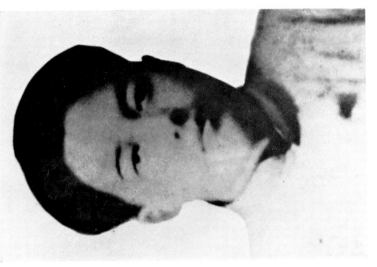

6 Mao Tse-t'an who was killed in action, east of Juichin, Kiangsi

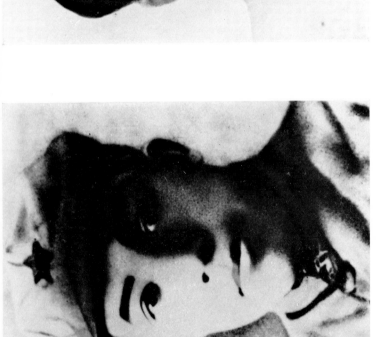

5 Mao Tse-min who was killed in Urumchi, Sinkiang

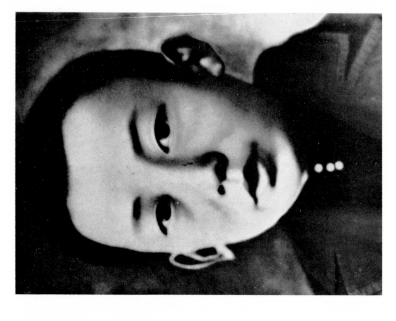

8 Mao Ch'u-hsiung (1927–46), Mao Tse-t'an's son

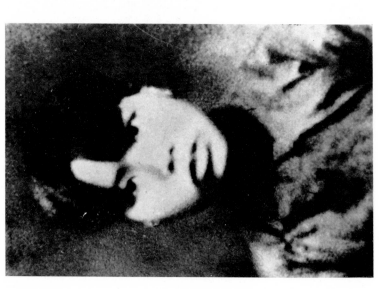

7 Mao Tse-chien (1905–29), Mao's cousin, who was killed in Hengshan

places has not even started—or, if it has started, most party committees concerned have a very poor understanding of the task of leadership in this great struggle and their leadership is far from conscientious and effective—the outline stresses again and again that the struggle must be conducted 'under direction', 'with prudence', 'with caution', and 'with the approval of the leading bodies concerned'. All this serves to place restrictions on the proletarian left, to impose taboos and commandments in order to tie their hands, and to place all sorts of obstacles in the way of the proletarian cultural revolution. In a word, the authors of the outline are rushing to apply the brakes and launch a counter-attack in revenge. As for the articles written by the proletarian left refuting the reactionary bourgeois 'authorities', they nurse bitter hatred against those already published and are suppressing those not yet published. But on the other hand, they give free rein to all the various ghosts and monsters who for many years have abounded in our press, radio, magazines, books, text-books, platforms, works of literature, cinema, drama, ballads and stories, the fine arts, music, the dance, etc., and in doing so they never advocate proletarian leadership or stress any need for approval. The contrast here shows where the authors of the outline really stand.

10. The present struggle centres on the issue of implementation of, or resistance to, Comrade Mao Tse-tung's line on the Cultural Revolution. Yet the outline states: 'Through this struggle, and under the guidance of Mao Tse-tung's thought, we shall open up the way for the solution of this problem (that is, "the thorough liquidation of bourgeois ideas in the realm of academic work").' Comrade Mao Tse-tung upened up the way for the proletariat on the cultural and ideological front long ago, in his *On New Democracy, Talks at the Yenan Forum on Literature and Art, Letter to the Yenan Peking Opera Theatre after Seeing the Performance of* 'Driven to Join the Liangshan Rebels', *On the Correct Handling of Contradictions among the People,* and *Speech at the Chinese Communist Party's National Conference on Propaganda Work.* Yet the outline maintains that Mao Tse-tung's thought has not yet opened up the way for us and that the way has to be opened up anew. Using the banner of 'under the guidance of Mao Tse-tung's thought' as cover, the outline actually attempts to open up a way opposed to Mao Tse-tung's thought, that is the

way of modern revisionism, the way for the restoration of capitalism.

In short, the outline opposes carrying the socialist revolution through to the end, opposes the line on the Cultural Revolution pursued by the Central Committee of the party headed by Comrade Mao Tse-tung, attacks the proletarian left and shields the bourgeois right, thereby preparing public opinion for the restoration of capitalism. It is a reflection of bourgeois ideology in the party; it is out-and-out revisionism. Far from being a minor issue, the struggle against this revisionist line is an issue of prime importance having a vital bearing on the destiny and future of our party and state, on the future complexion of our party and state, and on the world revolution.

Party committees at all levels must immediately stop carrying out the 'Outline Report on the Current Academic Discussion made by the Group of Five in Charge of the Cultural Revolution'. The whole party must follow Comrade Mao Tse-tung's instructions, hold high the great banner of the proletarian Cultural Revolution, thoroughly expose the reactionary bourgeois stand of those so-called 'academic authorities' who oppose the party and socialism, thoroughly criticize and repudiate the reactionary bourgeois ideas in the sphere of academic work, education, journalism, literature and art, and publishing, and seize the leadership in these cultural spheres. To achieve this, it is necessary at the same time to criticize and repudiate those representatives of the bourgeoisie who have sneaked into the party, the government, the army, and all spheres of culture, to clear them out or transfer some of them to other positions. Above all, we must not entrust these people with the work of leading the Cultural Revolution. In fact many of them have done and are still doing such work, and this is extremely dangerous.

Those representatives of the bourgeoisie who have sneaked into the party, the government, the army, and various cultural circles are a bunch of counter-revolutionary revisionists. Once conditions are ripe, they will seize political power and turn the dictatorship of the proletariat into a dictatorship of the bourgeoisie. Some of them we have already seen through, others we have not. Some are still trusted by us and are being trained as our successors, persons like Khrushchev, for example, who are still nestling beside us. Party committees at all levels must pay full attention to this matter.

This circular is to be sent, together with the erroneous document issued by the Central Committee on 12 February 1966, down to the level of county party committees, party committees in the cultural organizations, and party committees at regimental level in the army. These committees are asked to discuss which of the two documents is wrong and which is correct, their understanding of these documents, and their achievements and mistakes.

JMJP, 17.5.1967 and *RF*, 1967, no. 7.
This translation is taken from *PR*,
1967, no. 21, pp. 6–9.

33. 1.6.1966 The Big-character Poster at Peking University

This big-character poster at Peking University is a Marxist-Leninist one which should be at once broadcast and published in the newspapers.

Reported by K'ang Sheng on 8.9.1966,
NT, p. 15.

34. 2.6.1966 The Objective Existence of Class Struggle

Wind will not cease even if trees want to rest.

JMJP editorial, p. 1.

35. 8.6.1966 Construction and Destruction

Without destruction there can be no construction; without blockage there can be no flow; without stoppage there can be no movement.

JMJP editorial, p. 1.

36. 17.6.1966 The Exploiting and Exploited

The exploiters and reactionaries are, under any circumstance, the minority while the exploited and revolutionaries are

the majority. Therefore the dictatorship of the former is un-
justifiable, whereas that of the latter is fully justifiable.

JMJP, p. 3.

37. 26.6.1966 Comments on the Seven Good Examples of
the Manual Work of Chekiang Cadres

Class struggle, productive struggle, and scientific experiment
are three great revolutionary movements for the construction of
a great socialist country, the safeguard for a communist against
bureaucratism, revisionism, and dogmatism so that he can be
ever victorious, and the dependable guarantee for the proletariat to unite with other broad working masses to carry out
democratic dictatorship.

JMJP, p. 1.

38. 3.7.1966 Rely on the Left-wing Forces

In the great proletarian Cultural Revolution, it is imperative
to organize and enlarge proletarian left-wing forces, depending
on them to arouse, unite, and educate the masses.

JMJP, p. 1 and *RF*, 1966, no. 9.

39. 25.7.1966 The June 18th Incident in Peking[1]

The June 18th Incident was not counter-revolutionary, but
revolutionary.

Chiang Ch'ing's talk at Peking University,
25.7.1966, NT, p. 15.

40. 26.7.1966 Tidal Waves of Revolution

No need to be afraid of tidal waves; human society has been
evolved out of 'tidal waves'.

JMJP editorial, p. 1.

[1] The 'incident' refers to the fight between the students of Peking University
and the work team.

41. 26.7.1966 Swimming

Swimming has its rules. It is easy to learn once you know the rules.

ibid.

42. 29.7.1966 His Wish

My wish is to join all the comrades of our party to learn from the masses, to continue to be a school-boy.

JMJP editorial, p. 1.

43. 30.7.1966 Contradictions

Even the transformation from a quantitative to a qualitative change and the negation of negation are both unifications of contradictions. However you argue, they are still struggles of opposites. Dialectics can be made monistic, never pluralistic. Nature and society are full of contradictions. As soon as a contradiction is resolved, a new one emerges. There is no world or society without contradictions. Sometimes we may not be able to name a specific contradiction, but it exists all the same. Contradictions are the motivating force of the development of everything. This has been so in the past, is so at present, and will be so in future.

Reported by Ch'en Po-ta, 30.7.1966, NT, p. 16.

44. 1.8.1966 Letter to Red Guards

The action of the Red Guards expresses their indignation at, and accusation of the exploitation and oppression of the workers, peasants, revolutionary intellectuals, and revolutionary parties by the landlords, capitalists, imperialists, revisionists, and their lackeys. It fully justifies any rebellion against the reactionaries. I am firmly behind you.

We support you; we also ask you to unite with all those with whom you can unite. As for those who have made serious mistakes, you should give them work and let them rectify their mistakes, having pointed out their mistakes to them. Marx says: 'The proletariat should emancipate not only itself but also mankind as a whole. Its failure to emancipate mankind will eventually prevent it from emancipating itself.' I would like to draw your attention to this.

Yao Wen-yuan's speech at the Fifth Congress
of the Albanian Workers' Party, *JMJP*,
29.6.1967, p. 3.

45. 2.8.1966 The Anti-Japanese Military and Political University

The revolutionary and progressive characteristics of this university are due to the revolutionary and progressive characteristics of its staff and its courses.

The educational principles of the university are: 'Correct political orientation, plain, hard-working style, flexible strategy and tactics.'[1]

[We must] overcome difficulties, contact the masses, and heighten [our] militancy. Anyone who is corrupt and lazy does not deserve to be a student of this university, for he acts against the rules of this university.

To the second class of graduates: 'You must be brave, resolute, and tenacious. [You must] learn through struggles and be prepared to sacrifice your lives for the liberation of our nation.'

Written for the Production Drive of the university: 'Study on the one hand, produce on the other; overcome hardships and unnerve the enemies.' 'Now [you] study and produce. In future you will fight and produce.'

The style of the university: 'Unity, alertness, earnestness, and liveliness.'[2]

Reported by Yeh Chien-ying,
JMJP, p. 2.

46. 2.8.1966 Class Struggles

For our youth, the major subject of study is class struggle.

JMJP, p. 2.

---

[1] The 'three' of the 'Three-eight style'.
[2] The 'eight' of the 'Three-eight style'.

47. 5.8.1966 'Bombard the Headquarters—My Big-character Poster'

China's first Marxist-Leninist big-character poster and commentator's article on it in the *People's Daily* are indeed superbly
written! Comrades, please read them again. But in the last
fifty days or so some leading comrades from the central down
to the local levels have acted in a diametrically opposite way.
Adopting the reactionary stand of the bourgeoisie, they have
enforced a bourgeois dictatorship and struck down the surging
movement of the great Cultural Revolution of the proletariat.
They have stood facts on their head and juggled black and
white, encircled and suppressed revolutionaries, stifled opinions
differing from their own, imposed a white terror, and felt very
pleased with themselves. They have puffed up the arrogance of
the bourgeoisie and deflated the morale of the proletariat. How
poisonous! Viewed in connection with the right deviation in
1962 and the wrong tendency of 1964 which was 'left' in form
but right in essence, shouldn't this make one wide awake?

JMJP, 5.8.1967, p. 1 and
PR, no. 33, 11.8.1967.

48. 8.8.1966 The Resolutions of the Eleventh Plenum of the
Central Committee of the CCP—the sixteen
Articles

1. The great proletarian Cultural Revolution now unfolding
is a great revolution that touches people to their very souls and
constitutes a new stage in the development of the socialist revolution in our country, a deeper and more extensive stage.

At the Tenth Plenary Session of the Eighth Central Committee of the Party, Comrade Mao Tse-tung said: To overthrow
a political power, it is always necessary, first of all, to create
public opinion, to do work in the ideological sphere. This is true
for the revolutionary class as well as for the counter-revolutionary
class. This thesis of Comrade Mao Tse-tung's has been proved
entirely correct in practice.

Although the bourgeoisie has been overthrown, it is still
trying to use the old ideas, culture, customs and habits of the
exploiting classes to corrupt the masses, capture their minds and

endeavour to stage a come-back. The proletariat must do just the opposite: it must meet head-on every challenge of the bourgeoisie in the ideological field and use the new ideas, culture, customs and habits of the proletariat to change the mental outlook of the whole of society. At present, our objective is to struggle against and crush those persons in authority who are taking the capitalist road, to criticize and repudiate the reactionary bourgeois academic 'authorities' and the ideology of the bourgeoisie and all other exploiting classes and to transform education, literature and art and all other parts of the superstructure that do not correspond to the socialist economic base, so as to facilitate the consolidation and development of the socialist system.

2. The masses of the workers, peasants, soldiers, revolutionary intellectuals and revolutionary cadres form the main force in this great Cultural Revolution. Large numbers of revolutionary young people, previously unknown, have become courageous and daring pathbreakers. They are vigorous in action and intelligent. Through the media of big-character posters and great debates, they argue things out, expose and criticize thoroughly, and launch resolute attacks on the open and hidden representatives of the bourgeoisie. In such a great revolutionary movement, it is hardly avoidable that they should show shortcomings of one kind or another, but their main revolutionary orientation has been correct from the beginning. This is the main current in the great proletarian Cultural Revolution. It is the main direction along which the great proletarian Cultural Revolution continues to advance.

Since the Cultural Revolution is a revolution, it inevitably meets with resistance. This resistance comes chiefly from those in authority who have wormed their way into the party and are taking the capitalist road. It also comes from the old force of habit in society. At present, this resistance is still fairly strong and stubborn. However, the great proletarian Cultural Revolution is, after all, an irresistible general trend. There is abundant evidence that such resistance will crumble fast once the masses become fully aroused.

Because the resistance is fairly strong, there will be reversals and even repeated reversals in this struggle. There is no harm in this. It tempers the proletariat and other working people, and especially the younger generation, teaches them lessons and gives them experience, and helps them to understand that the revolutionary road is a zigzag one, and not plain sailing.

3. The outcome of this great Cultural Revolution will be determined by whether the party leadership does or does not dare boldly to arouse the masses.

Currently, there are four different situations with regard to the leadership being given to the movement of cultural revolution by party organizations at various levels:

(1) There is the situation in which the persons in charge of party organizations stand in the van of the movement and dare to arouse the masses boldly. They put daring above everything else, they are dauntless communist fighters and good pupils of Chairman Mao. They advocate the big-character posters and great debates. They encourage the masses to expose every kind of ghost and monster and also to criticize the shortcomings and errors in the work of the persons in charge. This correct kind of leadership is the result of putting proletarian politics in the forefront and Mao Tse-tung's thought in the lead.

(2) In many units, the persons in charge have a very poor understanding of the task of leadership in this great struggle, their leadership is far from being conscientious and effective, and they accordingly find themselves incompetent and in a weak position. They put fear above everything else, stick to outmoded ways and regulations, and are unwilling to break away from conventional practices and move ahead. They have been taken unawares by the new order of things, the revolutionary order of the masses, with the result that their leadership lags behind the situation, lags behind the masses.

(3) In some units, the persons in charge, who made mistakes of one kind or another in the past, are even more prone to put fear above everything else, being afraid that the masses will catch them out. Actually, if they make serious self-criticism and accept the criticism of the masses, the party and the masses will make allowances for their mistakes. But if the persons in charge don't, they will continue to make mistakes and become obstacles to the mass movement.

(4) Some units are controlled by those who have wormed their way into the party and are taking the capitalist road. Such persons in authority are extremely afraid of being exposed by

the masses and therefore seek every possible pretext to suppress the mass movement. They resort to such tactics as shifting the targets for attack and turning black into white in an attempt to lead the movement astray. When they find themselves very isolated and no longer able to carry on as before, they resort still more to intrigues, stabbing people in the back, spreading rumours, and blurring the distinction between revolution and counter-revolution as much as they can, all for the purpose of attacking the revolutionaries.

What the Central Committee of the party demands of the party committees at all levels is that they persevere in giving correct leadership, put daring above everything else, boldly arouse the masses, change the state of weakness and incompetence where it exists, encourage those comrades who have made mistakes but are willing to correct them to cast off their mental burdens and join in the struggle, and dismiss from their leading posts all those in authority who are taking the capitalist road and so make possible the recapture of the leadership for the proletarian revolutionaries.

4. In the great proletarian Cultural Revolution, the only method is for the masses to liberate themselves, and any method of doing things on their behalf must not be used.

Trust the masses, rely on them and respect their initiative. Cast out fear. Don't be afraid of disorder. Chairman Mao has often told us that revolution cannot be so very refined, so gentle, so temperate, kind, courteous, restrained and magnanimous. Let the masses educate themselves in this great revolutionary movement and learn to distinguish between right and wrong and between correct and incorrect ways of doing things.

Make the fullest use of big-character posters and great debates to argue matters out, so that the masses can clarify the correct views, criticize the wrong views and expose all the ghosts and monsters. In this way the masses will be able to raise their political consciousness in the course of the struggle, enhance their abilities and talents, distinguish right from wrong and draw a clear line between the enemy and ourselves.

5. Who are our enemies? Who are our friends? This is a question of the first importance for the revolution and it is likewise a question of the first importance for the great Cultural Revolution.

Party leadership should be good at discovering the left and developing and strengthening the ranks of the left, and should firmly rely on the revolutionary left. During the movement this is the only way to isolate thoroughly the most reactionary rightists, win over the middle and unite with the great majority so that by the end of the movement we shall achieve the unity of more than 95 per cent of the cadres and more than 95 per cent of the masses.

Concentrate all forces to strike at the handful of ultra-reactionary bourgeois rightists and counter-revolutionary revisionists, and expose and criticize to the full their crimes against the party, against socialism and against Mao Tse-tung's thought so as to isolate them to the maximum.

The main target of the present movement is those within the party who are in authority and are taking the capitalist road.

Care should be taken to distinguish strictly between the anti-party, anti-socialist rightists and those who support the party and socialism but have said or done something wrong or have written some bad articles or other works.

Care should be taken to distinguish strictly between the reactionary bourgeois scholar despots and 'authorities' on the one hand and people who have the ordinary bourgeois academic ideas on the other.

6. A strict distinction must be made between the two different types of contradictions: those among the people and those between ourselves and the enemy. Contradictions among the people must not be made into contradictions between ourselves and the enemy; nor must contradictions between ourselves and the enemy be regarded as those among the people.

It is normal for the masses to hold different views. Contention between different views is unavoidable, necessary and beneficial. In the course of normal and full debate, the masses will affirm what is right, correct what is wrong and gradually reach unanimity.

The method to be used in debates is to present the facts, reason things out, and persuade through reasoning. Any method of forcing a minority holding different views to submit is impermissible. The minority should be protected, because sometimes the truth is with the minority. Even if the minority is wrong, they should still be allowed to argue their case and reserve their views.

When there is a debate, it should be conducted by reasoning, not by coercion or force.

In the course of debate, every revolutionary should be good at thinking things out for himself and should develop the communist spirit of daring to think, daring to speak and daring to act. On the premise that they have the same main orientation, revolutionary comrades should, for the sake of strengthening unity, avoid endless debate over side issues.

7. In certain schools, units, and work teams of the Cultural Revolution, some of the persons in charge have organized counter-attacks against the masses who put up big-character posters against them. These people have even advanced such slogans as: opposition to the leaders of a unit or a work team means opposition to the party's Central Committee, means opposition to the party and socialism, means counter-revolution. In this way it is inevitable that their blows will fall on some really revolutionary activists. This is an error on matters of orientation, an error of line, and is absolutely impermissible.

A number of persons who suffer from serious ideological errors, and particularly some of the anti-party and anti-socialist rightists, are taking advantage of certain shortcomings and mistakes in the mass movement to spread rumours and gossip, and engage in agitation, deliberately branding some of the masses as 'counter-revolutionaries.' It is necessary to beware of such 'pick-pockets' and expose their tricks in good time.

In the course of the movement, with the exception of cases of active counter-revolutionaries where there is clear evidence of crimes such as murder, arson, poisoning, sabotage or theft of state secrets, which should be handled in accordance with the law, no measures should be taken against students at universities, colleges, middle schools and primary schools because of problems that arise in the movement. To prevent the struggle from being diverted from its main objective, it is not allowed, whatever the pretext, to incite the masses to struggle against each other or the students to do likewise. Even proven rightists should be dealt with on the merits of each case at a later stage of the movement.

8. The cadres fall roughly into the following four categories:

(1) good;

(2) comparatively good;

(3) those who have made serious mistakes but have not become anti-party, anti-socialist rightists;

(4) the small number of anti-party, anti-socialist rightists.

In ordinary situations, the first two categories (good and comparatively good) are the great majority.

The anti-party, anti-socialist rightists must be fully exposed, hit hard, pulled down and completely discredited and their influence eliminated. At the same time, they should be given a way out so that they can turn over a new leaf.

9. Many new things have begun to emerge in the great proletarian Cultural Revolution. The cultural revolutionary groups, committees and other organizational forms created by the masses in many schools and units are something new and of great historic importance.

These cultural revolutionary groups, committees and congresses are excellent new forms of organization whereby under the leadership of the Communist Party the masses are educating themselves. They are an excellent bridge to keep our party in close contact with the masses. They are organs of power of the proletarian Cultural Revolution.

The struggle of the proletariat against the old ideas, culture, customs and habits left over from all the exploiting classes over thousands of years will necessarily take a very, very long time. Therefore, the cultural revolutionary groups, committees and congresses should not be temporary organizations but permanent, standing mass organizations. They are suitable not only for colleges, schools and government and other organizations, but generally also for factories, mines, other enterprises, urban districts and villages.

It is necessary to institute a system of general elections, like that of the Paris Commune, for electing members to the cultural revolutionary groups and committees and delegates to the cultural revolutionary congresses. The lists of candidates should be put forward by the revolutionary masses after full discussion, and the elections should be held after the masses have discussed the lists over and over again.

The masses are entitled at any time to criticize members of the cultural revolutionary groups and committees and delegates elected to the cultural revolutionary congresses. If these members or delegates prove incompetent, they can be replaced through election or recalled by the masses after discussion.

The cultural revolutionary groups, committees and congresses in colleges and schools should consist mainly of representatives of the revolutionary students. At the same time, they should have a certain number of representatives of the revolutionary teaching staff and workers.

10. In the great proletarian Cultural Revolution a most important task is to transform the old educational system and the old principles and methods of teaching.

In this great Cultural Revolution, the phenomenon of our schools being dominated by bourgeois intellectuals must be completely changed.

In every kind of school we must apply thoroughly the policy advanced by Comrade Mao Tse-tung, of education serving proletarian politics and education being combined with productive labour, so as to enable those receiving an education to develop morally, intellectually and physically and to become labourers with socialist consciousness and culture.

The period of schooling should be shortened. Courses should be fewer and better. The teaching material should be thoroughly transformed, in some cases beginning with simplifying complicated material. While their main task is to study, students should also learn other things. That is to say, in addition to their studies they should also learn industrial work, farming and military affairs, and take part in the struggles of the Cultural Revolution as they occur to criticize the bourgeoisie.

11. In the course of the mass movement of the Cultural Revolution, the criticism of bourgeois and feudal ideology should be well combined with the dissemination of the proletarian world outlook and of Marxism-Leninism, Mao Tsetung's thought.

Criticism should be organized of typical bourgeois representatives who have wormed their way into the party and typical reactionary bourgeois academic 'authorities,' and this should include criticism of various kinds of reactionary views in philosophy, history, political economy and education, in works and theories of literature and art, in theories of natural science, and in other fields.

Criticism of anyone by name in the press should be decided after discussion by the party committee at the same level, and in some cases submitted to the party committee at a higher level for approval.

12. As regards scientists, technicians and ordinary members of working staffs, as long as they are patriotic, work energetically, are not against the party and socialism, and maintain no illicit relations with any foreign country, we should in the present movement continue to apply the policy of 'unity, criticism, unity.' Special care should be taken of those scientists and scientific and technical personnel who have made contributions. Efforts should be made to help them gradually transform their world outlook and their style of work.

13. The cultural and educational units and leading organs of the Party and government in the large and medium cities are the points of concentration of the present proletarian cultural revolution.

The great Cultural Revolution has enriched the socialist education movement in both city and countryside and raised it to a higher level. Efforts should be made to conduct these two movements in close combination. Arrangements to this effect may be made by various regions and departments in the light of the specific conditions.

The socialist education movement now going on in the countryside and in enterprises in the cities should not be upset where the original arrangements are appropriate and the movement is going well, but should continue in accordance with the original arrangements. However, the questions that are arising in the present great proletarian Cultural Revolution should be put to the masses for discussion at a proper time, so as to further foster vigorously proletarian ideology and eradicate bourgeois ideology.

In some places, the great proletarian Cultural Revolution is being used as the focus in order to add momentum to the socialist education movement and clean things up in the fields of politics, ideology, organization and economy. This may be done where the local party committee thinks it appropriate.

14. The aim of the great proletarian Cultural Revolution is to

revolutionize people's ideology and as a consequence to achieve greater, faster, better and more economical results in all fields of work. If the masses are fully aroused and proper arrangements are made, it is possible to carry on both the Cultural Revolution and production without one hampering the other, while guaranteeing high quality in all our work.

The great proletarian Cultural Revolution is a powerful motive force for the development of the social productive forces in our country. Any idea of counterposing the great cultural revolution against the development of production is incorrect.

15. In the armed forces, the Cultural Revolution and the socialist education movement should be carried out in accordance with the instructions of the Military Commission of the Central Committee and the General Political Department of the People's Liberation Army.

16. In the great proletarian Cultural Revolution, it is imperative to hold aloft the great red banner of Mao Tse-tung's thought and put proletarian politics in command. The movement for the creative study and application of Chairman Mao Tse-tung's works should be carried forward among the masses of the workers, peasants and soldiers, the cadres and the intellectuals, and Mao Tse-tung's thought should be taken as the guide for action in the Cultural Revolution.

In this complex great Cultural Revolution, Party committees at all levels must study and apply Chairman Mao's works all the more conscientiously and in a creative way. In particular, they must study over and over again Chairman Mao's writings on the cultural revolution and on the Party's methods of leadership, such as *On New Democracy, Talks at the Yenan Forum on Literature and Art, On the Correct Handling of Contradictions Among the People, Speech at the Chinese Communist Party's National Conference on Propaganda Work, Some Questions Concerning Methods of Leadership,* and *Methods of Work of Party Committees.*

Party committees at all levels must abide by the directions given by Chairman Mao over the years, namely that they should thoroughly apply the mass line of 'from the masses and to the masses' and that they should be pupils before they become teachers. They should try to avoid being one-sided or narrow. They should foster materialist dialectics and oppose metaphysics and scholasticism.

The great proletarian Cultural Revolution is bound to achieve brilliant victory under the leadership of the Central Committee of the party headed by Comrade Mao Tse-tung.

JMJP, 9.8.1966 and
PR, no. 33, 12.8.1966.

49.   12.8.1966   To the Revolutionary Masses of Peking

You must concern yourselves with the affairs of the country and carry the great proletarian Cultural Revolution right through to the end.

JMJP, p. 1.

50.   17.8.1966   Serving the Masses

We must never detach ourselves from the masses, so that we may know them, understand them, be with them, and serve them well.

JMJP editorial, p. 1.

51.   19.8.1966   To the Masses of the Great Proletarian Cultural Revolution

This movement is of a colossal scale and has truly mobilized the masses. It is highly significant to their ideological revolutionization.

Conversation with Lin Piao, *JMJP*, p. 1.

52.   20.8.1966   Communists and Masses

A communist must never stay aloof from or above the masses like a bureaucrat. He ought to be like an ordinary worker in the presence of the masses, join them, and become one of them.

JMJP editorial, p. 1.

53.   21.8.1966   Peking and the Rest of the Country

Let the rest of the country come to Peking or Peking go to

the rest of the country. . . . Let [those who live] at other places come and see. After all, the trains are free now, are they not?

> Reported by Comrade X in a speech to the
> students of the University of Communications,
> Sian, and of Chungking and
> Szechwan Universities, NT, p. 18.

54.   22.8.1966   Work Teams

Almost ninety per cent of the work teams throughout the whole country have committed general mistakes in their orientation.

> Reported by Chou En-lai in a speech to the
> students at Tsinghua University, *NT*, p. 16.

55.   26.8.1966   Work Teams

It will not do to depend on the work teams coming from the Navy, Air Force, and governmental agencies. They neither teach nor learn. How can they understand the conditions in the schools? There is Chien Po-tsan[1] at Peking University who has written many books and essays. Have you read them? You see, how do you [begin to] criticize them? The Cultural Revolution at schools must not depend on work teams; nor must it depend on you [those attending the eleventh plenum—Ed.] or me. It must depend on the revolutionary teachers and students at schools.

> Reported by the first secretary of the
> Szechwan provincial committee of the
> CCP [Liao Chih-kao] at Szechwan University,
> NT, p. 16.

56.   30.8.1966   Dunce Caps and Fist-fights

(I [Ch'en Yi] did things like this in the past. I beat people up and put dunce caps on landlords and local ruffians.) But

---

[1] An eminent historian who was severely criticized at the beginning of the Cultural Revolution. See p. 26, n. 1.

Chairman said: 'We must not do it this way. This is the peasants' way, not our way.'

> Reported by Ch'en Yi in a speech to the
> students of the Foreign Language School,
> [Peking], NT, p. 17.

57. 31.8.1966 Violent Struggles

(Chairman Mao wrote these eight characters in the Sixteen Articles): *'yao yung wen-tou; pu yung wu-tou'* (wage peaceful, not violent, struggles). (These eight characters were added by Chairman Mao personally; the original draft [of the 16 Articles] did not have them. . . . Words to the effect 'Do not beat people up' were copied from the 23 Articles and they were crossed out by the Chairman who personally wrote these eight characters.)

> Reported by the first secretary of the
> Hunan provincial committee of the CCP
> at a meeting of the staff and students
> of the colleges in Ch'angsha, NT, pp. 16–17.

58. 2.9.1966 Repressing Students

None of those who repressed student movements has ended well. The Manchu government repressed them; how did it end? The Northern warlords did the same. How did they end? Chiang Kai-shek repressed them; how did he end? Lu P'ing of Peking University and Chiang Nan-hsiang of Tsinghua University did exactly the same; how did they end? The work teams sent out later also repressed them. Now they have met their doom. Of course, we must add that the blame goes to those who sent them.

> Report by the first secretary of the
> Hunan provincial committee of the CCP
> at the meeting of the cadres of the
> provincial government and party
> organizations, NT, p. 16.

59.   5.9.1966   Violent Struggles

The great proletarian Cultural Revolution is a revolution that touches the souls of the people.

To realize [the goals of] this revolution, [we must] resort to peaceful, not violent, struggles.

JMJP, p. 1.

60.   7.9.1966   Tsingtao, Ch'angsha, and Sian

Lin Piao, Chou En-lai, T'ao Chu, [Ch'en] Po-ta, [Wang] Jen-chung, and Chiang Ch'ing:

I have read the attached document. The incidents in Tsingtao, Ch'angsha, and Sian are similar. They are caused by the opposition of organized workers and peasants against students and are all wrong. They must not be allowed to continue. Try to issue a directive from the Centre to stop them and then publish editorials to tell the workers and peasants to cease interfering with student movements. Nothing like this has happened in Peking, except that the People's Congress drafted 600 peasants into the city to protect Kuo Ch'iu-ying. Pass the experience of Peking on to other places.

I think the views of T'an Ch'i-lung and the vice-mayor [of Tsingtao?] are correct.

SHWS, p. 42.

61.   7.9.1966   Causes of Revolution

In any revolution, its internal causes are fundamental and its external ones are supplementary.

Reported by Chou En-lai at the Chinese
People's University, NT, p. 18.

62.   7.9.1966   Leadership of Revolution

A revolution depends on an inner core. This, the bourgeois faction in authority and the faction in authority [*sic*] which has committed mistakes know best; [their] peripheral organizations merely add fuel to the fire.

Reported by Chou En-lai at the Academy
of Sciences, NT, p. 18.

63.   10.9.1966   Educational System

The more you study, the more stupid you become. You are now at a crucial time of transition; you must learn the right way.

> Reported by Chou En-lai at a university
> and college Red Guard meeting, NT, p. 18.

64.   13.9.1966   Mistakes

Young people should be permitted to make mistakes. As long as their general orientation is correct, let them make minor mistakes. I believe that they can correct themselves in practical work.

> Reported by Hsieh Fu-chih at a reception
> of the Red Guards of Peking School of
> Politics and Law, NT, p. 18.

65.   24.9.1966   Basic Contradictions in the Cultural Revolution

The basic contradiction the great proletarian Cultural Revolution is trying to resolve is the one between the proletariat and the bourgeoisie, between the proletarian and bourgeois roads. The main point of the movement is to struggle against the capitalist roaders in authority in the party.

> *JMJP*, p. 3.

66.   26.9.1966   Youth

Young people can look at problems this way and that way. The like-minded of them often club together; this is nothing unusual.

> Reported by Chou En-lai in a speech at
> Rebel Headquarters of the College and University
> Students, Peking, NT, p. 17.

67.   1.10.1966   Class Struggle

As soon as [you] grasp the class struggle, it works [for you].

> *JMJP* editorial, p. 1.

68.   1.10.1966   Attributes of the Peoples of the World

The peoples of the world must have courage, dare to fight, and fear no hardships. When the ones in front fall, the others behind must follow up. In this way, the world will belong to the people and all the demons will be eliminated.

Reported by Lin Piao, *JMJP*, p. 2.

69.   October 1966   Party Members and Resolutions

[One can] never be sure that what is written in a resolution will be carried out by all our comrades; some of them will not.

Reported by Ch'en Po-ta, 'Summing up the Past Two Months,' said to be remark made at the eleventh plenum, NT, p. 17.

70.   24.10.1966   Grasp Revolution and Promote Production

Sent direct to Comrade [Ch'en] Po-ta:

I have read the revised draft [of your 'Summing up the Past Two Months']. It is very good. Please consider the insertion at some place of the two phrases: 'Grasp the Revolution; Promote Production.' [The 'Summing Up'] should be printed in pamphlets in large quantities and each party cell and each red guard group must have at least one copy.

SHWS, p. 42.

71.   12.11.1966   Support the Red Guards

I strongly support you.

to the Red Guards of the Tsinghua Middle School, *JMJP*, p. 1.

Long live comrades!
You must let politics take command, go to the masses, and be with the masses. You must conduct the great proletarian Cultural Revolution even better.

Spoken in front of a microphone on the rostrum
of the T'ienanmen, on the occasion of the
seventh review of the great armies of the Cultural
Revolution, ibid. [Since the beginning of the
Cultural Revolution, these have been the only
words spoken by Mao directly to the public
below the rostrum of the T'ienanmen. Ed.]

72. 28.11.1966 Literature

The overthrown bourgeoisie tries by hook or by crook to use
literature and arts to corrupt the masses, thus paving the way
for a capitalist restoration. This makes our tasks in literature and
art heavier rather than lighter. Our leadership on the literary
and art front should be strengthened instead of weakened. To
carry out their glorious tasks, our literary and art organizations must carry the great proletarian Cultural Revolution
through to the end.

Reported in a speech by Ch'en Po-ta,
RF, 1966, no. 5, p. 6.

73. 31.12.1966 Military Training

The idea of training revolutionary teachers and pupils by
army cadres is a good one. The training will make a great
difference. By it, [the teachers and pupils] can learn from the
PLA, politics, military affairs, the four firsts, and three-eight
style, the three great disciplines and eight points of attention,
and strengthen the discipline of their organizations.

JMJP, 16.5.1967, p. 1.

1967

74. 1.1.1967 Leadership and Democracy

Mistaken leadership which is harmful to the cause of the
revolution should not be unconditionally accepted; instead, it
should be resolutely rejected.

Democracy sometimes looks like an end in itself, but in fact
it is merely a means to an end.

JMJP editorial, p. 1.

75. Before 11.1.1967   Power Struggle at the Broadcasting
                        Station

The comrades of the Broadcasting Station have won the power of control. It is a good thing that power is now in the hands of proletarian revolutionaries. I have heard that the comrades there are split. This can be dealt with according to the [way] the contradictions among the people are handled: differences in opinion can be discussed and resolved.

Reported by Wang Li, NT, p. 12.

76. Before 23.11.1967   PLA's Support of the Left

To Lin Piao,

(The Chairman having read the document from x x of Anhwei and Comrade Lin Piao's comment on it.)

You must despatch troops to support the broad left-wing revolutionary masses. Later on, whenever true revolutionaries need support from the PLA, you should do likewise. The so-called 'non-interference' is untrue. [The PLA] has been involved for some time. I think on this matter you should issue new orders; the old ones should be cancelled.

NT, pp. 12–13.

77. 26.1.1967   Supporting the Left

The PLA should actively support the broad left-wing masses.

The PLA Daily, p. 1.

78. 26.1.1967   Economy and Revolution

Economize on consumption and carry on revolution. Protect the property of the country.

JMJP editorial, p. 1.

79. 27.1.1967   To the PLA

1. I think [we] must have an order of priorities; [we] must not carry on in all the military districts simultaneously.

2. The great revolution is being ferociously developed in the regions and the struggles for power are continuing. Our armed forces should support the left-wing revolutionaries there in their power struggle, and therefore they must not be involved in local cultural revolutions.

3. Internationally, both imperialism and revisionism are making use of our great Cultural Revolution to carry on their anti-Chinese activities. For instance, the Soviet Union is suppressing [our] students; [Soviet] aeroplanes near the Sinkiang border are more active; and [Soviet] ground forces are mobilized. All the armed units stationed in the big military districts along the frontiers such as Tsinan, Nanking, Foochow, and Kunming should be alerted and made ready. Therefore the time schedule of the great Cultural Revolution must be slightly postponed on account of the general situation, but it will be carried out in future.

NT, pp. 13–14.

80.   28.1.1967   Comment on the Decree of the Military Commission Issued on This Day

The eight articles are excellent, to be issued as they are.

WCHP, p. 56.

81. February 1967   The PLA and the Left

The PLA should actively give support to the truly proletarian revolutionary groups and resolutely oppose the right-wing.

RF, 1967, no. 3, p. 18.

82.   6.2.1967   The PLA, Production, and Revolution

The armed forces advance [an inch];
Production grows an inch.
Tighten the discipline [so that]
Revolution is always successful.

WCHP, pp. 64–5.

83.   8.2.1967   Public Opinion and Revolution

In order to overthrow a regime, [we] must first of all take control of the superstructure, the ideology, by preparing public opinion.

JMJP, p. 3.

84.   23.2.1967   Reform the Wrong

Permit them to reform themselves and redeem their mistakes by making contributions, as long as they are not anti-party and anti-socialist elements who stubbornly refuse to correct their mistakes in spite of repeated exhortations.

JMJP editorial, p. 2.

85.   7.3.1967   The PLA and Schools

This document (dated 8.3.1967) may be issued to the whole country. The PLA should separately and in sessions give military training to university students and children of middle schools and the upper formers of primary schools. They should also take part in the work of re-opening schools, re-adjusting school organization, setting up leadership bodies of the three-way alliance, and carrying out struggle, criticism, and reform. They should set up experimental points first and then apply the experience so acquired to a wider scope. They ought to convince students and children [to accept] what Marx taught us—'The proletariat must emancipate mankind as a whole before it can emancipate itself.' In military training, they must not reject teachers and cadres who have made mistakes. These people must be allowed to take part so as to facilitate their reform; the only exceptions to this are the aged and sick. All this is quite easy, if it is conscientiously carried out.

JMJP, p. 2 and *WCHP*, document of the Centre, no. 98–9, p. 98.

86.   10.3.1967   Three-way Alliance

At the places and in the organizational units where power struggle is necessary, there the principle of the revolutionary three-way alliance should be applied to setting up a revolutionary, representative, and proletarian provisional power structure which may be called a revolutionary committee.

JMJP editorial, p. 1.

87.   27.3.1967   School Work

Resume classes and carry on revolution.

JMJP editorial, p. 1.

88.   1.4.1967   The Film—'The Secret History of the Ch'ing Court'

'The Secret History of the Ch'ing Court' is regarded as a patriotic film, but as traitorous, traitorous through and through, by me.

Ch'i Peng-yü's article, *JMJP*, p. 1.

89.   1.4.1967   Imperialism and China (on the same film)

Was it the Chinese people who organized the Boxer groups and sent them to Europe, America, and Japan to rebel [against the governments there] and to kill and burn? Was it the imperialist powers which came to invade China and exploit the Chinese people, thus provoking the Chinese people to fight imperialism and its lackeys, to corrupt officials of China? This is a grave matter of right and wrong and should be made absolutely clear.

ibid., p. 2.

90.   6.4.1967   Comment on the Decree of the Military Commission on This Day

To Comrade Lin Piao,

This is excellent.

WCHP, p. 116.

91.   7.4.1967   Broadcast Comrade Lin Piao's Talk

The recording of Comrade Lin Piao's talk on 20 March 1967 should be broadcast to all the members of the PLA and the red guards of the whole country. Comrade Lin Piao's talk is a report of the utmost importance to Marxism-Leninism and Mao Tse-tung's thought; it is highly significant in guiding the current great proletarian Cultural Revolutionary movement and in promoting further victories for the proletarian revolutionaries in their struggles at two fronts. The party committees of all the military districts, party committees at various levels, revolutionary committees of all the provinces and cities, all the military control committees, and all the revolutionary mass organizations must organize themselves and study conscientiously Comrade Lin Paio's talk and must put it into practice meticulously.

WCHP, pp. 118–19.

92.   30.4.1967   Revolution, War, Work, Production, etc.

Grasp the revolution, hasten the preparation for war [defence?], speed up work, promote production, and support the army and cherish the people.

JMJP, p. 3.

93.   End of April or Beginning of May 1967

Three Pillars of the Revolution

The masses, the army, and the cadres are the three pillars on which we rely.

BTA 3.5.1967 reporting a big-character poster,
BBC/FE/2458/C1.

94.   7.5.1967   Szechwan Problems

It is difficult to avoid mistakes; the point is to correct them honestly. Too many people have been arrested in Szechwan and many mass organizations are branded as reactionary. All these are wrong, but they have been quickly rectified.

> The Resolution on Szechwan adopted by the
> Centre of the CCP (the Ten Red Articles),
> 7.5.1967.

95. 7.5.1967   China's Contribution to the World

With the growth of such vigour in socialist China, a country with a quarter of the world's population, we shall be able to make a great internationalist contribution.

Our goals will and certainly can be fulfilled.

> *JMJP* editorial, p. 1.

96. 12.5.1967   Three-way Alliance

Trust and rely on the masses; trust and rely on the PLA; trust and rely on the majority of the cadres.

> *JMJP* editorial, p. 1.

97. 12.5.1967   The Army and People

When the army and the people unite as one,
Who in the world is their equal?

> *JMJP* editorial, p. 1.

98. 18.5.1967   Uninterrupted Revolution

The present great Cultural Revolution is merely the first one; there will inevitably be more to follow. Comrade Mao said often in recent years: 'The victory or defeat of the revolution can be determined only over a long period of time. If it is badly handled, there is always the danger of a capitalist restoration. All members of the party and all the people of our country must not think that after one, two, three, or four great cultural revolutions there will be peace and quiet. They must always be on the alert and must never relax their vigilance.'

> *JMJP* editorial, p. 1.

99. 19.5.1967   Guard Against Revisionism

Guard against revisionism, particularly the emergence of revisionism at the party Centre.

JMJP, p. 1.

100. 28.5.1967   Novels and Anti-party Activities

The idea of carrying out anti-party activities through writing novels is new. The overthrow of any regime requires the preparation of public opinion, beginning with ideological work. This is true with the revolutionaries; it is also true with the reactionaries.

JMJP, p. 1.

101. 29.5.1967   Hai Jui and P'eng Teh-huai

The crux of the dismissal of Hai Jui lies in the dismissal itself. Emperor Chia-ching dismissed Hai Jui; in 1959 we sacked P'eng Teh-huai. P'eng Teh-huai *is* a Hai Jui.

JMJP, p. 3.

102. 1.6.1967   Friend and Foe

Who are our enemies and who are our friends? This is the first and foremost question of a revolution and it is also the first and foremost question of the great Cultural Revolution.

JMJP, p. 1.

103. 1.6.1967   Old Cadres

Old cadres have made their contributions in the past, but they must not live on that 'capital'. They should reform themselves and make fresh contributions in the great proletarian Cultural Revolution.

Jen Li-hsin's article, *JMJP*, p. 4.

104. 11.6.1967   Support the Left

Protect the left-wing; support the left-wing; form and enlarge left-wing units.

Jen Li-hsin's article, *JMJP*, p. 2.

105.   11.6.1967   Major Reasons and Minor Reasons[1]

Everything has its major and minor reasons; all the major ones govern the minor ones. People of our country must think in terms of major reasons if they want to think and act properly.

A Red Guard letter, *JMJP*, p. 3.

106.   12.6.1967   Class Struggle and Cadres

Everything must be handled and reasoned out from the point of view of class and class struggle and with the method of class analysis; all leading cadres should be treated in the same way. The method of simply rejecting everything and negating everything, of directing the struggle against the cadres who shoulder most of the responsibility and do most of the work or against the 'heads' [of departments] must be abandoned.

JMJP editor's note, p. 1.

107.   21.6.1967   Let People Speak Up

Let people speak up. The sky will not fall and you yourself will not be deposed as a result of it. [What if you] do not let people speak up? You may be deposed one day.

JMJP editorial, p. 1.

108.   21.6.1967   Progress

Do not stop half way and do not ever go backward. There is no way behind you.

The Peking Daily, 21.6.1967, reproduced in the *JMJP*, 23.6.1967, p. 3.

109.   25.6.1967   Petty Bourgeois Thought

[We] must skilfully direct the petty bourgeois ideology in our ranks on to the path of the proletarian revolution. This is the key to the victory of the great proletarian Cultural Revolution.

JMJP editor's note, p. 3.

[1] The style of this quotation is dated; it may have been composed by Mao a long time ago, perhaps before 1919.

110.   27.6.1967   Standpoint of the People

[We] must stand on the side, not on the opposing side, of the masses. This is a fundamental problem of the standpoint of a Marxist-Leninist.

The PLA Daily, 27.6.1967, reproduced in the *JMJP*, 28.6.1967, p. 1.

111.   27.6.1967   Trust the Majority of the Cadres and Masses

Trust the majority of the cadres and the masses. This is essential.

The PLA Daily, 27.6.1967, p. 1.

112.   29.6.1967   Heart-to-heart Talks

Popularize the work of heart-to-heart talks. It is a good method.

Jen Li-hsin's article, *JMJP*, p. 6.

113.   4.7.1967   Party Members

We, the communists, do not want official positions; we want revolution. We must have a thoroughly revolutionary spirit and must be with the masses every hour, every minute. As long as we are with the masses, we shall always be victorious.

Jen Li-hsin's article, *JMJP*, p. 4.

114.   5.7.1967   Organize the Masses

The organization of millions of people and the mobilization of a tremendous revolutionary force are what the present revolution needs in its offensive against the reactionaries.

JMJP, p. 3.

115.   7.7.1967   Mass Organizations of Two Factions

Whenever acute opposition exists between the mass organizations of two factions, there will be the need for careful political ideological work which can help to resolve all the differences. Careful political ideological work is needed even when [we] are dealing with conservative and reactionary organizations.

Jen Li-hsin's article, JMJP, p. 3.

116.   3.8.1967   Revolution and Productive Force

Revolution is the emancipation of productive force; it promotes the development of productive force.

The PLA Daily editorial, 3.8.1967,
reproduced in the JMJP, 3.8.1967, p. 2.

117.   8.8.1967   Cadres in the Wrong

Cadres who have made mistakes can re-establish themselves, provided that they do not persist with their mistakes, but reform them, and are forgiven by the revolutionary masses.

Jen Li-hsin's article, JMJP, p. 3.

118.   13.8.1967   Political Power

The basic problem of a revolution is the problem of political power. The possession of political power means the possession of everything; the loss of it means the loss of everything.

JMJP, p. 2.

119.   17.8.1967   Power Struggle

All proletarian revolutionaries unite and fight for political power against the handful of capitalist roaders in authority.

JMJP editorial, p. 1.

120.   17.8.1967   Socialist Economy

If our country does not build up a socialist economy, what is it going to be? It will be like Yugoslavia, a capitalist country in fact. The proletarian dictatorship will be transformed into a bourgeois dictatorship, worse still, a reactionary and fascist dictatorship. This problem deserves our fullest attention and [I] hope our comrades will give it their thought.

RF, 1967, no. 13, p. 9.

121.   21.8.1967   Mistakes

It is difficult not to make mistakes. The thing is to correct them conscientiously.

JMJP, p. 1.

122.   24.8.1967   News Service

They [the revisionists] deny the party and class characteristics of a newspaper; they overlook the differences in principle between proletarian and bourgeois news services; they confuse the news service which reflects the collective economy of a socialist country with that which reflects the economic anarchy and group competition of a capitalist country.

Wen Hung-pin's article, *JMJP*, p. 4.

123.   25.8.1967   News Service

Newspapers in a socialist country are fundamentally different from those in a capitalist country. In a socialist country, newspapers reflect the planned socialist economy based on public ownership. This is quite different from newspapers in a capitalist country which reflect economic anarchy and group competition. As long as class distinction exists in the world, newspapers are a means of class struggle.

JMJP, p. 3.

124.   26.8.1967   Residual Ideology

Although the socio-economic system has been transformed, reactionary thought, bourgeois and upper-petty-bourgeois thought inherited from the past, still exists in the minds of a considerable number of people, and cannot be transformed

quickly. Its transformation needs time, a long period of time.
This is the class struggle in [our] society.

JMJP, p. 2.

125. 30.8.1967 Train a Large Number of Revolutionary
                 Vanguards

[We] must train a large number of revolutionary vanguards
who have political vision, militant spirit, and readiness to make
sacrifices. They are frank, honest, active, and upright. They
seek no self-interest; they are completely dedicated to national
and social emancipation. They fear no hardships; they are
always firm and brave in the face of hardships. They are never
boastful; they covet no limelight. They are unpretentious,
realistic people. With a large number of people like this, the
tasks of the Chinese revolution can be easily fulfilled.

JMJP, p. 1.

126. 1.9.1967 Think Hard

Think hard!

JMJP, p. 1.

127. 2.9.1967 Class Struggle

Throughout the socialist stage, there exist classes and class
struggle. The struggle is protracted and complicated, sometimes even fierce. [Therefore] the instruments of our dictatorship must not be weakened; on the contrary, they should be
strengthened.

JMJP editorial, p. 1.

128. 2.9.1967 Support the Army and Cherish the People

Develop still further the movement of supporting the army
and cherishing the people.

JMJP editorial, p. 1.

129.   7.9.1967   Creativeness of Lin Piao

The four firsts are good; they are original. Since Comrade Lin Piao put forward the four firsts and the three-eight style, the PLA's political and military work has taken a giant step forward. It has become more concrete and theoretically [more advanced].

JMJP, p. 3.

130.   12.9.1967   Fake Left but Actually Right

Reactionaries who appear in disguise show people their false image and hide away their true faces. However since they are counter-revolutionaries, they can never cover up their true faces completely.

JMJP, p. 3.

131.   14.9.1967   Revolutionary Alliance

Within the working class, there is no basic clash of interests. Under the proletarian dictatorship, the working class has absolutely no reason to split into two hostile factional organizations.

JMJP editorial, p. 1.

132.   17.9.1967   From Unity to Unity

Unity—criticism and self-criticism—unity.

RF, 1967, no. 14.

133.   22.9.1967   Grand Alliance

Some of our comrades toddle along like women with bound feet. They complain about others: 'Too fast, too fast!'

JMJP editorial, p. 1.

134.   September 1967   Better Situation

In a few more months the entire situation will be even better.

JMJP editorial, 1.1.1968, p. 1.

135. 1.10.1967   Grand Alliance

The revolutionary red guards and revolutionary student organizations must form a grand alliance. As long as they are revolutionary mass organizations, they must form a great alliance according to revolutionary principles.

JMJP, p. 3.

136. 1.10.1967   Selfishness and Revisionism

Combat selfishness and criticize revisionism.

Lin Piao's speech, *JMJP*, 2.10.1967, p. 1.

137. 17.10.1967   Be More Alert

We must preserve a high degree of alertness in all departments of our work. We must be good at distinguishing fake supporters of the revolution who are actually reactionaries and douse them away from all our battlefronts, so that we may preserve the victories which are already won and will be won.

JMJP, p. 2.

138. 19.10.1967   Form of Revolutionary Organization

The form of revolutionary organization is determined by the requirements of revolutionary struggle. If an organizational form does not meet the requirements of a revolutionary struggle, it must be abandoned.

JMJP editorial, p. 1.

139. 20.10.1967   Cadre Education

The cadre problem must be tackled through education by widening educational work.

JMJP, p. 1.

140. 21.10.1967   Cadre Problem

The correct handling of the cadres is the crux of the revolutionary three-way alliance, the strengthening of the revolutionary grand alliance, and the improvement in the work of the 'struggle, criticism, and reform' in the basic unit. This must be done well.

JMJP editorial, p. 1.

141. 22.10.1967 Education and Attack

Expand education and reduce attack.

JMJP, p. 2.

142. 26.10.1967 Fake Left

What is fake is fake. Strip off the disguise!

Ho Hsiao's article, *JMJP*, p. 6.

143. 4.11.1967 Education

To carry on the proletarian Cultural Revolution, [we] must depend on the broad masses of revolutionary students and teachers in schools and on the revolutionary workers. We must depend on the activists among them, i.e. the proletarian revolutionaries who are determined to carry the great proletarian Cultural Revolution to the end.

JMJP, p. 1.

144. 6.11.1967 Nature of the Cultural Revolution

Therefore the great proletarian Cultural Revolution is a great revolution that touches the souls of the people and solves the problem of a world view for the people.

JMJP, p. 2.

145. 6.11.1967 Revolutionary Party

A revolutionary party and the revolutionary people must repeatedly undergo both positive and negative education.[1] Through comparison and contrast, they become tempered and mature, thus making sure of victory. To belittle the role of the negative teacher is not to be a thorough dialectical materialist.

JMJP, p. 1.

[1] That is, to learn from both the good and the bad.

148

146.   6.11.1967   Faction in Power

The handful of capitalist roaders in power in our party are the representatives of the bourgeoisie in our party.

JMJP, p. 2.

147.   6.11.1967   Combat Selfishness and Criticize Revisionism

The basic ideological programme of the great proletarian Cultural Revolution is 'to combat selfishness and criticize revisionism.'

JMJP editorial, p. 2.

148.   6.11.1967   Emancipation of the Masses

The Cultural Revolution can only be the emancipation of the masses by the masses.

JMJP editorial, p. 2.

149.   6.11.1967   Three-way Alliance

This great Cultural Revolution, using the great democratic methods of the proletarian dictatorship, has mobilized the masses from below. At the same time, it puts into practice the grand alliance of the proletarian revolutionaries, the three-way alliance between the revolutionary masses, the PLA, and the revolutionary cadres.

JMJP editorial, p. 2.

150.   9.11.1967   Excellent Situation

The situation in the great proletarian Cultural Revolution is not just good, but excellent. The over-all situation is better than at any time in the past. The important sign of the excellent situation is that the masses have been fully aroused. Never before has a mass movement been aroused so extensively and penetratingly as it is at present.

JMJP, p. 1.

151.   16.11.1967   The Relationship between the High and Low Levels

The relationship between the levels should be properly handled; the relationship between the cadres and masses should also be handled well. In future, cadres should go individually and see what is happening below. They must hold fast to the mass line, discuss with the masses whenever a problem crops up, and be the pupils of the masses. In a certain sense, the fighters who have the richest practical experience are the most intelligent and the ablest.

JMJP, p. 1.

152.   12.12.1967   Study Classes

The study classes organized by the PLA must have the participation of soldiers.

JMJP, p. 1.

153.   22.12.1967   Criticism and Self-criticism

The two factions should talk less of each other's weaknesses and mistakes. Let the others talk about their own weaknesses and mistakes. Each side ought to do more self-criticism— seeking general agreement and leaving minor differences intact.

JMJP, p. 1.

154.   Date uncertain, 1967   Four Instructions at a Standing Committee Meeting [of the Politburo]

1. We must step forward to meet the masses, to accept their criticism, and to do our own self-criticism. This is to get oneself near the fire [so to speak].

2. We must step forward to explain our policies to the masses. Those who have had to wear a dunce cap or had their face blackened should take the cap off, clean their face, and go straight to work.

3. Think of long-term interests and unite the majority. The freaks and monsters are the landlords, rich peasants, re-

actionaries, bad elements, and rightists—the minority. Even some who have made serious mistakes should be saved by letting them correct their errors. Otherwise, how can we unite more than ninety-five per cent [of the people].

4. Convince the cadres and make them understand. Do not let everyone who has been through the test [criticism] become ashen with despair. We must go out, not with the word 'fear' (*p'a*) but with the word 'dare' (*kan*) [in our minds]. In this way we can solve questions of any magnitude. If we go out with the word 'fear', [the opponents] will make more and more demands.

NT, p. 12.

1968

155. 12.1.1968 Reshape the World

The struggle to reshape the world by the proletariat and revolutionary peoples consists of these tasks: to reshape the objective world and also to reshape their own subjective world.

JMJP commentator, p. 1.

156. 17.1.1968 Cunningness of the Reactionaries

How do the counter-revolutionaries play their game of duplicity? How do they manage to present a false image to deceive us while clandestinely carrying on [activities] we do not even suspect? Millions of good people do not know this and therefore many counter-revolutionaries have wormed their way into our ranks. Our people do not have good eye-sight: they are unable to differentiate the upright from the crooked. They may be able to tell the good from the bad in the light of their activities under normal conditions. Nevertheless, we are rather inept at singling out certain people in the light of their activities under special conditions.

The New Anhwei Daily, 17.1.1968,
reproduced in the *JMJP*, 24.1.1968, p. 1.

157.   19.1.1968   Party Organization

The party organization must consist of the advanced elements of the proletariat. As a vigorous vanguard organization, it should be able to lead the proletarian revolutionary masses in their struggle against class enemies.

JMJP, p. 1.

158.   5.2.1968   Study Classes

Setting up study classes is a good procedure, because many problems can be solved in them.

JMJP, p. 1.

159.   9.2.1968   People's Air Force

Form a strong people's air force to defend the fatherland and to prepare for the repulsion of invaders.

JMJP, p. 6.

160.   12.2.1968   Inscription for the New Chingkangshan District (originally Chian, Kiangsi)

Develop the revolutionary tradition and win even greater victory.

JMJP, p. 1.

161.   1.3.1968   Anarchy

Resolutely overcome lack of discipline or even, in many places, anarchy.

Anarchy is detrimental to the interests of the people and against their wishes.

JMJP, p. 1.

162.   30.3.1968   Experiences of the Revolutionary Committees

The experience of the revolutionary committees is threefold:
1. they have representatives from the revolutionary cadres;

2. they have representatives from the PLA; and 3. they have representatives from the revolutionary masses. They have carried out the revolutionary three-way alliance. The revolutionary committees must achieve a unified leadership by cutting through duplicated administrative structures. [Following the principles of] eliminating incompetent soldiers and simplifying the administration, the committees should organize a revolutionized leading core to make contacts with the masses.

JMJP, p. 1.

163.   1.4.1968   Three-way Alliance

The 'three-way alliance' revolutionary committee is an invention of the working class and the masses in this great Cultural Revolution.

The essential point of reforming the state agencies is to make contact with the masses.

JMJP, p. 1.

164.   10.4.1968   Nature of the Cultural Revolution

The great proletarian Cultural Revolution is in essence a great political revolution under socialist conditions by the proletariat against the bourgeoisie and all other exploiting classes. It is the continuation of the long struggle against the Kuomintang reactionaries waged by the CCP and the broad revolutionary masses under its leadership. It is the continuation of the struggle between the proletariat and bourgeoisie.

JMJP, p. 1.

165.   27.4.1968   Left, Centre, and Right

Except in the deserts, at every place of human habitation there is the left, the centre, and the right. This will continue to be so 10,000 years hence.

JMJP, p. 1.

166.   13.5.1968   Good Cadres—a reaffirmation

We must believe that more than ninety per cent of our cadres are good or comparatively good. The majority of those who have made mistakes can be reformed.

JMJP, p. 1.

167.   3.6.1968   Protect the Masses

Protect or, on the contrary, repress the masses: this is the basic distinction between the CCP and the KMT, between the proletariat and the bourgeoisie, and between the proletarian and bourgeois dictatorships.

JMJP, p. 1.

168.   10.6.1968   Struggle Against the Revisionists

The old Social Democrats in the past decades, and modern revisionists in the past dozen years or so . . . have formed a group of anti-communist, anti-people, and counter-revolutionary elements against whom we are waging a life-and-death struggle. There is no equality between us and them. Therefore the fight against them is a fight for our preservation and their extinction. The relationship between us and them can never be one of equality; it is a relationship of one class oppressing another— i.e. proletarian dictatorship over the bourgeoisie.

The day when the people are happy will be the day when the counter-revolutionaries begin their misery.

JMJP, p. 5.

169.   21.7.1968   Scientific and Technological Training

We must still run colleges. Here I must stress that we should still run physics and engineering colleges, but the period of schooling ought to be shortened, the education revolutionized, proletarian politics put in command, and the way of training technical personnel from the ranks of the workers advocated by the Shanghai Machine-Tool Factory adopted. Students must be selected from workers and peasants with practical experience, and after their study at school for several years they should return to practical production.

BBC/FE/2828/B/2.

170. 14.8.1968 Leading Role of the Working Class

Our country has a population of 700 million people and the working class is the leading class. The leading role of the working class in the Cultural Revolution and all fields of work should be developed. The working class should also constantly raise its own political consciousness in the course of the struggle.

JMJP, p. 1 and BBC/FE/2849/B/1.

171. 26.8.1968 Steps to be Taken

Set up three-way alliance revolutionary committees, conduct thorough criticisms, purify the ranks of the class, reform the party, simplify the administration, revise unreasonable rules and regulations, send down office personnel, and carry out 'struggle-criticism-transformation' in factories. Roughly speaking, these are the stages [we shall] pass through.

Yao Wen-yuan's article, *JMJP*, p. 1.

172. 27.8.1968 Educational Revolution

To carry out the proletarian educational revolution, it is imperative to have the leadership of the working class and its participation, together with the revolutionary three-way alliance of the soldiers of the PLA, students, and teachers, and the activists among the workers who have resolved to carry the proletarian educational revolution through to the end. Workers' propaganda teams should remain at the schools for a long time to share the task of 'struggle-criticism-transformation' and to perpetuate their leadership there. In the countryside, schools are to be run by the most reliable allies of the working class— the poor, lower, and middle peasants.

JMJP, p. 1.

173. 12 and 14.9.1968 Re-educating Intellectuals

This physician who has moved from the city to the country-side proves that the majority, even overwhelming majority, of students educated in old-style schools are capable of integrating with workers, peasants, and soldiers. Some of them can even be inventive and creative. However, they must be re-educated by workers, peasants, and soldiers under the guidance of the correct line [so that] their old thinking may be reformed thoroughly. Such intellectuals are welcomed by workers, peasants, and soldiers.

JMJP, 12.9.1968, p. 1 and
14.9.1968, p. 2.

174. 8.10.1968 Reforming Cadres

It is an excellent opportunity for the great number of cadres to learn anew by being sent down to do manual work. Only the aged and sick are exempted from taking this opportunity. Cadres who hold offices should be sent down on a rota basis.

JMJP, p. 1.

175. 16.10.1968 Party Rectification

I. A human being has arteries and veins and his heart makes the blood circulate. He breathes through the lungs, exhaling carbon dioxide and inhaling oxygen afresh, that is, getting rid of the waste and letting in the fresh. A proletarian party must also get rid of the waste and let in the fresh, for only in this way can it be full of vigour. Without eliminating waste and getting fresh blood the party has no vigour.

II. Our power—who gives it to us? The working class gives it to us and the masses of labouring people who comprise over ninety per cent of the population give it to us. We represent the proletariat and the masses, and have overthrown the enemies of the people. The people therefore support us. One of the basic principles of the communist party is to rely directly on the revolutionary masses.

BBC/FE/2901/B/1.

176. 30.10.1968 The Cultural Revolution

For consolidating the dictatorship of the proletariat, preventing a capitalist restoration, and constructing socialism, the

Great Proletarian Cultural Revolution has been absolutely necessary and timely.

> Quoted from the communique of the Twelfth
> Plenum of the Eighth Central Committee,
> *JMJP*, 2.11.1968, p. 1.

177.   25.11.1968   Historical Experience

Historical experience is noteworthy. A line or a view must be constantly and repeatedly explained. It will not do to explain it only to a few; it must be made known to the broad revolutionary masses.

> *JMJP*, p. 1.

178.   22.12.1968   Re-educating the Young

It is absolutely necessary for educated young people to go to the countryside to be re-educated by the poor and lower-middle peasants. Cadres and other city people should be persuaded to send their sons and daughters who have finished junior or senior middle school, college, or university to the countryside. Let us mobilize. Comrades throughout the countryside should welcome them.

> *JMJP*, 23.12.1968, p. 1.

179.   31.12.1968   Purifying Class Ranks

In purifying our class ranks, it is necessary to take a firm hold first and then pay attention to the policy.

In treating the counter-revolutionary elements and those who had made mistakes, it is necessary to pay attention to the policy. The target of attack must be narrowed and more people must be helped through education. Evidence, investigation, and study should be stressed. It is strictly forbidden to extort confessions and accept such confessions. As for good people who have made mistakes, we must give them more help through education. When they are awakened, we must liberate them without delay.

> NCNA and BBC/FE/2963/B/3.

1969

180. 21.2.1969   Policy and Planning

a. Serious attention should be given to policy in this stage of the struggle-criticism-transformation in the great proletarian Cultural Revolution.

b. In formulating plans it is necessary to mobilize the masses and carefully leave some leeway.

JMJP editorial, 22.2.1969, p. 1.

181. 13.3.1969   Russian Revisionism

The broad masses and the majority of the party members and cadres in the Soviet Union are good and revolutionary; so revisionist domination will not long survive.

JMJP, p. 1.

182. 17.3.1969   Summing up Experience

It is necessary to sum up experience conscientiously.

When one goes to a unit to get to know the situation there, one must become acquainted with the whole process of the movement—its inception, its development, and its present state; how the masses have acted and how the leadership has acted; what contradictions and struggles have emerged and what changes have occurred in these contradictions; and what progress people have made in their knowledge—so as to find out its laws.

BBC/FE/3026/B/5.

183. 22.3.1969   Spring Farming

The present is the time of spring farming. Let us hope that leading comrades, responsible personnel, and the popular masses will seize the opportunity to grasp the links in the chain of production in order to overtake last year's records.

JMJP editorial, p. 1.

184.   24.3.1969   Russian Revisionism

The poisonous pests have arranged their own grave-diggers.
Their date of burial will not be too far away.

JMJP, p. 6.

185.   15.4.1969   The Ninth Congress

We hope the present Congress will be a congress of unity and
victory and after its conclusion, even greater victories will be
won throughout the country.

NCNA, BBC/FE/3049/C/2.

186.   15.4.1969   The Proletariat

The proletariat is the greatest class in human history.
Ideologically, politically, and numerically it is the greatest
revolutionary class. It can and must unite the overwhelming
majority of people around itself in order to isolate as much as
possible and attack a handful of enemies.

Quoted in Lin Piao's Political Report,
JMJP, 28.4.1969.

187.   15.4.1969   The Chinese and World Revolutions

We have won a great victory. But the defeated class will
continue to struggle. Its members are still about and it still
exists. Therefore we cannot speak of the final victory, not for
decades. We must not lose our vigilance. From the Leninist
point of view, the final victory in one socialist country not only
requires the efforts of the proletariat and the broad popular
masses at home, but also depends on the victory of the world
revolution and the abolition of the system of exploitation of
man by man on this earth so that all mankind will be emanci-
pated. Consequently, it is wrong to talk about the final victory
of the revolution in our country light-heartedly; it runs counter
to Leninism and does not conform to facts.

Quoted in Lin Piao's Political Report,
JMJP, 28.4.1969.

INDEX TO THE INSTRUCTIONS

PART III

A Chronological Bibliography of Mao's Writings (in both English and Chinese) 1917–1968

compiled by the editor

1917

1 Notes from reading taken when Mao was at the First Teachers' Training College, over 10,000 characters, unpublished; only one volume survived the fire of the 'Horse Day Incident' (21.5.1927), Ch'angsha. See Li Jui, p. 37; Hsieh Chüeh-tsai, 'My first meeting with Comrade Mao Tse-tung,' *New Observers*, 1952, no. 11. n. tr.

2 'A study of physical education,' signed '28-Stroke Student,' *New Youth*, III, no. 2, 1.4.1917. SRS, Mao Zedong: *Une étude de l'éducation physique*, Paris: Mouton, 1962, and excerpts in SRS, *PT*, pp. 94–102.

3 'A letter to Hakuro Toten,' reproduced in Miyazaki Ruke, 'Mo Taku-to no tegami,' *Asahi Shimbun*, 3.7.1967.

1918

. . .   . . .

1919

4 *The Hsiang River Review* (Weekly) ed. Mao, first issue 14.7.1919, suspended at the beginning of August 1919, altogether five issues and one supplement.

5 'Events in the West—comments' and 'World miscellany' in each issue. n. tr.

6 'The Germans painfully signed the Treaty,' no. 2. n. tr.

7 'The great union of the popular masses,' nos. 2, 3, and 4, reproduced in *Sunday*, Ch'engtu, nos. 19, 20, and 21. SRS, *PT*, pp. 105–6 and 170–1.

8 'The founding of the Society for Health Studies,' supplement, 21.7.1919. n. tr.

9   'Ch'en Tu-hsiu, his arrest and rescue,' date uncertain. n. tr.

10   'What does a radical party mean?' date uncertain. n. tr.

11   A new-style poem, date uncertain. n. tr.

12   *The New Hunan* (Weekly) ed. Mao from no. 7 to no. 10 immediately before its suspension, first issue 5.6.1919, which is the only issue extant. n. tr.

13   'The regulations of the Problem Study Society,' *Peking University Monthly*, 23.10.1919. n. tr.

14   'Students' work,' *Hunan Education Monthly*, I, no. 2, 1.11.1919. n. tr.

In the *Ta Kung Pao*, Ch'angsha

15   'A critique of Miss Chao's suicide,' 16.11.1919.

16   'The evils of society and Miss Chao,' date uncertain.

17   'Advice to boys and girls on the marriage problem,' 19.11.1919.

18   'The problem of love—young people and old people,' date uncertain.

19   'The problem of Miss Chao's personality,' date uncertain.

20   'Against suicide,' 30.11.1919. rf. in the *Hunan Li-shih Tzu-liao*, 1959, no. 4, pp. 27–32 and Roxane Witke, 'Mao Tse-tung, women and suicide in the May Fourth era,' *CQ*, no. 31. Also SRS, *PT*, pp. 226–8.

1920

21   'Self-determination of the people of Hunan,' *T'ien-wen*, ed. P'eng Huang, Shanghai (from 1.2.1920 to 11.7.1920), no. 23. n. tr.

22   'Introducing *The Communist Monthly*, *Ta Kung Pao*, Ch'ang-sha, 11–12.1920. n. tr.

23   'More than 10 articles on the self-government of Hunan,' *Ta Kung Pao*, dates uncertain. n. tr.

1921

Correspondence of the members of the New Citizens' Study Society, issued by the Culture Bookstore, Ch'angsha, 1921. The letters are dated from 6.1918 to 1.1921.

24   The first series, 13 letters, three by Mao. n. tr.

25   The second series, 31 letters, eight by Mao. n. tr.

26   The third series, 7 letters, correspondence between Ts'ai Ho-sen and Mao on the questions of communism and the founding of a party. n. tr.

1922

27 Popular readers compiled with Li Liu-ju, 2nd half, 1922. n. tr.
28 'Letter to the *Ta Kung Pao* correspondent, Tun, from the Compositors Union,' *Ta Kung Pao*, Ch'angsha, 14.12.1922. n. tr.

1923

29 'Statement on the inauguration of the Hunan Self-education University,' *Tung-fang Tsa-chih*, XX, no. 6, 25.3.1923. n. tr.
30 'External pressure, warlords, and revolution,' *New Era*, no. 1. n. tr.

In the *Guide Weekly*
31 'The Peking *Coup d'état* and the merchants,' nos. 31–2, 11.7.1923. SRS, *PT*, 139–42 and 266.
32 'The provincial constitution *sutra* and Chao Heng-t'i,' no. 36, 15.8.1923. n. tr.
33 'The English and Liang Ju-hao,' no. 38, 29.8.1923. n. tr.
34 'Cigarette tax,' no. 38, 29.8.1923. n. tr.

1924

. . . . . .

1925

35 *The Political Weekly* ed. Mao, published by the *Political Weekly* Society, Department of Propaganda, the KMT, Canton, n. tr.

In the first issue (5.12.1925)
36 'Reasons for publication of the *Political Weekly*'
37 'The three-three-three-one system'
38 'Yang K'un-ju's public notice and Liu Chih-lu's telegram'
39 'Those anti-communists who are opposed to the same enemies are also our friends'
40 'Praises from all countries'
41 'Long live the grand alliance of the anti-communist Chinese people's armies!'
42 'Communist programme and "not really communist" '
43 'Tsou Lu and revolution'

In the second issue (13.12.1925)

44   'To the left or to the right?'
45   'So, this is communism!'

In the third issue (20.12.1925)

46   'The Peking right wing and imperialism'
47   'The last tool of imperialism'
48   'The worst trick of the right wing'

(No more articles by Mao appeared in this periodical after the third issue.)

1926

In the *Chinese Peasants*, Canton

49   'Analysis of the various classes of the Chinese peasantry and their attitude towards revolution,' I, no. 1, 1.1926. SRS, *PT*, pp. 172–7.

50   'Analysis of the classes in Chinese society,' I, no. 2, 19.2.1926; *Chinese Youth*, no. 116, 13.3.1926; *SW*, I, 1.

51   'Report on propaganda,' *Political Weekly*, nos. 6–7, 4.1926. n. tr.

52   *Ch'angsha*—to the melody of *Shen Yuan Ch'un*, JC, p. 320.

53   'The bitter sufferings of the peasants in Kiangsu and Chekiang, and their movements of resistance,' *Guide Weekly*, no. 179, 25.11.1926; SRS, *PT*, pp. 178–9.

54   'The class basis of Chao Heng-t'i and the tasks before us,' a pamphlet, Ch'angsha, 12.1926, rf. in J. Rue, *Mao Tse-tung in Opposition*, Stanford, 1966, p. 48.

1927

55   'Report on an investigation of the peasant movement in Hunan,' *Fighters Weekly* (the organ of the Hunan CP), Ch'angsha, 5.3.1927; *Guide Weekly*, no. 191, 12.3.1927; Supplement (no. 7) of the *Wuhan Central Daily*, 28.3.1927; the third section on the 14 Great Achievements, *SW*, 1947 supplement, pp. 12–39; *SW*, I, 2.

56   'Case study of the lives of Chinese tenant peasants,' Canton, 1927(?). Chang Ching-lu, *Historical Material of Modern Publications*, I, p. 77 gives the date, 1937; this is likely to be a mistake.

57   *Huang Ho Lou* (Yellow Crane Tower), to the melody of *P'u Sa Man*, summer 1927, JC, p. 322.

58   Lost: 'Investigation of the villages in Ch'angsha, Hsiangt'an, Hsianghsiang, Hengshan, and Liling in Hunan,' unpublished, n. tr. rf. Liberation Publishing Society, *Village Investigations*, Central China edition, 1949, preface 1; *SW*, III, p. 12.

1928

59   *Chingkang Mountain*—to the melody of *Hsi Chiang Yüeh*, summer 1928, JC, p. 323.
60   'Two letters from the Front Committee to the Centre,' *Central Correspondence*, nos. 2 and 5, 12 and 30, 8.1928. n. tr.
61   'Political problems and the tasks of the party of the border region—the resolutions of the second conference of the CP in the Hunan-Kiangsi border region,' 5.10.1928, *SW*, 1947 supplement, pp. 101–8; *SW*, I, 3.
62   'Report from the Chingkangshan Front Committee to the Centre,' 25.11.1928, *SW*, 1947 supplement, pp. 63–87; *SW*, I, 4.
63   'The land law of Chingkangshan,' 12.1928, Liberation Publishing Society, *Rural Survey*, 1949, pp. 91–3. n. tr.
64   Lost: 'Investigation of the villages of Ningkang and Yunghsin of Chingkangshan,' unpublished, n. tr. rf. Liberation Publishing Society, *Rural Survey*, 1949, preface 1; *SW*, III, p. 12.

1929

65   *New Year's Day*—to the melody of *Ju Meng Ling*, JC, p. 324.
66   *Huich'ang*—to the melody of *Ch'ing P'ing Lo*, 1.1929, JC, p. 325.
67   'The second anniversary of An Wu-ch'ing's martyrdom,' 1.1929, *SHWS*, p. 6.
68   'The land law of Hsingkuo,' 4.1929, Liberation Publishing Society, *Rural Survey*, 1949, pp. 94–5. n. tr.
69   *Advance to Fukien*—to the melody of *Ch'ing P'ing Lo*, 9 or 10.1929, JC, p. 326.
70   *The double ninth day*—to the melody of *Ts'ai Sang Tzu*, 11.10.1929, JC, p. 327.
71   'The resolutions of the 9th conference of the representatives of the 4th Army of the CCP,' *SW*, 1944, III, pp. 135–183; *SW*, I, 5.

1930

72 'A letter to Comrade Lin Piao,' 5.1.1930, *SW*, 1947 supplement, pp. 88–100; *SW*, I, 6.

73 *March on Chian*—to the melody of *Chien Tzu Mu Lan Hua*, 2.1930, JC, p. 328.

74 'Oppose book worship,' 5.1930, *SR*, pp. 33–41.

75 *Attack on Nanch'ang*—to the melody of *Tieh Lien Hua*, 6.1930, JC, p. 329.

76 'Investigation at Hsingkuo,' 9.1930 (completed on 26.1.1931), *SW*, 1947, I, pp. 23–94; Liberation Publishing Society, *Rural Survey*, 1949, pp. 7–62. n. tr.

77 'Investigation at Tungt'ang and other places,' 30.10.1930, Liberation Publishing Society, *Rural Survey*, pp. 63–70. n. tr.

78 'Investigation at Muk'ou Village,' 18.11.1930, ibid., pp. 71–73.

79 'Land redistribution in west Kiangsi,' 12.11.1930, ibid., pp. 74–8. n. tr.

80 'Mistakes in the land struggles of Kiangsi,' 14.11.1930, ibid., pp. 79–82. n. tr.

81 'Questions of sharing the green [shoots] and land tenure,' 15.11.1930, ibid., pp. 83–8. n. tr.

82 'The problem of the rich peasants after land redistribution,' (situation in Yunghsin and the northern route, recorded by Mao Tse-tung based on the report by Wang Huai and Ch'en Cheng-jen) ibid., pp. 89–90. n. tr.

83 'A letter to Ku Po,' 12.1930, copy made by the party branch of P'ihsia, Hsiao Tso-liang, *Power Relations within the Chinese Communist Movement 1930–1934*, I, p. 104, and II, p. 264. The authenticity of this letter is suspect.

1931

84 *The First Encirclement*—to the melody of *Yü Chia Ao*, 1.1931, JC, p. 330.

85 *The Second Encirclement*—to the melody of *Yü Chia Ao*, 5.1931, JC, p. 332.

1932

86 'A letter to Yuan Kuo-p'ing on mass work,' 6.3.1932, Ch'en Ch'eng, R. 14.

87 'Stop the civil war and resist Japan,' Juichin, 1932, 4 pp. in Nym Wales collection.

1933

88 *Tapoti*—to the melody of *P'u Sa Man*, 2.1933, JC, p. 333.

89 'How to analyse the classes,' 7.6.1933, *Collected Subversive Documents of the Red Bandits*, III, pp. 946–9; *SW*, I, 8.

In the *RC*

90 'Land investigation is the major task in many areas,' no. 86, 17.6.1933. n. tr.

91 'The first step in land investigation—widely mobilizing the organizations,' no. 87, 20.6.1933. n. tr.

92 'Develop land investigation campaign according to the differences in the evolvement of village class struggle,' no. 88, 23.6.1933. n. tr.

93 'New situation and new tasks,' no. 97, 29.7.1933. n. tr.

94 'Crush the 5th Encirclement and the tasks of soviet economic reconstruction—a report to the economic reconstruction conference of the 17 southern counties,' no. 102, 16.8.1933; *SW*, I, 7.

95 'A preliminary survey of land investigation campaign,' *Struggle*, no. 24, 29.8.1933; *Red Flag*, no. 61, 30.10.1933; *Collected Subversive Documents of the Red Bandits*, III, pp. 970–88. n. tr.

96 'This year's elections,' *RC*, no. 108, 6.9.1933. n. tr.

97 'Foreword to the *Work of Ch'angkang Village Soviet*,' 15.12.1933, Ch'en Ch'eng, R. 10. n. tr.

98 'Mass work in land investigation campaign,' *Red Flag*, no. 63, 12.1933. n. tr.

99 'Work of the Ch'angkang village soviet in Hsingkuo,' *Struggle*, nos. 42, 43, and 44 on 12, 19, and 26.1.1934; *Young People's Honest Words*, no. 6, 14.1.1934; Liberation Publishing Society, *Rural Survey*, 1949, pp. 96–132. n. tr.

100 'Survey of Ts'aihsi village,' 1933, *SW*, 1947, I, pp. 151–74. n. tr.

101 Lost: 'Survey of Hsunwu,' 1933. n. tr. rf. Liberation Publishing Society, *Rural Survey*, 1949, preface 2; *SW*, III, p. 12.

1934

102 'Opening speech at the second national congress of soviet representatives,' *RC*, no. 2, 24.1.1934. n. tr.

103 'Report to the second national congress of soviet representatives on behalf of the Central Executive and People's Committees of Chinese Soviet Republic,' 24–5.1.1934, *RC*, no. 6. 14.1.1934; *SW*, I, 9; *DH*, pp. 226–39.

104 'Be concerned with the well-being of the masses, pay attention to methods of work,' 27.1.1934, *SR*, pp. 42–7; *SW*, I, 10.

105 'Conclusion on the Central Executive Committee's report to the second national congress of soviet representatives,' *RC*, no. 5, 31.1.1934.

106 'Report on urgent mobilization to the second national congress of soviet representatives,' *RC*, no. 6, 1.2.1934.

107 'Closing speech of the second national congress of soviet representatives,' *RC*, no. 7, 3.2.1934.
(The second national congress documents, see *Red China*, N.Y.: International Publishers, 1934 and London: Martin Lawrence, 1934.)

108 'Work of the Ts'aihsi village soviet in Shanghang,' *Struggle*, no. 49, 2.3.1934. n. tr.

109 'How does a village soviet work?' 10.4.1934, Chang Wen-t'ien and Mao Tse-tung, *How do a district soviet and a village soviet work?* Ch'en Ch'eng, R. 10. n. tr.

110 'May Day declaration of the Central Government of Chinese Soviet Republic,' *RC*, no. 179, 24.4.1934. n. tr.

111 'The scheme of Japanese imperialism,' (interview with a *Red China* correspondent) *RC*, no. 181, 28.4.1934; *Chieh-pao*, 15.5.1934 in Hatano, IV, pp. 807–10. n. tr.

112 'Interview on present situation and the anti-Japanese vanguard of the Red Army,' *RC*, no. 221, 1.8.1934. n. tr.

1935

113 *Loushan Pass*—to the melody of *Yi Ch'in O*, 1.1935, JC, p. 334.

114 *Three Short Poems*—to the melody of *Shih Liu Tzu Ling*, 3–4.1935, JC, p. 335.

115 'Proclamation on the northward march of the Chinese Workers' and Peasants' Red Army to fight Japan,' *National Battle Front*, no. 2, 10.8.1935; SRS, *PT*, pp. 152–4.

116 *The Long March* (*lü shih*) 9.1935, JC, p. 336.

117 *Mount Liup'an*—to the melody of *Ch'ing P'ing Lo*, 10.1935, JC, p. 337.

118 *K'unlun*—to the melody of *Nien Nu Chiao*, 10.1935, JC, pp. 338–9.

119 'On tactics against Japanese imperialism,' 27.12.1935, *SW*, I, 11.

1936

120 'Letter to Comrade Lin Piao,' before 6.1936 (the Anti-Japanese Military and Political University was founded in 6.1936 and this letter discusses its foundation), *SHWS*, pp. 1–2.

121 'The Central Soviet Government's appeal to the Elder Brothers Soviety,' *Struggle*, no. 105, 12.7.1936; SRS, *PT*, pp. 189–90; SRS, 'Mao Tse-tung and Secret Societies,' *CQ*, no. 27.

122 'Problems of strategy in Chinese revolutionary war,' autumn 1936, *SW*, 1947 supplement, pp. 109–83; *SW*, I, 12.

123 'Letter to Shen Chun-ju, Chang Nai-ch'i, Tsou T'ao-fen, and T'ao Hsing-chih,' 10.8.1936, *Struggle*, no. 13; Hatano, VI, pp. 566–71; *China, the march toward unity*, N.Y., 1937.

124 'Important statement on the cessation of the civil war and resistance to Japan—Stop all hostile activities against the National Revolutionary Army,' 15.10.1936, *Mao Tse-tung on the Sino-Japanese War*, pp. 47–9, n. tr.

125 'Statement on Chiang Kai-shek's statement,' 28.12.1936, *SW*, I, 13.

1937

126 'Letter to the old comrade, Hsü [T'eh-li], 30.1.1937, *SHWS*, p. 5.

127 'Interview with Agnes Smedley,' 1.3.1937, *Essays by Mao Tse-tung*.

128 'Letter to Edgar Snow,' 10.3.1937, MS. at Hoover Institution.

129 'The tasks of the Chinese national anti-Japanese united front,' *Liberation*, no. 2, 1.5.1937; *SW*, I, 14.

130 'Win the masses in their millions for the anti-Japanese national united front,' 7.5.1937, *Liberation*, no. 4, 24.5.1937; *SW*, I, 15.

131 'Letter to the Spanish people,' 15.5.1937, *Essays by Mao Tse-Tung*; SRS, *PT*, pp. 290 f.

132 'Letter to Comrade E. Browder,' 24.6.1937, *Essays by Mao Tse-tung*; SRS, *PT*, p. 291.

133 'On practice,' 7.1937, *JMJP*, 29.12.1950; *SW*, I, 16.

134 'Declaration of the CCP,' 23.7.1937, *Mao Tse-tung on the Sino-Japanese War*, pp. 50–2. n. tr.

135 'Policies, measures, and perspectives for resisting the Japanese invasion,' *Liberation*, no. 12, 15.8.1937; *SW*, II, 18.

136 'On contradiction,' 8.1937 (probably based on his lecture notes of dialectical materialism, rf. Chang Ju-hsin, 'Learn and grasp Mao Tse-tung's theory and strategy,' *LD*, 18–19.2.1942); *JMJP*, 1.4.1952; *SW*, I, 17.

137 'For the mobilization of all the nation's forces for victory in the war of resistance,' 25.8.1937, *SW*, II, 19.

138 'Combat liberalism,' 7.9.1937, *SW*, II, 20.

139 'Urgent tasks following the establishment of KMT-CCP co-operation,' *Liberation*, no. 18, 2.10.1937; *SW*, II, 21.

140 'Speech at the meeting celebrating the completion of the buildings of the Anti-Japanese Military and Political University,' *Our Great Task* (the university's official organ), no. 14, 17.10.1937; *SHWS*, p. 2.

141 'Inscriptions for the founding of the North Shensi Public School,' *Mobilization*, no. 10, 23.10.1937; *SHWS*, pp. 5–6.

142 'Interview with the British journalist James Bertram,' 25.10.1937, *Liberation*, no. 23, 23.11.1937; *SW*, II, 22.

143 'The situation and tasks in the Anti-Japanese War after the fall of Shanghai and T'aiyuan,' 12.11.1937, *SW*, II, 23.

144 *Essays by Mao Tse-tung*, Shanghai, 1937, n. tr.

145 *Mao Tse-tung on Guerilla Warfare*, tr. Samuel Griffith II, N.Y.: Praeger, 1961.

1938

146 'On "one-party dictatorship",' *Liberation*, no. 28, 11.1.1938. n. tr.

147 'Interview with an Associated Press correspondent on the future of the Anti-Japanese War,' 11.2.1938, Hatano, VII, pp. 427–33.

148 *Basic Tactics*, Hankow: Self-strengthening Publishing House, 3.1938; tr. SRS, N.Y.: Praeger, 1966. Authenticity disputable.

149 'Speech commemorating the 13th anniversary of the death of Dr. Sun Yat-sen and the deaths of officers and soldiers in the Anti-Japanese War,' *Liberation*, no. 33, 1.4.1938. n. tr.

150 'Proclamation by the government of the Shensi-Kansu-Ninghsia Border Region and the Rear Headquarters of the Eighth Route Army,' 15.5.1938, *SW*, II, 24.

151 'Problems of strategy in guerilla war against Japan,' *Liberation*, no. 40, 30.5.1938; *SW*, II, 25.

152 'On protracted war,' *Liberation*, nos. 43–4, 1.7.1938; *SW*, II, 26.

153 'Interview with the representatives of the World Students Union,' *Liberation*, no. 46, 23.7.1938. n. tr.

154 'Our views on the People's Political Council,' *Liberation*, no. 47, 1.8.1938. n. tr.

155 'The New Stage,' *Liberation*, no. 57, 25.11.1938; *Documents*, Shanghai, III, IV; Chungking: New China Information Committee, 1938; ch. 7, *SW*, II, 27.

156 'Letter to Mr. Chiang Kai-shek,' unpublished, rf. Chiang Kai-shek, *Soviet Russia in China*, London, 1957, p. 87.

157 'The question of independence and initiative within the united front,' 5.11.1938, *SW*, II, 28.

158 'Problems of war and strategy,' 6.11.1938, *SW*, II, 29.

159 'Interview with a Yenan *New China Daily* correspondent, Ch'i-kuang,' Far Eastern Publishing House, 1938, n. tr.

160 'On Lu Hsün,' *July*, 3.1938; *Documents*, II, pp. F. 8–10; *SHWS*, pp. 2–4 (the speech was made at the meeting commemorating the first anniversary of the death of Lu Hsün in the North Shensi Public School, 19.10.1937.).

1939

161 'Introducing the *Military and Political Journal* of the Eighth Route Army,' inaugural issue, 15.1.1939. n. tr.

162 'Speech at the May Day celebration in Yenan,' 1.5.1939, *New China Daily*, 10.5.1939; *Quotations*, p. 147. n. tr.

163 'The May the 4th Movement,' *Liberation*, no. 70, 1.5.1939; *SW*, II, 30.

164 'The orientation of the youth movement,' 4.5.1939, *SW*, II, 31.

165 'The political orientation of the national spiritual mobilization,' *Liberation*, no. 71, 15.5.1939; *Masses*, III, no. 3, 11.6.1939. n. tr.

166 'Inscription for the Anti-Japanese Military and Political University,' 4.1939, *JMJP*, 2.8.1966, p. 2.

167 'To be attacked by the enemy is not a bad thing but a good thing,' 26.5.1939 for the celebration of the third anniversary of the Anti-Japanese Military and Political University, *SR*, pp. 130–2.

168 'The Chinese and British peoples stand on the same front,' 1.6.1939, *Masses*, III, no. 10, 23.7.1939.

169 'The gravest danger at the moment,' *Liberation*, nos. 75–6, 10.7.1939; *SW*, II, 32.

170 'Punish the reactionaries according to law,' *Liberation*, no. 81, 20.8.1939; *SW*, II, 33.

171 'Interview with a *New China Daily* correspondent on the new international situation,' 1.9.1939, *SW*, II, 34.

172 'On the Russo-German Non-aggression Pact,' Chungking *New China Daily*, 6.9.1939; Wang Chien-min, *Draft History*, III, pp. 385–7. n. tr.

173 'Outline of a speech on the second imperialist war,' *Liberation*, no. 85, 30.9.1939 (the speech was given at a meeting of party cadres in Yenan, 14.9.1939). n. tr.

174 'Mr. Mao Tse-tung's statement on the present international situation and China's Resistance War,' *Liberation*, nos. 83–4, 20.9.1939; *SW*, II, 35.

175 'Introducing *the Communist*,' 4.10.1939, *SW*, 1947 supplement; *SW*, II, 37. (Apart from a reference to this monthly in Chang Ching-lu, *Historical Material of Modern Publications*, IV, 1st part, no other Chinese writer has either mentioned it or cited any article published in it. Earl Browder, however, refers to Ch'en Po-ta's review of *China's Destiny* by Chiang Kai-shek, in its January issue in 1944, in his preface to *On New Democracy*. The Chinese translation of Browder's preface is carried in the *LD*, 1.11.1944.)

176 'Youth needs experience,' 5.10.1939, *Selected Essays on the Youth Movement*, Chinese Youth Publishing House, 1940; SRS, *PT*, p. 230.

177 'Interview with correspondents,' *Liberation*, nos. 87–8, 20.10.1939. n. tr.

178 'The CCP Centre's decisions on the current situation and the party's tasks,' *Liberation*, nos. 87–8, 20.10.1939; *SW*, II, 38.

179 'The identity of interests between the Soviet Union and all mankind,' *Liberation*, no. 86, 10.10.1939; *SW*, II, 36.

180 'Recruit large number of intellectuals,' 1.12.1939, *SW*, II, 39.

181 'Speech at the meeting celebrating the 4th anniversary of the December 9th students movement organized by Yenan Schools and youth organizations,' unpublished, rf. *Comrade Mao Tse-tung on Youth and Youth Work*, Peking, 1964, pp. 9–10 and 14. n. tr.

455 'Instruction issued at the Hupei Iron-Steel Works,' 9.1958, *SHWS*, p. 18.

456 'Interview with a NCNA correspondent,' 29.9.1958, *RF*, no. 10, 16.10.1958; *JMJP*, 1.10.1958; *PR*, no. 32, 7.10.1958.

457 'Talk at the Wuch'ang meeting of the Politburo of the Central Committee of the CCP,' 1.12.1958, *Quotations*, pp. 72–4.

1959

458 'Letter to Comrade William Z. Foster,' 17.1.1959, *SHWS*, p. 19.

459 'Talk at the enlarged Chengchow meeting of the Politburo of the Centre of the CCP,' 2.1959, *Anti-party Clique*, p. 5.

460 'Talk at the 2nd meeting of the Politburo at Chengchow,' 3.1959, *Anti-party Clique*, p. 6.

461 'Statement on international and domestic situations, and problems in Tibet at the 16 Supreme State Conference,' *JMJP*, 6.4.1959.

462 *Return to Shaoshan (lü-shih)* 6.1959, JC, p. 350.

463 *Lushan (lü-shih)* 1.7.1959, JC, p. 351.

Anti-party Clique

464 'Statements before and after the Lushan plenum,' 10.7. and 16.8.1959, pp. 11–12.

465 'Criticism of P'eng Teh-huai's statement on 14.7.1959,' 7.1959, p. 13.

466 'Criticism on a letter,' (criticism on Li Chung-yün's statement) 26.7.1959, p. 13.

467 'Comments on the circulation of three essays,' (refutation of Khrushchev's views on rural communes) 29.7.1959, p. 14.

468 'Letter to Wang Chia-hsiang,' (refutation of Khrushchev's views on rural communes) 1.8.1959, p. 14.

469 'Talk at the 8th plenum of the 8th Central Committee,' 2.8.1959, pp. 16–17.

470 'Comments on an article—"The dissolution and resumption of mess halls of Taochu Brigade, T'anling Commune, P'ingchiang, Hunan",' 5.8.1959, p. 17.

471 'Comments on two articles—"Situations in Wang Kuo-fan Commune have always been excellent" and "Who are the gossips in the villages now?",' 6.8.1959, p. 18.

1962

489 'Talk on democratic centralism,' 30.1.1962, *SHWS*, pp. 22–5.
490 'Talk at the 10th plenum of the 8th Central Committee,' 24.9.1962, *Anti-party Clique*, pp. 24–7.
491 'Resolutions of the 10th plenum of the 8th Central Committee: further consolidating the collective economy of communes,' *JMJP*, 29.9.1962.
492 'Notes on Comrade K'o Ch'ing-shih's report,' 12.12.1962, *SHWS*, p. 25.
493 *Winter Clouds (lü-shih)*, 26.12.1962, JC, p. 358.

1963

494 *Reply to Kuo Mo-jo*—to the melody of *Man Chiang Hung*, 9.1.1963, JC, p. 359.
495 'Where do correct ideas come from?' 5.1963, *SR*, pp. 405–6.
496 'Statement supporting the American Negroes' just struggle against imperialist racial discrimination,' *JMJP*, 9.8.1963; *People of the World, Unite and Defeat the US Aggressors and All Their Lackeys*, Peking: FLP, 1964.
497 'Statement opposing aggression against southern Vietnam and slaughter of its people by the US-Ngo Dinh Diem clique,' *JMJP*, 30.8.1963; *People of the World, Unite and Defeat the US Aggressors and All Their Lackeys*, 1964.
498 'Instruction concerning literature and art,' 9.1963, *SHWS*, p. 26.
499 'Instruction concerning literature and art,' 12.12.1963, *JMJP*, 28.5.1967; *Five Documents on Literature and Art*, Peking, 1967.
500 'The Centre's instruction on intensifying mutual learning and overcoming complacency and conceit,' (excerpts) 13.12.1963, NT, pp. 4–7.

1964

501 'Statement on the Chinese people's firm support of the Panamanian people's just patriotic struggle against US imperialism,' *JMJP*, 13.1.1964; *People of the World, Unite and Defeat the US Aggressors and All Their Lackeys*, Peking, 1964.
502 'Statement on the Chinese people's support of the Japanese people's great patriotic struggle,' *JMJP*, 28.1.1964;

People of the World, Unite and Defeat the US Aggressors and All Their Lackeys, Peking, 1964.

503 'Spring Festival instruction on education,' 13.2.1964, *SHWS*, pp. 26–8.

504 *Quotations from Chairman Mao Tse-tung*, 5.1964, Peking, 1966.

505 'Instruction concerning literature and art,' 27.6.1964, *JMJP*, 28.5.1967; *Five Documents on Literature and Art*, Peking, 1967.

506 *Selected Readings from the Works of Mao Tse-tung*, 9.7.1964, Peking, 1967.

507 'Instruction on literature and art,' 8.1964, *SHWS*, p. 26.

508 'Statement supporting the people of the Congo (L) against US aggression,' 28.11.1964, *New China Monthly*, no. 242; *People of the World, Unite and Defeat the US Aggressors and All Their Lackeys*, Peking, 1964.

509 'Talk on education at the reception of the Nepalese education delegation,' *SHWS*, pp. 28–9.

510 'Comments on the directive on learning from the PLA and intensifying political work,' *SHWS*, p. 30.

1965

511 '23 Articles on rural socialist education,' 14.1.1965, *JMJP*, 31.3.1965; Fukien, 18.1.1965.

512 'Comments on Comrade Hsü Yin-sheng's article: "How to play table tennis",' 1.1965, *SHWS*, p. 31.

513 'Comments on Comrade Ch'en Cheng-jen's report on his "squatting point",' 29.1.1965, *SHWS*, p. 31.

514 'Talk at a work conference of the Politburo,' 1.1965, unpublished, rf. *JMJP*, 3.6.1965. n. tr.

515 'Interview with Edgar Snow,' 1.1965, London *Sunday Times* and *Washington Post*, 14.2.1965.

516 *Chingkangshan Revisited*—to the melody of *Shui Tiao Ko T'ou*, Takeuchi Minoru, 'A poem by Mao Tse-tung,' *Asahi Shimbun* (evening edition), 19.1.1967; JC, *CQ*, no. 34 and MTT, pp. 112–13.

517 'Statement supporting the Dominican people's resistance against US armed aggression,' *JMJP*, 12.5.1965.

518 'Instruction on public health work,' 6.1965, NT, p. 9.

519 'Interview with the French Minister of Culture, André Malraux,' André Malraux, *Antimemoires*, Paris: Gallimard, 1967, pp. 522–53; excerpts, JC, MTT, pp. 28–9.

520 'Talk at Hangchow,' 21.12.1965, *SHWS*, pp. 31–4; NT, pp. 1–3.

1966

521 'Comments on the report on further improving the agricultural work of the PLA by the Rear Service Department of the Military Commission—a letter to Comrade Lin Piao,' 7.5.1966, *SHWS*, pp. 34–5.

522 'A circular of the CCP Centre,' 16.5.1966, *RF*, 1967, no. 7, 20.5.1967; *PR*, no. 21, 1967.

523 'Talk at a conference,' 21.7.1966, NT, pp. 8–9.

524 'Talk at a meeting with district party secretaries and members of the Central Cultural Revolution Team,' 22.7.1966, *SHWS*, pp. 43–4.

525 'Letters to the red guards of Tsinghua Middle School,' 1.8.1966, *SHWS*, pp. 35–6.

526 'Bombard the headquarters,' (My big-character poster) 5.8.1966, *JMJP*, 5.8.1967; *PR*, no. 33, 1967.

527 'Resolutions on the great Cultural Revolution of the 11th plenum of the Central Committee of the CCP,' (the 16 articles) 8.8.1966, *JMJP*, 9.8.1966; Peking, FLP, 1966; SCMP, no. 3761.

528 'Closing speech at the 11th plenum of the 8th Central Committee,' 8.8.1966, *SHWS*, pp. 37–8.

529 'Talk at an enlarged work conference of the Centre,' end of August 1966(?), *SHWS*, pp. 38–40.

530 'Talk at a work conference of the Centre,' 23.8.1966, *SHWS*, p. 40.

531 'Instruction on the problems in Tsingtao, Ch'angsha, and Sian,' 7.9.1966, *SHWS*, p. 42.

532 'Comments on Comrade Ch'en Po-ta's *Two months summary*,' 24.10.1966, *SHWS*, p. 42.

533 'Talk at a general report conference,' 24.10.1966, *SHWS*, pp. 44–6; NT, p. 10; excerpts, *Anti-party Clique*, p. 27; JC, MTT, pp. 91–7.

534 'Talk at the work conference of the Centre,' 25.10.1966, *SHWS*, pp. 40–2.

535 'Message of greetings to the 5th Congress of the Albanian Workers' Party,' *RF*, 1966, no. 15, 13.12.1966.

1967

536 'Talk at a Central Cultural Revolution conference,' 8.1.1967, NT, p. 11.

537 'Talk at a Central Cultural Revolution conference,' 9.1.1967, NT, pp. 11–12.

538 'Instruction to Comrade Lin Piao,' 9.1.1967, NT, pp. 12 and 13.

539 'Four-point instruction at a Standing Committee meeting,' 1.1967(?), NT, p. 12.

540 'Instruction on the power struggle at the Broadcasting Station,' (issued through Comrade Wang Li) 1.1967, NT, p. 12.

541 'Talk at an enlarged meeting of the Military Commission,' (reported by Premier Chou) 27.1.1967, NT, p. 13.

542 'Instruction to the PLA,' (issued through Yeh Chien-ying) 27.1.1967, NT, pp. 13–14.

543 'Conversation with Premier Chou on power struggle,' 1967, NT, p. 14.

544 'Telegram to Chairman Nhuyen Huu Tho on the 7th anniversary of the Vietnam Liberation Front,' *JMJP*, 19.12.1967; SCMP, No. 4084.

Addenda

545 'Summing up the campaign against the enemy's Fifth "Encirclement", Resolutions of the Centre of the CCP adopted by the Conference of the Politburo, Tsunyi, 8 January 1935 *SW*, Chin-Chi-Lu-Yü edition, 1948 and reproduced in the *History of the Chinese Revolution—Reference Material* edited by the Seminar Room of the Department of History, Chinese People's University, 1957 (manuscript copy); translation and commentary by Jerome Ch'en, the *China Quarterly*, no. 40, October–December 1969.

546 To P'eng Teh-huai (a poem) *The Case of Peng Teh-huai 1959–1968*, edited by Union Research Institute, Hong Kong, 1968 (back cover).

547 *Selected Works of Mao Tse-tung*, apart from those already referred to in entries 258–62, there are:

548 Vol. 1 Central Kiangsu Publishing Society, 1945

549 Vol. 5 Hsinhua Bookshop, East Shantung, 1946

550 Central Bureau of the Chin-Chi-Lu-Yü Border Region, 1948

Suggestions were made to have the 5th and 6th volumes of the *SW* published before the 9th Congress of the CCP, see CP Centre Document, Centre-Issue (67) 358, quoted in the *T'ien-shan Hung-ch'i* (Red Flag on Tienshan), Sinkiang, 15.1.1968, p. 1.

551   *On the Chinese Revolution,* Political Department of the North-East Military Region, 1948.

552   *Selected Essays,* Hsinhua Bookshop, P'u-hai Region, 1948.

553   'A talk at the conference of the heads of propaganda and culture-education departments of the provinces and cities on 6.3.1957,' (unpublished) see *JMJP,* 1.9.1968.

554   'A criticism of the *People's Daily,*' 4.1957 (unpublished), see *JMJP,* 1.9.1968.

555   'The *Wen-hui Pao's* bourgeois tendencies in a period of time,' published under the name of the Editorial Board of the *JMJP,* 14.6.1957 and see *JMJP,* 1.9.1968.

556   'A talk on the *People's Daily,*' 1.1958, see *JMJP,* 1.9.1968.

557   'An introduction on how to run a newspaper,' (unpublished) see *JMJP,* 1.9.1968

558   'An inscription for the Japanese workers,' 18.9.1962

559   'A talk in January 1964,' (unpublished) see *JMJP,* 1.9.1968.

560   'On educational revolution,' see Union Research Institute, *CCP Documents of the Great Proletarian Cultural Revolution 1966–1967,* Hong Kong, 1968, p. 635.

1917

1 　讀書筆記　　　　　第一師範時所記，一萬餘字，未發表。1927.5.21 長沙'馬日事變'中燒毀，僅存一本。見李銳，頁37；謝覺哉，'第一次會見毛澤東同志'，新觀察，1952，11期。

2 　'體育之研究'　　　署名二十八畫生，新青年，3卷，2號，1917.4.1.

3 　'給宮時滔天的信'　見宮時電介，'毛沢東の手紙'，朝日新聞 1967.7.3.

1918

─────────

1919

4 　湘江評論（週刊）　　毛澤東主編，1919.7.14 創刊，八月上旬被封，共五期，臨時增刊一期。

5 　'西方大事述評'，'世界雜評'　　見各期。

6 　'德意志人沈痛簽約'　　　　　　2期。

7 　'民眾的大聯合'　　　2,3,4期，（成都，星期日 19, 20, 21期轉載。）

8 　'健學會之成立'　　　增刊，1919.7.21.

9 　'陳獨秀之被捕及營救'　不詳

10 　'請問什麼叫過激黨'

11 　'新詩一首'

12 　新湖南週刊　　　　自第7期至10期（封）由毛澤東主編，1919.6.5 創刊。只存1卷1期。

13 　'問題研究會章程'　　北京大學月刊，1919.10.23.

14 　'學生之工作'　　　　湖南教育月刊 1卷，2期，1919.11.1.

　　長沙大公報

15 　'對趙女士自殺的批評'　　1919.11.16.

16 　'社會萬惡與趙女士'　　　不詳

17 　'婚姻問題敬告男女青年'　1919.11.19.

18 　'戀愛問題──少年人與老年人'不詳

19 　'趙女士的人格問題'

20 　'非自殺'　　　　　　　　1919.11.30.

1920

21 　'湖南人民的自決'　　上海天問週刊（1920.2.1─7.11），彭璜主編，23期。

　　長沙大公報

22 　'介紹"共產黨月刊"'　　1920.11─12.

23 　十餘篇關於湖南自治的文章

1921

　　新民學會會員通訊集　1918.6～1921.1　長沙文化書店發行

24　　第一集十三封　　　　毛澤東三封

25　　第二集三十一封　　　毛澤東八封

26　　第三集七封　　　　　蔡和森與毛澤東關於共產主義及建黨問題通訊.

　　　1922

27 平民讀本　　　與李六如合編　　　1922 下半年.

28 '鉛印活版工會致大公報記者留書.'　　　長沙大公報 1922. 12. 14.

　　　1923

29 '湖南自修大學創立宣言.'　　　東方雜誌 20卷, 6號, 1923. 3. 25.

30 '外力軍閥與革命.'　　　新時代 1 期.

　　　嚮導週報

31　　'北京政變與商人.'　　　31-2 期, 1923. 7. 11.

32　　'消憲經與趙恒惕.'　　　36 期, 1923. 8. 15.

33　　'英國人與梁如浩.'　　　38 期, 1923. 8. 29.

34　　'紙烟稅.'　　　38 期, 1923. 8. 29.

　　　1924

　　　1925

35 政治週報　　　毛澤東主編, 中國國民黨中央宣傳部廣州政治週報社出版.

　　　第一期 (1925. 11. 30)　　　毛澤東的文章:

36　　'政治週報發刊理由.'

37　　'三三三一制.'

38　　'楊坤如的佈告與劉志陸的電報.'

39　　'如果討赤 志同仇雖亦吾良友.'

40　　'頌聲來於萬國.'

41　　'反共產中國國民軍大同盟萬歲.'

42　　'共產章程與實非共產.'

43　　'鄉魯與革命.'

　　　第二期

44　　'向左還是向右.'

45　　'赤化原來如此.'

　　　第三期 (1925. 12. 20)

46　　'北京右派會議與帝國主義.'

47　　　　'帝國主義的最後工具.'
48　　　　'右派的最大本領.'
　　　　（人民日報出版社，十九種影印革命期刊索引，1958 第三版，
　　　　有政治週報全部論文索引，但未得見.）

1926

廣州中國農民
49　'中國農民各階級分析及其對革命的態度.'　　1卷，1期，1926.1.
50　'中國社會各階級分析.'　　　　1卷，2期，1926.2；中國青年 116 期，1926.3.13
　　　　　　　　　　　　　　　　HC，I，1.
51　'宣傳報告.'　　　　　　　政治週報 6-7 期，1926.4.10
52　沁園春（長沙）　　　　　　　　　　1926 秋.
53　'江浙農民的痛苦及其反抗運動.'　嚮導週報，179 期，1926.11.25.
54　趙恆惕之階級基礎與我們當前的任務（小冊子）　長沙，1926.12.

1927
55　'湖南農民運動考察報告.'　　長沙戰士週報（中共湖南省委刊物），
　　　　　　　　　　　　　　1927.3.5；嚮導週報，191 期，1927.3.12；
　　　　　　　　　　　　　　武漢中央日報副刊，1927.3.28（第七
　　　　　　　　　　　　　　號）；第三段（十四件大事），HC，1947.
　　　　　　　　　　　　　　續編，頁 12-39；HC，I，2.
56　'中國佃農生活舉例.'　　廣州，1927（?）. 張靜廬，現代出版史料
　　　　　　　　　　　　　　甲編，頁 77 作 1937 出版，恐誤.
57　菩薩蠻（黃鶴樓）　　　　1927 夏.
58　遺失，'湖南長沙，湘潭，湘鄉，衡山，醴陵農村調查.'　未發表
　　　　　　　　　　　　　　見解放社，農村調查，華中版，1949，
　　　　　　　　　　　　　　序言一；HC，III，頁 810.

1928
59　西江月（井崗山）　　　　1928 夏.
60　'前委致中央的兩封信.'　　1928.8.12 與 30，中央通訊 2，5 期.
61　'政治問題和邊界黨的任務 —— 湘贛邊區第二次黨大會的決議案.'
　　　　　　　　　　　　　　1928.10.5，HC，1947 續編，頁 101-8；HC，I，3.
62　'井崗山前委對中央的報告.'　1928.11.25，HC，1947 續編，頁 63-87；HC，I，4.
63　'井崗山土地法'　　　　　1928.12，解放社，農村調查，1949，頁 91-3.
64　遺失，'井崗山寧岡，永新農村調查.'　未發表，見解放社，農村調
　　　　　　　　　　　　　　查，1949，序言一；HC，III，頁 810.

1929

65　如夢令（新卡）

66　清平樂（會昌）　　　　　　　　1929.1.

67　'安吳青絢難兩週卆紀念，'　　　1929.1, 思想萬歲, 頁6.

68　'興國縣土地法，'　　　　　　　1929.4, 解放社, 農村調查, 1949, 頁94-5.

69　清平樂（進軍福建）　　　　　　1929. 9-10.

70　採桑子（重陽）　　　　　　　　1929. 10.11.

71　'中國共產黨紅軍第四軍第九次代表大會決議案，'（古田會議決議案）, HC, 1944, Ⅲ, 頁135-183; HC, Ⅰ, 5.

1930

72　'給林彪同志的信，'　　　　　　1930.1.5, HC, 1947 續編, 頁88-100; HC, Ⅰ, 6.

73　減字木蘭花（進軍吉安）　　　　1930.2.

74　'反對本本主義，'　　　　　　　1930.5, 選讀, 甲, 上.

75　蝶戀花（攻南昌）　　　　　　　1930.6.

76　'興國調查，'　　　　　　　　　1930.9.（1931.1.26 整理完畢）, HC, 1947, Ⅰ, 頁23-94; 解放社, 農村調查, 1949, 頁7-62.

77　'東塘等處調查，'　　　　　　　1930.10.30, 解放社, 農村調查, 1949, 頁63-70.

78　'木口村調查，'　　　　　　　　1930.11.18, 解放社, 農村調查, 1949, 頁71-73.

79　'贛西土地分配情形，'　　　　　1930.11.12, 解放社, 農村調查, 1949, 頁74-78.

80　'江西土地鬥爭中的錯誤，'　　　1930.11.14, 解放社, 農村調查, 1949, 頁79-82.

81　'分青和出租問題，'　　　　　　1930.11.15, 解放社, 農村調查, 1949, 頁83-88.

82　'分田後的富農問題，'（永新反北路的情形. 王懷 陳正人報告. 毛澤東紀錄）, 解放社, 農村調查, 1949, 頁89-90.

83　'致古柏的信，'　　　　　　　　1930.12,「波下支部抄」. Hsiao Tso-Liang, Power Relations within the Chinese Communist Movement 1930-1934, Ⅰ, 頁104, Ⅱ, 264. （此件可靠性頗成問題.）

1931

84　漁家傲（第一次圍剿）　　　　　1931.1.

85　漁家傲（第二次圍剿）　　　　　1931.5.

1932.

86　'給袁國平的信. 關於群眾工作的指示，'　　　1932.2.6, 陳誠, R. 14.

87　'關於停戰抗日之談話，'　　　瑞金, 1932. 共四頁, Nym Wales Collection.

1933

88 菩薩蠻 (大柏地)　　　　　　　1933. 2.

89 '怎樣分析階級,'　　　　　　1933. 6. 7. 赤匪反動文件彙編, III, 頁946-9; HC, I, 8.
紅色中華

90 '查田運動是廣大區域內的中心任務,'　　8B期, 1933. 6. 17.

91 '查田運動的第一步, 組織上的大規模動員,'　87期, 1933. 6. 20.

92 '依據農村中階級鬥爭的發展狀態的差別去展開查田運動,'　8B期, 1933. 6. 23.

93 '新的形勢與新的任務,'　　　97期, 1933. 7. 29.

94 '粉碎五次圍剿與蘇維埃經濟建設任務 ── 在南部十七縣經濟建設
大會上的報告,'　　　　　102期, 1933. 8. 16; HC, I, 7.

95 '查田運動的初步總結,'　　　鬥爭, 24期, 1933. 8. 29; 紅旗, 61期, 1933. 10. 30;
赤匪反動文件彙編, III, 頁970-88.

96 '今年的選舉,'　　　　　　紅色中華, 108期, 1933. 9. 6.

97 '寫在前頭 ── 長岡鄉鄉蘇工作序言.'　　1933. 12. 15, 陳誠, R. 10.

98 '查田運動的群眾工作,'　　紅旗, 63期, 1933. 12.

99 '興國長岡鄉的蘇維埃工作.'　1933. 12. 15, 鬥爭, 42, 43, 44期, 1934. 1. 12, 19, 26;
青年實話, 6號, 1934. 1. 14; 解放社, 農村調查,
頁96-132.

100 '才溪鄉調查,'　　　　　解放社, 農村調查, 頁133-50; HC, 1947, I, 頁151-74.

101 遺失, '尋鄔調查,'　　　1933, 見解放社, 農村調查, 序言二, HC, III, 頁809.

1934

102 '第二次全蘇大會開幕詞,'　紅色中華, 2期, 1934. 1. 24.

103 '中華蘇維埃共和國中央執行委員會與人民委員會對第二次全國蘇維埃
代表大會的報告,'　　1934. 1. 24-5, 紅色中華, 3期, 1934. 1. 26; HC, I. 9.

104 '關心群眾生活, 注重工作方法,'　1934. 1. 27, 選讀, 甲, 上; HC, I, 10.
紅色中華

105 '全蘇第二次大會關於中央執行委員報告的結論,'　5期, 1934. 1. 31.

106 '全蘇第二次大會關於緊急動員的報告,'　6期, 1934. 2. 1.

107 '全蘇第二次大會閉幕詞,'　　7期, 1934. 2. 3.

108 '上杭才溪鄉的蘇維埃工作,'　鬥爭, 49期, 1934. 3. 2.

109 '鄉蘇怎樣工作,'　　1934. 4. 10, 張聞天, 毛澤東, 區鄉蘇維埃怎
樣工作, 陳誠, R. 10.

110 '中華蘇維埃共和國中央政府五一勞動節宣言,'　紅色中華, 179期, 1934. 4. 24.

111 '論日本帝國主義的陰謀 —— 與 "紅色中華" 記者談話,'　　紅色中華, 181期.
　　　　　　　1934. 4. 28 ; 捷報, 1934. 5. 15, 波多野, Ⅳ, 頁 807-10.

112 '與記者談目前局勢與抗日先遣隊,'　　　　紅色中華, 221期, 1934. 8. 1.
1935

113 憶秦娥 (婁山關)　　　　1935. 1.

114 十六字令三首　　　　1935. 3-4.

115 '中國工農紅軍北上抗日宣言,'　　民族戰線自報, 2期, 1935. 8. 10.

116 律詩 (長征)　　　　1935. 9.

117 清平樂 (六盤山)　　　　1935. 10.

118 念奴嬌 (崑崙)　　　　1935. 10.

119 論反對日本帝國主義的策畧,'　　　1935. 12. 27 ; HC, Ⅰ, 11.
1936

120 '與林彪同志的信,'　　　1936. 6 以前 (抗日軍政大學成立於 1936. 6 ; 此信
　　　　　　　　討論抗大籌備事), 思想萬歲, 頁 1-2.

121 '蘇維埃中央政府對哥老會宣言,'　　鬥爭, 105期, 1936. 7. 12.

122 '中國革命戰爭的戰畧問題,'　　1936. 秋, HC, 1947 續編, 頁 109-83; HC, Ⅰ, 12.

123 '致沈鈞儒, 章乃器, 鄒韜奮, 陶行知書,'　　　1936. 8. 10. 鬥爭, 13期;
　　　　　　　波多野, Ⅵ, 頁 566-71.

124 '關於停戰抗日之重要談話, 停止對國民革命軍任何攻擊行動,'
　　　　　　　1936. 10. 15, 毛澤東論中日戰爭, 頁 47-9.

125 '關於蔣介石聲明的聲明,'　　　1936. 12. 28, HC, Ⅰ, 13.
1937

126 '給徐 [特立] 老同志的信,'　　　1937. 1. 30, 思想萬歲, 頁 5.

127 '與史沫特勒的談話,'　　　1937. 3. 1, 毛澤東論文集.

128 '致斯沿山,'　　　1937. 3. 10, 手稿, 胡佛圖書館.

129 '中國抗日民族統一戰線在目前階段的任務,' 解放, 2期, 1937. 5. 1; HC, Ⅰ, 14.

130 '為爭取千百萬群眾進入抗日民族戰線而鬥爭,'　1937. 5. 7, 解放, 4期,
　　　　　　　1937. 5. 24 ; HC, Ⅰ, 15.

131 '致西班牙人民書,'　　　1937. 5. 15, 毛澤東論文集.

132 '致白勞德同志書,'　　　1937. 6. 24, 毛澤東論文集.

133 '實踐論,'　　　1937. 7, 人民日報, 1950. 12. 29 ; HC, Ⅰ, 16.

134 '中國共產黨宣言,'　　　1937. 7. 23, 毛澤東論中日戰爭, 頁 50-2.

135 論反對日本帝國進攻的方針辦法與前途,'　　解放, 12期, 1937. 8. 15;
　　　　　　　HC, Ⅱ, 18.

136 '矛盾論.' 1937. 8 (或根據 '辯證唯物論講授提綱' 寫成. 由八路軍出版. 見張如心, '學習和掌握毛澤東的理論和策畧.' 解放日報, 1942. 2. 18, 19); 人民日報, 1952. 4. 1; HC, I, 17.

137 '為動員一切力量爭取抗戰勝利而鬥爭.' 1937. 8. 25, HC, II. 19.

138 '反對自由主義.' 1937. 9. 7, HC, II, 20.

139 '國共兩黨統一戰線成立後中國革命的迫切任務.' 解放, 14期, 1937. 10. 2; HC, II, 21.

140 '在抗大校舍落成大會上的訓詞.' 抗大校刊 "我們的偉大事業." 14期, 1937. 10. 17; 思想萬歲, 頁 2.

141 '為陝北公學成立與開學紀念題詞.' 動員, 10期, 1937. 10. 23; 思想萬歲, 頁 5-6.

142 '與英國記者貝蘭特之談話.' 1937. 10. 25, 解放, 23期, 1937. 11. 23; HC, II, 22.

143 '上海太原失陷後抗日戰爭的形勢和任務.' 1937. 11. 12, HC, II, 23.

144 毛澤東論文集 上海 1937.

145 論游擊戰 (Mao Tse-tung on Guerrilla Warfare, tr. Samuel Griffith II. New York: Praeger, 1961).

1938

146 論 "一黨專政." 解放, 28期, 1938. 1. 11.

147 '與美聯社記者談抗日前途.' 1938. 2. 11, 波多野, III, 頁 427-33.

148 游擊戰爭的戰畧問題 漢口自強出版社, 1938. 3.

149 '在紀念孫總理逝世十三週年及追悼抗敵陣亡將士大會上的演說詞.' 解放, 33期, 1938. 4. 1.

150 '陝甘寧邊區政府, 第八路軍後方留守處佈告.' 1938. 5. 15, HC, II, 24.

151 '抗日游擊戰爭的戰畧問題.' 解放, 40期, 1938. 5. 30; HC, II, 25.

152 '論持久戰.' 解放, 43-4期, 1938. 7. 1, HC, II, 26.

153 '與世界學聯代表柯樂滿先生, 雅德先生, 傅路德先生, 雷克難先生之談話.' 1938. 7. 2, 解放, 46期, 1938. 7. 23.

154 '我們對於國民參政會的意見.' 解放, 47期. 1938. 8. 1.

155 '論新階段.' 解放, 57期, 1938. 11. 25; 上海 "文獻", III, IV; 第七章 HC, II, 27.

156 '致蔣介石先生函.' 未發表. 見 Chiang Kai-shek, Soviet Russia in China, London, 1957. 頁 87.

157 '統一戰線中的獨立自主問題.' 1938. 11. 5, HC, II, 28.

58 '戰爭和戰略問題,' 1938.11.6, HC, II, 29.

59 '毛澤東先生對延安新華日報記者其光先生談話,' 遠東出版社. 1938.

60 '魯迅論,' 七月半月刊, 1938.8, 文獻, II, 頁 F 8-10; 思想萬歲, 頁 2-4.
(在陝北公學魯迅逝世週年大會上講話, 1937.10.19.)

1939

61 '八路軍軍政雜誌發刊詞.' 軍政雜誌創刊號, 1939.1.15.

62 '在延安慶祝五一國際勞動節大會上的講話,' 1939.5.1, 新中華報,
1939.5.10; 語錄, 頁 128.

63 '五四運動,' 解放, 70期, 1939.5.1; HC, II, 30.

64 '青年運動的方向,' 1939.5.4, HC, II, 31.

65 '國民精神總動員的政治方向,' 解放, 71期, 1939.5.15; 群眾, III, 3期,
1939.6.11.

66 '為抗大題詞,' 1939.4, 人民日報, 1966.8.2, 頁 2.

67 '被敵人反對是好事而不是壞事,' 1939.5.26 為抗大成立三週年而作, 選讀, 甲, 上.

68 '中英兩國人民站在一條戰線上,' 1939.6.1, 群眾, III, 10期, 1939.7.23.

69 '當前時局最大危機,' 解放, 75-6期. 1939.7.10; HC, II, 32.

70 '用國法制裁反動分子,' 解放, 81期. 1939.8.20; HC, II, 33.

71 '關於國際形勢對新華社記者的談話,' 1939.9.1, HC, II, 34.

72 '德蘇互不侵犯協定,' 重慶新華日報, 1939.9.6; 王健民, 史稿, III, 頁 385-7.

73 '第二次帝國主義戰爭講演提綱,' 解放, 85期, 1939.9.30 (1939.9.
14 在延安黨幹部會上的演說).

74 '毛澤東先生關於目前國際形勢與中國抗戰的談話,' 解放, 83-4
期, 1939.9.20; HC, II, 35.

75 '"共產黨人"發刊詞,' 1939.10.4, HC, 1947 續編, HC, II, 37. (張靜廬,
現代出版史料,丁,上; 此外則未見中國任何人
提及或引用此刊物中的文章. Earl Browder 之
"新民主義論"序' 1944.11.1 提及 1944. 1月號
之"共產黨人" 有陳伯達關於"中國之命運"
的文章.)

76 '青年需要經驗,' 1939.10.5, 中國青年社, 中國青運文選, 1940.

77 '毛澤東先生與新聞記者的談話,' 解放, 86期, 1939.10.10.

78 '中共中央關於目前形勢與黨的任務的決定,' 解放, 87-8期, 1939.10.20;
HC, II, 38.

79 '蘇聯利益與全世界人民利益一致,' 解放, 86期, 1939.10.10; HC, II, 36.

180 '大量吸收知識分子,'   1939. 12. 1, HC, II, 39.
181 '在延安各學校及青年團體紀念一二.九學生運動四週年大會上講話,' 未
         發表. 見毛澤東同志論青年和青年工作, 北京, 1964.
         頁 9-10, 14.
182 '中國革命與中國共產黨,'   1939. 12. 15, HC, II, 40.
183 '抗戰與外援的關係,'   八路軍軍政雜誌, 2 期, 1939. 12. 15.
184 '斯大林是中國人民的朋友,'   1939. 12. 21, 解放, 95 期, 1939. 12. 30; HC, II, 41
185 '紀念白求恩,'   1939. 12. 21, HC, II, 42.
   1940

186 '吳玉章同志六十壽辰祝詞,'   1940. 1. 15, 新中華報, 1940. 1. 24; 語錄, 頁 215.
187 '駁斥某戰區司令長官部造謠的談話,'   解放, 96 期, 1940. 1. 20.
188 '新民主主義論,'   1940. 1, 解放, 98-9 期, 1940. 2. 20; HC, II, 43.
189 '克服投降危險, 力爭時局好轉,'   1940. 1. 28; HC, II, 44.
190 '延安民眾討汪擁蔣通電,'   1940. 2. 1, 解放, 98-9 期, 1940. 2. 20, HC, II, 46.
191 '在邊區自然科學研究會成立大會上的講話,'   1940. 2. 5, 新中華報
         1940. 3. 15; 語錄, 頁 175.
192 '"中國工人" 發刊詞,'   1940. 2. 7, HC, II, 47. (見張靜廬, 現代出版史料,
     丁, 上, 頁 296. 此為毛澤東論工人運動唯一的文章.)
193 '相持階段中的形勢與任務,'   解放, 98-9 期, 1940. 2. 20; HC, II, 45.
194 '必須強調團結和進步,' 1940. 2. 10, HC, II, 48.
195 '參政員毛澤東等致國民參政會通電,' 解放, 98-9 期, 1940. 2. 20.
196 '新民主主義的憲政—延安各界憲政促進會成立大會上的演講,'
         1940. 2. 20, 解放, 101 期, 1940. 3. 8; HC, II, 49.
197 '抗日根據地的政權問題,' 1940. 3. 6, HC, II, 50.
198 '目前統一戰線中的策略問題,'   1940. 3. 11, HC, II, 51.
199 '放手發展抗日力量, 抵抗反共頑固派的進攻,'   1940. 5. 4; HC, II, 52.
200 '團結到底,'   1940. 7. 播種社. 1941; HC, II, 53.
201 '論政策,'   1940. 12. 25, HC, II, 54.
202 '辯證法唯物論,'   民主, I, 1-2 期.
   1941

203 '為皖南事變發表的命令和談話,'   1941. 1, HC, II, 55.
204 '農村調查序言和跋,' 1941. 3. 17, HC, 1944, V; 解放社, 農村調查, 1949,
         序言二, 頁 151-2; HC, III, 58.

182 'The Chinese revolution and the CCP,' 15.12.1939, *SW*, II, 40.

183 'The Resistance and its connexion with foreign aid,' *Military and Political Journal* of the Eighth Route Army, no. 2, 15.12.1939. n. tr.

184 'Stalin, friend of the Chinese people,' 21.12.1939, *Liberation*, no. 95, 30.12.1939; *SW*, II, 41.

185 'In memory of Norman Bethune,' 21.12.1939, *SW*, II, 42.

1940

186 'Message of greetings on the 60th birthday of Comrade Wu Yü-chang,' 15.1.1940, *New Chinese Daily*, 24.1.1940; *Quotations*, p. 250, n. tr.

187 'Refute the fabrications of the headquarters of the commander-in-chief of a certain war-zone,' *Liberation*, no. 96, 20.1.1940, n. tr.

188 'On new democracy,' 1.1940, *Liberation*, nos. 98–9, 20.2.1940; *SW*, II, 43.

189 'Overcome the danger of capitulation and strive for a turn for the better,' 28.1.1940, *SW*, II, 44.

190 'Denounce Wang Ching-wei and support Chiang Kai-shek, a telegram from the people of Yenan,' 1.2.1940, *Liberation*, nos. 98–9, 20.2.1940; *SW*, II, 46.

191 'Speech at the inaugural meeting of the Natural Science Research Society of the Border Region,' 5.2.1940, *New Chinese Daily*, 15.3.1940; *Quotations*, pp. 204–5.

192 'Introducing *the Chinese Worker*,' 7.2.1940, *SW*, II, 47. (The periodical is referred to in Chang Ching-lu, *Historical Material of Modern Publications*, IV, 1st part, p. 296. This is Mao's only article on the workers' movement.)

193 'Situation and tasks in the stalemate,' *Liberation*, nos. 98–9, 20.2.1940; *SW*, II, 45.

194 'We must stress unity and progress,' 10.2.1940, *SW*, II, 48.

195 'Mao Tse-tung and other councillors' telegram to the People's Political Council,' *Liberation*, nos. 98–9, 20.2.1940. n. tr.

196 'New democratic constitutional government—a speech at the inaugural meeting of the Yenan Constitutional Government Promotion Society,' 20.2.1940, *Liberation*, no. 101, 8.3.1940; *SW*, II, 49.

197 'On the question of political power in the anti-Japanese base areas,' 6.3.1940, *SW*, II, 50.

198 'Current problems of tactics in the Anti-Japanese united front,' 11.3.1940, *SW*, II, 51.

199 'Freely expand the anti-Japanese forces and resist the on-slaughts of the anti-communist die-hards,' 4.5.1940, *SW*, II, 52.

200 'Unity to the very end,' 7.1940, Sowing Publishing House, 1941; *SW*, II, 53.

201 'On policy,' 25.12.1940, *SW*, II, 54.

202 'Dialectical materialism,' *Democracy*, I, nos. 1–2; SRS, *PT*, 120–4; Dennis J. Doolin and Peter J. Golas, *CQ*, no. 19; Karl A. Wittfogel, *Studies in Soviet Thought*, III, no. 4 and *Modern Chinese History Project*, University of Washington, reprint series no. 25.

1941

203 'Order and statement on the Southern Anhwei Incident,' 1.1941, *SW*, II, 55.

204 'Preface and postscript to *Rural Survey*, 3–4.1941, *SW*, 1944, V; *SW*, III, 58; Liberation Publishing Society, *Rural Survey*, 1949, preface 2 and pp. 151–2.

205 'The situation after the repulse of the second anti-communist onslaught,' 18.3.1941, *SW*, II, 56.

206 'Conclusions on the repulse of the second anti-communist on-slaught,' 8.5.1941, *SW*, II, 57.

207 'Reform our study,' 5.1941, *SW*, 1944, V; *SW*, III, 59.

208 'Expose the plot for a Far Eastern Munich,' 25.5.1941, *SW*, III, 60.

209 'On the international united front against Fascism,' 23.6.1941, *SW*, III, 61.

210 'Comrade Mao Tse-tung received the student delegations from Suite and Michih,' *LD*, 15.8.1941. n. tr.

211 'Telegram of condolence to Chang Ch'ung's family,' *LD*, 16.8.1941. n. tr.

212 'Notes on Lu Chung-ts'ai's *Long March*,' *LD*, 14.9.1941. n. tr.

213 'At the Eastern Anti-Fascist Congress, Comrade Mao Tse-tung called the whole nation to strengthen unity,' *LD*, 31.10.1941. n. tr.

214 'Comrade Mao Tse-tung's broadcast speech,' (at the Border Region Council conference) *LD*, 7.11.1941. n. tr.

215 'Speech at the Shensi-Kansu-Ninghsia Border Region Coun-cil,' *LD*, 22.11.1941; *Important Documents of the Second Session of the Shensi-Kansu-Ninghsia Border Region Council*, Yenan, 1944, pp. 17–21; *SW*, III, 62.

1942

216 'Chairman Mao's directive,' 23.1.1942, *LD*, 15.4.1942 (This is 'Chairman Mao calls all the armed units in the Border Region to study "the resolutions of the 9th conference of the representatives of the 4th Army of the CCP" and the garrison headquarters in its directive lays down the method study,' and the resolutions, Item 68 in this bibliography, are also known as 'the resolutions of the Kut'ien conference'. This was the first time that the *LD* used 'Chairman Mao' in its headlines.).

217 'Oppose stereotyped party writing,' 8.2.1942, *LD*, 18.6.1942; *SW*, III, 64.

218 'The Propaganda Department of the Centre called a meeting on reforming the style of writing. Mao Tse-tung: "The elimination of the stereotyped party writing is a precondition of the elimination of subjectivism and factionalism." ' *LD*, 10.2.1942. n. tr.

219 'Celebrating the 24th anniversary of the Red Army,' *LD*, 23.2.1942. n. tr.

220 'At a discussion on the reform of this paper, Comrade Mao Tse-tung calls for the use of newspapers to reform the three styles and criticizes absolute egalitarianism and the resort to sarcasm and slander.' *LD*, 2.4.1942. n. tr.

221 'Rectify the styles of study, party work, and writing,' *LD*, 27.4.1942; *SW*, III, 63.

222 'Talks at the Yenan forum on literature and art,' 2 and 23.5.1942, *LD*, 19.10.1943; East China edition, 1947; *SW*, III, 65.

223 'A most important policy,' 7.9.1942. *SW*, III, 66.

224 'The turning point in World War II,' 12.10.1942, *SW*, III, 67.

225 'In celebration of the 25th anniversary of the October Revolution,' 7.11.1942, *SW*, III, 68.

226* 'The CCP's views on the 10th plenum of the KMT,' *LD*, 30.11.1942. n. tr.

227 'Economic and financial problems,' 12.1942, *SW*, 1944, IV, pp. 3–204; a small part of it, *SW*, III, 69.

1943

228 'Chairman Mao calls for speeding up productive education,' *LD*, 4.1.1943. n. tr.

229 'Letter criticizing P'eng Teh-huai's talk on democratic education,' 6.5.1943, *Anti-party Clique*, p. 1. n. tr.

230* 'The CCP Central Committee's decision on the proposal to dissolve the Communist International by the presidium of the Executive Committee of the Communist International,' *LD*, 26.5.1943. n. tr.

231 'Comrade Mao Tse-tung's detailed report on the question of the dissolution of the Communist International,' *LD*, 28.5.1943; SRS, *PT*, p. 288; Stuart Gelder, *The Chinese Communists*, London: Victor Gollancz, 1946, pp. 169–73.

232 'The CCP Centre's resolution on some questions concerning methods of leadership,' 1.6.1943, *LD*, 4.6.1943; *SW*, III, 70; *SR*, pp. 234–9.

233 'Summing up 22 years of heroic struggles,' 1.7.1943, *LD*, 3.7.1943; Stuart Gelder, op. cit., pp. 150–4.

234 'On co-operatives,' *Productive Organization and Rural Survey*, 1946.

235 'Some pointed questions for the KMT,' (editorial) *LD*, 12.7.1943; *SW*, III, 71.

236 'The CCP Politburo: Spread the campaigns to reduce rent, increase production and "support the government and cherish the people",' *LD*, 1.10.1943; *SW*, III, 72.

237 'Comments on the KMT 11th plenum and the second conference of the third session of the People's Political Council,' *LD*, 5.10.1943; rf. Chang Ching-lu, *Historical Material of Modern Publications*, IV, 1st part, p. 293; *SW*, III, 73.

238 'Talk at the cadres' evening meeting celebrating the October Revolution,' *LD*, 7.11.1943. n. tr.

239 'Message of greetings to Stalin on the occasion of the October Revolution celebration,' *LD*, 8.11.1943. n. tr.

240 'Get organized!' (a talk at the reception of the labour heroes of the Shensi-Kansu-Ninghsia Border Region) 29.11.1943, *LD*, 2.12.1943; *SW*, III, 74.

1944

241 'Letter to the Yenan Peking Opera Theatre after seeing *Driven to Join the Liangshan Mountain Rebels*,' 9.1.1944, *JMJP*, 25.5.1967; *Five Documents on Literature and Art*, Peking: FLP, 1967, pp. 1–2.

242 'Our study and the current situation,' 12.4.1944, *SW*, III, 75.

243 'Develop industries and down with Japanese bandits,' *LD*, 26.5.1944. n. tr.

244 'Yenan University should serve the Resistance War and the political, economic, and cultural reconstruction of the Border Region,' *LD*, 31.5.1944. n. tr.

245 'Interview with a group of journalists on international and domestic situations—statements, questions, and answers,' *LD*, 13.6.1944. n. tr.

246* 'Dangers after the fall of Ch'angsha,' (editorial) *LD*, 24.6.1944. n. tr.

247 'On the policy of co-operatives,' *LD*, 4.7.1944; *Documents on Production* (*Sheng-ch'an wen-hsien*), ed. Wang P'ing, Shantung: Hsinhua Book Co., 1946. n. tr.

248* 'Adopt new forms of organization and styles of work,' (editorial) *LD*, 5.9.1944. n. tr.

249 'Serve the people,' 8.9.1944, *LD*, 21.9.1944; *SW*, III, 76.

250* 'Yenan authoritative person comments on the KMT-CCP talks,' *LD*, 20.9.1944. n. tr. (For the first time, the *LD* used the term 'Yenan authoritative person' (*ch'uan-wei jen-shih*).)

251 'Yenan observer on the danger of Chiang Kai-shek's speech,' *LD*, 12.10.1944; *SW*, III, 77.

252 'Speech at the Border Region conference on culture and education—policy of the united front in cultural work,' *LD*, 1.11.1944; *Masses*, X, no. 2; *SW*, III, 78.

253 'Telegram to Roosevelt on his re-election,' *LD*, 10.11.1944. n. tr.

254 'No title,' (in memory of Tsou T'ao-fen) *LD*, 15.11.1944. n. tr.

255* 'Yenan authoritative person on the changes in KMT personnel,' *LD*, 23.11.1944. n. tr.

256 'Talks for 1945—speech at the Border Region Council meeting,' 15.12.1944, *LD*, 16.12.1944; *SW*, 1947, III, pp. 125–35.

257 *Snow*—to the melody of *Shen Yuan Ch'un*, winter 1944–5, JC, pp. 340–1.

258 *Selected Works* 1st ed. by the *Shansi-Chahar-Hopei Daily*, 1944.

259 —2nd ed. 1945.

260 —The Central Bureau of Shansi-Chahar-Hopei ed. 1947.

261 —2nd ed. 1948.

262 —Harbin edition, 1948. (See Addenda).

1945

263 'Fight for an early victory,' (New Year's Message) *LD*, 1.1.1945. n. tr.

264 'Strengthen unity and defeat Japanese bandits,' *LD*, 2.1.1945. n. tr.

265* 'Yenan authoritative person on Chiang Kai-shek's New Year Speech,' *LD*, 4.1.1945. n. tr.

266 'We must learn to do economic work in two or three years,' (Speech at a conference of labour heroes and model workers of the Border Region) *LD*, 12.1.1945; *SW*, III, 79.

267 'Production is also possible and necessary in the guerilla zones,' 31.1.1945, *SW*, III, 80.

268 'In memory of P'eng Hsüeh-feng,' *LD*, 8.2.1945. n. tr.

269 'Telegram to Marshal Stalin,' (on the Red Army Day) *LD*, 22.2.1945. n. tr.

270 'Telegram of condolence of the death of Roosevelt,' 13.4.1945.

271 'China's two possible destinies,' *SW*, III, 81.

272 'Let the whole party unite and fight to accomplish its tasks,' 24.4.1945, *SR*, pp. 254–9.

273 'On production by the Army for its own support and on the importance of the great movements for rectification and for production,' (editorial) *LD*, 27.4.1945; *SW*, III, 84.

274 'Opening speech at the 7th Congress of the CCP,' *LD*, 1.5.1945; *DH*, pp. 289–91.

275 'On coalition government,' 24.4.1945, *LD*, 3.5.1945; *SW*, III, 82.

276 'Telegram to Marshal Stalin on the triumphant liberation of Berlin by the Red Army,' *LD*, 4.5.1945. n. tr.

277 'The foolish old man who removed the mountains,' 11.6.1945, *SW*, III, 83.

278* 'Statement by a person of responsibility at the CCP Centre: non-participation in the present session of the People's Political Council,' *LD*, 17.6.1945. n. tr.

279 'The Hurley-Chiang duet is a flop,' 10.7.1945, *SW*, III, 85.

280 'On the danger of the Hurley policy,' 12.7.1945, *LD*, 13.7.1945; *SW*, III, 86.

281 'Telegram to Comrade William Z. Foster on the revival of the US communist party,' 29.7.1945, *Masses*, X, no. 16, 25.8.1945; *SW*, III, 87.

282 'Telegram to Marshal Stalin,' 9.8.1945, *LD*, 10.8.1945. n. tr.

283 'The last round of the Anti-Japanese War,' *LD*, 10.8.1945; *SW*, III, 88.

284 'Urgent tasks in front of us,' (editorial) *LD*, 13.8.1945; *SW*, IV, 89; *SR*, pp. 246–78.

285 'Chiang Kai-shek is provoking civil war,' 13.8.1945; *SW*, IV, 90.

286 'Two telegrams from the commander-in-chief of the 18th Group Army to Chiang Kai-shek,' 8.1945, *SW*, IV, 91.

287 'On a statement by Chiang Kai-shek's spokesman,' 16.8.1945, *SW*, IV, 92.

288 'On peace negotiations with the KMT—circular of the Central Committee of the CCP,' 26.8.1945, *SW*, IV, 93.

289 'Hope all anti-Japanese parties and patriots will fight for peace, democracy, unity, and the construction of a new China,' *LD*, 30.8.1945. n. tr.

290 'Hope the negotiations will produce good results,' *LD*, 14.9.1945. n. tr.

291 'Interview with a Reuter correspondent on China's need for peaceful reconstruction,' 27.9.1945, *LD*, 8.10.1945; *SW*, 1947, III, pp. 139–42.

292* 'The results of the KMT-CCP negotiations and our future tasks,' (editorial) *LD*, 13.10.1945. (On the third day after his return to Yenan.) n. tr.

293 'On the Chungking negotiations,' 17.10.1945, *SW*, IV, 94.

294 'The truth about the KMT attacks,' 5.11.1945, *SW*, IV, 95.

295 'Rent reduction and production are two important matters for the defence of the liberated areas,' 7.11.1945, *SW*, IV, 96.

296* 'Yenan authoritative person on the convocation of the National Assembly: this unilateral action of the KMT reveals its decision to wage a full-scale civil war,' *LD*, 17.11.1945. n. tr.

297 'Telegram to General Kao Shu-hsun,' (on Kao's surrender) *LD*, 18.11.1945. n. tr.

298 'Policy for work in the liberated areas for 1946,' 15.12.1945, *SW*, IV, 97.

299 'Build stable base areas in the northeast,' 18.12.1945, *SW*, IV, 98.

1946

300* 'Chiang Kai-shek's New Year's Day speech and the Political Consultative Conference,' (editorial) *LD*, 7.1.1946. n. tr.

301* 'On "the views on the enlargement of the Government",' (editorial) *LD*, 19.1.1946. n. tr.

302* 'Yenan authoritative person on the possibility of important results from the Political Consultative Conference,' *LD*, 1.2.1946. n. tr.

303* 'Refute Chiang Kai-shek,' *LD*, 7.4.1946; *A Catalogue of the Documents of the Political Consultative Conference*, Historical Document Publishers, 1946, pp. 179–86. n. tr.

304 'Some points in appraisal of the present international situation,' 4.1946, *SW*, IV, 99; *SR*, pp. 279–80.

305 'Salute the April 8th martyrs,' *LD*, 20.4.1946. n. tr.

306 'Telegram of condolence of the death of Kalinin,' *LD*, 5.6.1946. n. tr.

307* 'Yenan authoritative person's statement: Oppose the Byrnes Act in aid of Chiang Kai-shek,' *LD*, 17.6.1946. n. tr.

308 'Against the US Act to give military aid to Chiang Kai-shek,' *LD*, 23.6.1946; *Masses*, XI, no. 9; *SW*, 1947, III, pp. 145–6. n. tr.

309 'Telegram of comfort to Ma Hsu-lun,' *LD*, 6.7.1946. n. tr.

310 'Reply to some distinguished people in Chungking on united struggle for peace,' *LD*, 7.7.1946. n. tr.

311 'Telegram of condolence of the death of Li Kug-p'u,' *LD*, 13.7.1946. n. tr.

312 'Telegram of condolence to Wen I-to's family,' *LD*, 17.7.1946. n. tr.

313 'Smash Chiang Kai-shek's offensive by a war of self-defence,' 20.7.1946, *SW*, IV, 100.

314 'Telegram of condolence of the death of T'ao Hsing-chih,' *LD*, 25.7.1946. n. tr.

315 'Talk with the American correspondent Anna Louise Strong,' 8.1946, *SW*, IV, 101.

316 'Concentrate a superior force to destroy the enemy forces one by one,' 16.9.1946, *SW*, IV, 102.

317 'Interview with an American correspondent,' 29.9.1946, *LD*, 7.10.1946; *Masses*, XII, no. 12; *SW*, IV, 103.

318 'A three months' summary,' 1.10.1946, *SW*, IV, 104.

319 'Chairman Mao's reply to a telegram from the Perak branch of the Democratic League on the question of peace,' *LD*, 12.10.1946. n. tr.

320 'Telegram to General Kao Shu-hsun on the first anniversary of his surrender,' *LD*, 30.10.1946, n. tr.

321* 'On the war situation,' (editorial) *LD*, 4.11.1946. n. tr.

322 'Telegram to Marshal Stalin on the 29th anniversary of the USSR,' *LD*, 7.11.1946. n. tr.

323* 'The war situation is beginning to change,' (editorial) *LD*, 6.12.1946. n. tr.

1947

324 'New Year's message,' *LD*, 1.1.1947. n. tr.

325 'Celebrating the first anniversary of the Central China Democratic Allied Army,' 8.1.1947, *LD*, 9.1.1947. n. tr.

326 'Greet the new high tide of the Chinese revolution,' 1.2.1947, *SW*, IV, 105.

327 'On the temporary abandonment of Yenan and the defence of the Shensi-Kansu-Ninghsia Border Region—two documents issued by the Central Committee of the CCP,' *SW*, IV, 106.

328 'The concept of operations for the northwest war theatre,' 15.4.1947, *SW*, IV, 107.

329 'The Chiang Kai-shek Government is besieged by the whole people,' 30.5.1947, *SW*, IV, 108.

330 'Strategy for the second year of the war of liberation,' 1.9.1947, *SW*, IV, 109.

331 'Manifesto of the Chinese People's Liberation Army,' 10.1947, *SW*, IV, 110.

332 'On the reissue of the three main rules of discipline and the eight points for attention—instruction of the general headquarters of the Chinese People's Liberation Army,' 10.10.1947, *SW*, IV, 111.

333 'The present situation and our tasks,' 25.12.1947, the 6th section in *New Democratic Industrial and Commercial Policies*; *SW*, IV, 112.

334 *Selected Works*, supplement, printed by the Central Bureau of the CCP in Shansi-Chahar-Hopei, 12.1947. n. tr.

1948

335 'On setting up a system of reports,' 7.1.1948, *SW*, IV, 113.

336 'On some important problems of the party's present policy,' 18.1.1948, *SW*, IV, 114.

337 'The democratic movement in the Army,' 30.1.1948, *SW*, IV, 115.

338 'Different tactics for carrying out the land law in different areas,' 3.2.1948, *SW*, IV, 116.

339 'Correct the "left" errors in land reform propaganda,' 10.2.1948, *SW*, IV, 117.

1949

359 'Carry the revolution through to the end,' (NCNA editorial) *JMJP*, 1.1.1949; *SW*, IV, 136.

360 'Expose the war criminal's conspiracy of suing for peace,' (NCNA editorial) *JMJP*, 6.1.1949; *SW*, IV, 137.

361 'Statement on the present situation,' *JMJP*, 15.1.1949; *SW*, IV, 138.

362 'Comment by the spokesman of the Central Committee of the CCP on the resolution of the Nanking Executive Yuan,' *JMJP*, 23.1.1949; *SW*, IV, 139.

363 'A solemn warning by the CCP spokesman on the peace talk plot of the Nanking pseudo-government and on the release of the Japanese war criminal, Okamura Yasuji,' *JMJP*, 29.1.1949; *SW*, IV, 140.

364 'The CCP spokesman's second comment on peace terms,' *JMJP*, 6.2.1949; *SW*, IV, 141.

365 'The CCP spokesman's statement on the KMT traitorous "government" committing further crimes of treason —punishment of war criminals to include Japanese war criminals,' *JMJP*, 7.2.1949; *SW*, IV, 141.

366 'Turn the army into a working force,' 8.2.1949, *SW*, IV, 142.

367 'Why do the badly split reactionaries still idly clamour for "total peace"?' (NCNA comment) *JMJP*, 16–17.2.1949; *SW*, IV, 143.

368 'The KMT war criminal group vainly attempt to save their own skin by turning from an "appeal for peace" to an "appeal for war",' *JMJP*, 18.2.1949; *SW*, IV, 144.

369 'The KMT die-hards' deception is exposed: from an "appeal for peace" to an "appeal for war",' *JMJP*, 18.2.1949; *SW*, IV, 144.

370 'On the KMT's different answers to the question of responsibility for the war,' (NCNA editorial) *JMJP*, 19.2.1949; *SW*, IV, 145.

371 'Report to the second plenary session of the 7th Central Committee of the CCP,' 5.3.1949, *JMJP*, 3.10.1966; *SW*, IV, 146.

372 'Methods of work of party committees,' 13.3.1949, *SW*, IV, 147.

373 *The Occupation of Nanking by the PLA* (*lü-shih*) 4.1949, JC, p. 342.

374 *To Liu Ya-tzu* (*lü-shih*) 4.1949, JC, p. 343.

375 'Whither the Nanking government?' (NCNA editorial) *JMJP*, 5.4.1949; *SW*, IV, 148.

376 'Reply to Li Tsung-jen on the implementation of the eight principles,' *JMJP*, 10.4.1949. n. tr.

377 'Order to the Army for the country-wide advance,' 21.4.1949, *SW*, IV, 149.

378 'Proclamation of the Chinese People's Liberation Army,' 26.4.1949, *SW*, IV, 150.

379 'On the outrages by British warships—statement by the spokesman of the general headquarters of the Chinese People's Liberation Army,' *JMJP*, 1.5.1949; *SW*, IV, 151.

380 'On the May 4th Movement,' *JMJP*, 4.5.1949. n. tr.

381 'Address to the Preparatory Committee of the New Political Consultative Conference,' *JMJP*, 20.6.1949; *SW*, IV, 152.

382 'On the people's democratic dictatorship,' *JMJP*, 1.7.1949; *SW*, IV, 153.

383 'Cast away illusions, prepare for struggle,' (NCNA editorial) *JMJP*, 15.8.1949; *SW*, IV, 154.

384 'Farewell, Leighton Stuart!' *JMJP*, 19.8.1949; *SW*, IV, 155.

385 'Fourth comment on the White Paper,' *JMJP*, 29.8.1949; *SW*, IV, 156.

386 'Fifth comment on the White Paper,' *JMJP*, 31.8.1949; *SW*, IV, 157.

387 'Sixth comment on the White Paper,' *JMJP*, 17.9.1949; *SW*, IV, 158.

388 'Opening speech at the 1st plenary session of the New Political Consultative Conference,' *JMJP*, 22.9.1949; SRS, *PT*, pp, 109–110.

389 'Learn from Norman Bethune,' *JMJP*, 12.11.1949. n. tr.

390 'Telegram to the secretary-general of the Indian communist party,' *JMJP*, 20.11.1949; SRS, *PT*, p. 260.

391 'Speech at Stalin's birthday celebration in Moscow,' 21.12.1949, *SHWS*, pp. 8–9.

392 *Rural Survey*, Liberation Publishing Society, Central China Edition, 1949.

1950

393 'Interview with a correspondent of Tass,' *JMJP*, 3.1.1950. n. tr.

394 'Farewell speech at the Moscow railway station,' *JMJP*, 20.2.1950. n. tr.

395 'On self-criticism,' *JMJP*, 22.4.1950. n. tr.

396 'Report to the third plenum of the 7th Central Committee of the CCP—fight for a fundamental turn for the better in the financial and economic situation,' (the June 6th statement), 6.6.1950, *JMJP*, 13.6.1950; *New China Monthly*, 1950, no. 7; Peking, New China Bookstore, 1950; *Collected Important Documents of the Communist Bandits*, 1953, II, pp. 81–5; Peking, FLP, 1950.

397 'Opening speech at the 2nd meeting of the national committee of the People's Political Consultative Conference,' *JMJP*, 15.6.1950. n. tr.

398 'Closing speech at the 2nd meeting of the national committee of the People's Political Consultative Conference,' *JMJP*, 24.6.1950. n. tr.

399 'Talk at the eighth meeting of the Government Council,' 28.6.1950, *Shih-chieh chih-shih*, no. 20, 20.10.1958; *PR*, 1958, no. 37.

400 *Reply to Liu Ya-tzu*—to the melody of *Wan Hsi Sha*, 2.10.1950, *JMJP*, 2.10.1950; JC, p. 344.

1951

401 'Give serious attention to the discussion of the film *The Life of Wu Hsun*,' *JMJP*, 20.5.1951 and 26.5.1967; *Five Documents on Literature and Art*, Peking, 1967.

402 'Opening and closing speeches at the 3rd meeting of the national committee of the 1st People's Political Consultative Conference,' 10–11.1951, *New China Monthly*, no. 25. n. tr.

403 'Thought reform and industrialization,' *JMJP*, 24.10.1951. n. tr.

1952

404 'Address at the Soviet Embassy's banquet celebrating the 2nd anniversary of the Sino-Soviet Treaty of Friendship, Alliance, and Mutual Assistance,' *Shih-chieh chih-shih*, no. 20, 20.10.1958. n. tr.

405 'Against corruption and waste,' (excerpts from earlier writings) *New China Monthly*, no. 27.

406 *Selected Works of Mao Tse-tung*, vols. 1, 2, and 3.

1953

407 'Instructions to the 4th meeting of the national committee of the 1st People's Political Consultative Conference,' *JMJP*, 8.2.1953. n. tr.

408 'Telegram of condolence on the death of Stalin,' 6.3.1953, *New China Monthly*, no. 41.

409 'The greatest friendship,' 10.3.1953, *New China Monthly*, no. 42; NCNA, 10.3.1953.

410 'Instruction on the orientation of the Youth League's work,' 30.6.1953, *New China Monthly*, no. 46.

411 'Resolution on strengthening the unity of the party,' 24.12.1953, rf. the communiqué of the 4th plenum of the 7th Central Committee, unpublished, see *New China Monthly*, no. 53; excerpt, *SHWS*, p. 14. n. tr.

1954

412 *Peitaiho*—to the melody of *Lang T'ao Sha*, summer 1954(?), JC, p. 345.

413 'Opening speech at the 1st meeting of the 1st National People's Congress of the People's Republic of China,' *JMJP*, 16.9.1954; *New China Monthly*, no. 60. n. tr.

414 'Letter concerning studies of "The Red Chamber Dream",' 16.10.1954, *JMJP*, 27.5.1967; *Five Documents on Literature and Art*, Peking, 1967.

1955

415 'Opening speech at the emergency congress of the CCP,' 3.1955, unpublished, rf. *New China Monthly*, no. 67; excerpts, *SHWS*, p. 10.

416 'Comments on the second group of material on Hu Feng's counter-revolutionary clique,' *JMJP*, 24.5.1955; *Quotations*, p. 212; *SHWS*, p. 11.

417 'Comments on the third group of material on Hu Feng's counter-revolutionary clique,' *JMJP*, 10.6.1955; *SHWS*, p. 12.

418 'On the problems of agricultural co-operativization,' 31.7.1955, *JMJP*, 17.10.1955; FLP, 1956; *SR*, pp. 316–40.

419 'Selections from the introductory notes in *The Socialist Upsurge in China's Countryside*,' 27.12.1955, *JMJP*, 12.1.1956; *SR*, pp. 341–9.

1956

420 'Talk at the Centre's meeting on the problems of intellectuals,' 20.1.1956, *SHWS*, p. 13.

421 'On the ten great relationships,' (speech delivered at an enlarged meeting of the Politburo, 4.1956) rf. Liu Shao-ch'i's report, *People's Handbook*, 1959, p. 21; NT, pp. 19–28. JC, MTT, pp. 66–85.

422 *Swimming*—to the melody of *Shui Tiao Ko T'uo*, 5.1956, JC, p. 346.

423 'Opening speech at the 8th Congress of the CCP,' 15.9.1956, *Documents of the 8th Congress of the CCP*, Peking, 1956, pp. 9–10; *Collected Documents for Socialist Education*, I, second part, pp. 1121–4; *JMJP*, 16.9.1956; FLP, Peking, 1956.

424 'On the Ninetieth Anniversary of Dr. Sun Yat-sen's birth,' 12.11.1956, *JMJP*, 12.11.1956 and 13.11.1966.

425 'Statement at the 2nd plenum of the 8th Central Committee,' *JMJP*, 16.11.1956. n. tr.

1957

426 'Letter to Tsang K'e-chia and others on poetry,' 12.1.1957, *Nineteen Poems*, Peking: FLP, 1958; *SHWS*, p. 14.

427 'On the correct handling of contradictions among the people,' 27.2.1957, *JMJP*, 3.3.1957 and full text on 19.6.1957; *SR*, pp. 350–87.

428 'Speech at the CCP's national conference on propaganda work,' 12.3.1957, *SR*, pp. 388–402.

429 *The Immortals*—to the melody of *Tieh Lien Hua*, 11.3.1957, JC, p. 347.

430 'Speech at the banquet in honour of President Voroshirov,' 17.4.1957, *Collected Documents for Socialist Education*, I, second part, pp. 1125–7. n. tr.

431 'Things are changing,' 5.1957, *SHWS*, p. 15.

432 'Speech at the reception of the representatives to the 3rd national congress of the New Democratic Youth League,' 25.5.1957, *New China Fortnightly*, no. 12.

433 'The bourgeois orientation of the *Wen Hui Pao* should be criticized,' *JMJP*, 1.7.1957.

434 'The situation in the summer of 1957,' 7.1957, *SHWS*, p. 16.

435 'Talk at the 3rd plenum of the 8th Central Committee,' *JMJP*, 10.10.1957.

436 'Statement at the Moscow Airport,' *JMJP*, 3.11.1957.

437 'Speech at the celebration of the 40th anniversary of the October Revolution,' *JMJP*, 7.11.1957.

438 'Speech at the reception given by the Presidium of the CPSU,' *JMJP*, 19.11.1957.

439 'Conversation with Chinese students,' *JMJP*, 19.11.1957.

(The above four items, see *Chairman Mao's Statements in the Soviet Union*, Peking, 1957, and *Survey of China Mainland Press*, Hong Kong, no. 1856.)

1958

440 'Letter to a district party committee in Kwangsi on the question of running a newspaper,' 12.1.1958, *SHWS*, p. 19.

441 'Talk at a Supreme State Conference meeting,' (excerpts) 28.1.1958, *Anti-party Clique*, p. 1.

442 'Instruction on the question of red and expert,' 31.1.1958, *SHWS*, p. 17.

443 '60 points on working methods,' (draft) 31.1.1958, NT, pp. 29–38.

444 'Instruction on part-time work and part-time study,' 2.1958, *SHWS*, p. 17.

445 'Instruction on the question of minority nationalities,' 3.1958, *SHWS*, p. 18.

446 'Introducing a co-operative,' *RF*, no. 1, 15.4.1958; *SR*, pp. 403–4.

447 'Talk at the 2nd session of the 8th Congress of the CCP,' *JMJP*, 25.5.1958. n. tr.

448 'Talk at the team leaders' discussion of the enlarged meeting of the Military Commission,' (excerpts) 28.6.1958, *Anti-party Clique*, pp. 3–5.

449 *Farewell to the God of Plagues* (*lü-shih*), 30.6.1958, JC, p. 349.

450 'Letter to Chang Wen-t'ien,' 2.8.1958, *Anti-party Clique*, pp. 14–15.

451 'Instruction issued at Tientsin University,' 13.8.1958, *SHWS*, p. 18.

452 'On "Seven Advices" by Mei Sheng,' 16.8.1958, *Anti-party Clique*, pp. 15–16.

453 'Brilliantly analysed international and domestic situations at the 15th Supreme State Conference,' 8.9.1958, *JMJP*, 9.9.1958. n. tr.

454 'Instruction issued at Wuhan University,' 12.9.1958, *SHWS* p. 18.

205 '打退第二次反共高潮後的時局,' 1941.3.18, HC, II, 56.

206 '關於打退第二次反共高潮的總結,' 1941.5.8, HC, II, 57.

207 '改造我們的學習,' 1941.5, HC, 1944, V; HC, III, 59.

208 '揭破遠東慕尼黑的陰謀,' 1941.5.25, HC, III, 60.

209 '關於反法西斯的國際統一戰線,' 1941.6.23, HC, III, 61.

210 '毛澤東同志接見綏東學生代表,' 解放日報, 1941.8.15.

解放日報

211 '慰唁張沖家屬,' 1941.8.16.

212 '魯志才長征記的按語,' 1941.9.14.

213 '東方反法西斯大會上毛澤東同志號召民族加強團結,' 1941.10.31.

214 '毛澤東同志發表廣播演說,' (邊區參議會) 1941.11.7.

215 '在陝甘寧邊區參議會的演說,' 1941.11.22; 陝甘寧邊區第二屆參議會
重要文獻, 延安, 1944, 頁17-21; HC, III, 62.

1942

216 '毛主席批示,' 1942.1.23發出, 1942.4.15 (此即'毛主席號召全邊區部隊
研究"紅四軍九次黨代表大會決議," 留守兵團發出訓
令, 規定學習研究辦法.' 解放日報第一次用'毛主席'
標題.)

217 '反對黨八股,' 1942.2.8, 1942.6.18登載; HC, III, 64.

218 '中共中央宣傳部召集會議, 厲行整頓文風. 毛澤東:要肅清主觀主
義, 宗派主義, 必須肅清黨八股,' 1942.2.10.

219 '慶祝紅軍二十四週年,' 1942.2.23.

220 '在本報改版座談會上, 毛澤東同志號召整頓三風要利用報紙, 批
評絕對平均觀念, 和冷嘲暗箭辦法.' 1942.4.2.

221 '整頓學風, 黨風, 文風,' 1942.4.27; HC, III, 63.

222 '在延安文藝座談會上的講話,' 1942.5.2, 23, 1943.10.19刊登;
華東版, 1947; HC, III, 65.

223 '一個極其重要的政策,' 1942.9.7, HC, III, 66.

224 '第二次世界大戰的轉折點,' 1942.10.12, HC, III, 67.

225 '祝十月革命二十五週年,' 1942.11.7, HC, III, 68.

226 '對中國國民黨十中全會, 中國共產黨發表意見,' 解放日報, 1942.11.30.

227 '經濟問題與財政問題' 1942.12, HC, 1944, IV, 頁3-204; (原文之一小部
份) HC, II, 69.

1943

228 '毛主席號召加緊生產教育,'　　　解放日報, 1943. 1. 4.

229 '批判彭德懷,關於民主教育談話的一封信,' 1943. 5. 6. 反黨集團, 頁 1.

230 *'中國共產黨中央委員會關於共產國際執委主席團提議解散共產國際
的決定,'　　　　　　　解放日報, 1943. 5. 26.

解放日報

231 '關於共產國際解散問題, 毛澤東同志作詳盡報告,' 1943. 5. 28.

232 '中共中央關於領導方法的決議,' 1943. 6. 1, 1943. 6. 4 刊登; HC, Ⅲ, 70.
選讀, 甲, 下.

233 '總結策勇鬥爭的二十二年,' 1943. 7. 1, 1943. 7. 3 刊登.

234 '論合作社,'　　　　生產組織與農村調查, 1946.

解放日報

235 '質問國民黨,' (社論)　　1943. 7. 12; HC, Ⅲ, 71.

236 '中共中央政治局 關於減租生產擁政愛民及宣傳十大政策的指示,'
1943. 10. 1; HC, Ⅲ, 72.

237 '評國民黨十一中全會及三屆二次國民參政會,' 1943. 11. 5; (見張靜盧,
現代出版史料, 丁, 上, 頁 293); HC, Ⅲ, 73.

238 '在慶祝十月革命節幹部晚會上的講話,' 1943. 11. 7.

239 '電斯大林慶祝十月革命節,' 1943. 11. 8.

240 '組織起來: 在招待陝甘寧邊區勞動英雄會上講話,' 1943. 11. 29,
1943. 12. 2 刊登; HC, Ⅲ, 74.

1944

241 '看了"逼上梁山"以後寫給延安平劇院的信,' 1944. 1. 9, 人民日報, 1967. 5. 25.

242 '學習和時局,' 1944. 4. 12, HC, Ⅲ, 75; 選讀, 甲, 下.

解放日報

243 '發展工業 打倒日寇,' 1944. 5. 26.

244 '延大應為抗戰及邊區政治經濟文化建設服務,' 1944. 5. 31.

245 '接見記者團席上暢談國內外局勢 ── 致詞, 問題, 答覆,' 1944. 6. 13.

246 *'長沙失陷後的危機,' (社論) 1944. 6. 24.

247 '談合作社業務,' 1944. 7. 4.

248 *'採用新的組織形式與工作方式,' (社論) 1944. 9. 5.

249 '為人民服務,' 1944. 9. 8, 1944. 9. 21 刊登; HC, Ⅲ, 76.

250 *'延安權威人士評國共談判,' 1944. 9. 20 (第一次用 '權威人士' 名義.)

251 `延安觀察家評論　蔣介石演說具有危險性.' 1944. 10. 12; HC, III, 77.
252 `在邊區文教大會講演　文教統一戰線方針.' 1944. 11. 1; 群眾, 10卷.
　　　　2期; HC, III, 78.
253 `電賀羅斯福當選連任,' 1944. 11. 10.
254 `無題,' (紀念鄒韜奮會) 1944. 11. 15.
255 *`延安權威人士評國民黨人事調動,' 1944. 11. 23.
256 `一九四五年的任務 — 在邊區參議會上的演說,' 1944. 12. 15.
　　　　1944. 12. 16 刊登, HC, III, 1947, 頁 125-35.
257 沁園春 (雪) 1944-5 冬.
258 毛澤東選集　　晉察冀日報社初編本 1944. (參看補遺)
259 　　　　　　再版 1945.
260 　　　晉察冀中央局編印本 1947.
261 　　　　　　再版 1948.
262 　　　哈爾濱排印本 1948.
　 1945
　解放日報
263 `爭取勝利早日實現,' (新年獻詞) 1945. 1. 1.
264 `加強團結戰勝日冦,' 1945. 1. 2.
265 *`延安權威人士評蔣介石元旦廣播.' 1945. 1. 4.
266 `兩三年內完全學會經濟工作.' (在勞動英雄模範工作者大會上
　　　　講演.) 1945. 1. 12; HC, III, 79.
267 `游擊區也能夠生產, 也必須生產.' 1945. 1. 31; HC, III, 80.
　解放日報
268 `彭雪楓輓詞,' 1945. 2. 8.
269 `致斯大林元帥賀電,' 1945. 2. 22.
270 `弔唁羅斯福電文,' 1945. 4. 13.
271 `兩個中國之命運,' HC, III, 81.
272 `全黨團結起來, 為實現黨的任務而鬥爭.' 1945. 4. 24. 選讀, 甲, 下.
　解放日報
273 `論軍隊生產自給, 兼論整風和生產兩大運動的重要性.' (社論)
　　　　1945. 4. 27; HC, III, 84.
274 `中國共產黨第七次全國代表大會開幕詞,' 1945. 5. 1.
275 `論聯合政府,' 1945. 4. 24, 1945. 5. 3 刊登; HC, III, 82.

303 ＊‘駁蔣介石，’ 1946.4.7；歷史文獻社，政協文獻目錄, N.P., 1946, 頁179-86.

304 ‘關於目前國際形勢的幾點估計，’ 1946.4, HC, IV, 99；選讀，甲，下.
解放日報

305 ‘向"四·八"被難烈士致敬，’ 1946.4.20.

306 ‘弔唁李如璧寧電，’ 1946.6.5.

307 ＊‘延安權威人士聲明：反對貝爾納斯援蔣法案，’ 1946.6.17.

308 ‘反對美軍事援蔣法案，’ 1946.6.23；群眾, 11卷, 9期；HC, 1947, III, 頁145-6.

309 ‘電慰馬敘倫，’ 1946.7.6.

310 ‘電覆渝名流 同心協力爭取和平，’ 1946.7.7.

311 ‘弔唁李公樸，’ 1946.7.13.

312 ‘弔唁聞一多家屬，’ 1946.7.17.

313 ‘以自衛戰爭粉碎蔣介石的進攻，’ 1946.7.20, HC, IV. 100.
解放日報

314 ‘弔唁陶行知，’ 1946.7.25.

315 ‘和美國記者安娜·路易斯·斯特朗的談話，’ 1946.8, HC, IV, 101.

316 ‘集中優勢兵力，各個殲滅敵人，’ 1946.9.16, HC, IV, 102.
解放日報

317 ‘答美記者問，’ 1946.9.29, 1946.10.7 刊登；群眾, 12卷, 12期；HC, IV, 103.

318 ‘三個月的總結，’ 1946.10.1, HC, IV, 104.

319 ‘毛主席電覆民盟馬來霹靂分部促和平電，’ 1946.10.12.

320 ‘電賀高樹勳將軍起義週年，’ 1946.10.30.

321 ＊‘論戰局，’ (社論) 1946.11.4.

322 ‘電賀斯大林元帥 祝蘇聯二十九年國慶，’ 1946.11.7.

323 ＊‘戰局在開始變動，’ (社論) 1946.12.6.

1947

324 ‘新年祝詞，’ 1947.1.1.

325 ‘電賀華中民主聯軍成立週年，’ 1947.1.8, 1947.1.9 刊登.

326 ‘迎接中國革命的高潮，’ 1947.2.1, HC, IV, 105.

327 ‘中共中央關於暫時放棄延安和保衛陝甘寧邊區的兩個文件，’ HC, IV, 106.

328 ‘關於西北戰場的作戰方針，’ 1947.4.15, HC, IV, 107.

329 ‘蔣介石政府已處在全民的包圍中，’ 1947.5.30, HC, IV, 108.

330 ‘解放戰爭第二年的戰署方針，’ 1947.9.1, HC, IV, 109.

331 ‘中國人民解放軍宣言，’ 1947.10, HC, IV, 110.

332 '中國人民解放軍總部關於重行頒佈三大紀律八項注意的訓令.'
1947. 10. 10, HC, IV, 111.

333 '目前形勢和我們的任務,' 1947. 12. 25, 第六段刊於新民主義工商政策;
HC, IV, 112.

334 毛澤東選集 續編 中共晉察冀中央局印, 1947. 12.

1948

335 '關於建立報告制度,' 1948. 1. 7, HC, IV, 113.

336 '關於目前黨的政策中的幾個重要問題,' 1948. 1. 18, HC, IV, 114.

337 '軍隊內部的民主運動,' 1948. 1. 30, HC, IV, 115.

338 '在不同地區實施土地法的不同策器,' 1948. 2. 3, HC, IV, 116.

339 '糾正土地改革宣傳中的"左傾"錯誤,' 1948. 2. 10, HC, IV, 117.

340 '新解放區土地政策要點,' 1948. 2. 15, HC, IV, 118.

341 '關於工商業政策,' 1948. 2. 27, HC, IV, 119.

342 '關於民族資產階級和開明紳士問題,' 1948. 3. 1, HC, IV, 120.

343 '評西北大捷兼論解放軍的新式整軍運動,' 1948. 3. 7, HC, IV, 121.

344 '山西崞縣一篇土改通訊的序言,' 1948. 3. 13, 土改整黨典型經驗,
香港, 1948, 頁 4-5.

345 '關於情況的通知,' 1948. 3. 20, HC, IV, 122.

346 '在晉綏幹部會議上的講話,' 1948. 4. 香港, 1948; HC, IV, 123.

347 '對晉綏日報編輯人員的談話,' 1948. 4. 2, HC, IV, 124; 選讀, 甲, 下.

348 '再克洛陽後給洛陽前線指揮部的電報,' 1948. 4. 8, HC, IV, 125.

349 '新解放區農村工作的策器問題,' 1948. 5. 24, HC, IV, 126.

350 '一九四八年的土地改革工作和整黨工作,' 1948. 5. 25, HC, IV, 127.

351 '關於遼瀋戰役的作戰方針,' 1948. 9-10, HC, IV, 128.

352 '關於建全黨委制,' 1948. 9. 20, HC, IV, 129; 選讀, 甲, 下.

353 '中共中央關於九月會議的通知,' 1948. 10. 10, HC, IV, 130.

354 '關於淮海戰役的作戰方針,' 1948. 10. 11, HC, IV, 131.

355 '全世界革命力量團結起來, 反對帝國主義的侵略' 人民, 1948. 11. 7; HC, IV, 132.

356 '中共中央負責人評論中國軍事形勢,' 人民, 1948. 11. 16; HC, IV, 133.

357 '關於平津戰役的作戰方針,' 1948. 12. 11. HC, IV, 134.

358 '不投降就要被消滅,' 人民, 1948. 12. 22; HC, IV, 135.

1949

359 '將革命進行到底,' (新華社社論) 人民, 1949. 1. 1; HC, IV, 136.

360 '揭露戰犯求和陰謀,' (新華社社論)　　　人民, 1949.1.6; HC, IV, 137.

361 '關於時局的聲明,'　　　　　　　　　　人民, 1949.1.15; HC, IV, 138.

362 '中共中央發言人評南京行政院的決議,'　1949.1.21, 人民, 1949.1.23; HC, IV, 139.

363 '就南京偽政府"和談陰謀"及釋放日本戰犯岡村寧次, 中共發言人表示嚴正
　　　意見,'　　　　　　　　　　　　　人民, 1949.1.29; HC, IV, 140.

364 '中共發言人再談和平條件,'　　　　　　人民, 1949.2.6; HC, IV, 141.

365 '對國民黨賣國"政府"又犯嚴重賣國罪, 中共發言人發表聲明. 懲和戰
　　　犯一項必須加上懲辦日本戰犯,'　　　人民, 1949.2.7; HC, IV, 141.

366 '把軍隊變為工作隊,'　　　　　　　　　1949.2.8, HC, IV, 142.

367 '四分五裂的反動派, 為什麼空喊全面和平?' (新華社評論)
　　　　　　　　　　　　　　　　　　　人民, 1949.2.16-17; HC, IV, 143.

368 '國民黨戰犯集團妄圖拯救他們自己, 由呼吁"和平"改為呼吁戰爭,'
　　　　　　　　　　　　　　　　　　　人民, 1949.2.18; HC, IV, 144.

369 '國民黨九硬派騙人把戲無法再演, "呼吁和平"變為"呼吁戰爭",'
　　　　　　　　　　　　　　　　　　　人民, 1949.2.18; HC, IV, 144.

370 '評國民黨對於戰爭責任問題的幾種答案,' (新華社社論)
　　　　　　　　　　　　　　　　　　　人民, 1949.2.19; HC, IV, 145.

371 '在中國共產黨第七屆中央委員會第二次全體會議上的報告,' 1949.3.5.
　　　　　　　　　　　　　　　　　　　人民, 1966.10.3; HC, IV, 146.

372 '黨委會的工作方法,'　　　　　　　　　1949.3.13, HC, IV, 147.

373 律詩 (解放軍攻佔南京)　　　　　　　　1949.4.

374 律詩 (贈柳亞子)　　　　　　　　　　　1949.4.

375 '南京政府向何處去?' (新華社社論)　　人民, 1949.4.5; HC, IV, 148.

376 '覆李宗仁　關於具體實現八項原則問題,' 人民, 1949.4.10.

377 '向全國進軍令,'　　　　　　　　　　　1949.4.21, HC, IV, 149.

378 '中國人民解放軍總部宣佈約法八章,'　　人民, 1949.4.26; HC, IV, 150.

379 '中國人民解放軍總部發言人為英國軍艦暴行發表聲明,'
　　　　　　　　　　　　　　　　　　　人民, 1949.5.1; HC, IV, 151.

380 '論五四運動,'　　　　　　　　　　　　人民, 1949.5.4.

381 '在新政治協商會議籌備會上的講詞,'　　人民, 1949.6.20; HC, IV, 152.

382 '論人民民主專政,'　　　　　　　　　　人民, 1949.7.1; HC, IV, 153.

383 '丟掉幻想, 準備鬥爭,' (新華社社論)　 人民, 1949.8.15; HC, IV, 154.

384 '別了, 司徒雷登,'　　　　　　　　　　人民, 1949.8.19; HC, IV, 155.

385 '四評白皮書,'　　　　　　　　　人民, 1949. 8. 29; HC, Ⅳ, 156.

386 '五評白皮書,'　　　　　　　　　人民, 1949. 8. 31; HC, Ⅳ, 157.

387 '六評白皮書,'　　　　　　　　　人民, 1949. 9. 17; HC, Ⅳ, 158.

388 '中國人民政協第一屆會議上開幕詞,' 人民, 1949. 9. 22.

389 '學習白求恩,'　　　　　　　　　人民, 1949. 11. 12.

390 '致印度共產黨總書記電,'　　　　人民, 1949. 11. 10.

391 '在莫斯科慶祝斯大林壽辰大會上的祝詞,'　1949. 12. 21, 思想萬歲, 頁 8-9.

392 農村調查, 解放社華中版, 1949.

　　　1950

393 '答塔斯社記者問,'　　　　　　　人民, 1950. 1. 3.

394 '在莫斯科車站上的臨別演說,'　　人民, 1950. 2. 20.

395 '論自我批評,'　　　　　　　　　人民, 1950. 4. 22.

396 '在中國共產黨七屆中央委員會第三次全體會議上的報告 —— 為爭取國
　　家財政經濟狀況的基本好轉而鬥爭,' (六六文告), 1950. 6. 6,
　　　　　　　　　　　　　　　　　人民, 1950. 6. 13; 新華月報, 1950, 7期,
　　　　　　　　　　　　　　　　　北京新華書店, 1950; 共匪重要資料
　　　　　　　　　　　　　　　　　彙編, 1953, Ⅱ, 頁 81-5.

397 '在人民政協全國委員會第二次會議上致開幕詞,'　人民, 1950. 6. 15.

398 '在政協第二次會議上致閉幕詞,' 人民, 1950. 6. 24.

399 '在中央人民政府委員會第八次會議上講話,'　1950. 6. 28, 世界知識, 20
　　　　　　　　　　　　　　　　　期, 1958. 10. 20.

400 浣溪紗 (和柳亞子)　　　　　　人民, 1950. 10. 2.

　　　1951

401 '應當重視電影 "武訓傳" 的討論,' 人民, 1951. 5. 20, 1967. 5. 26.

402 '中國人民政治協商會議第一屆全國委員會第三次會議開會詞及閉會詞,'
　　　　　　　　　　　　　　　　　1951. 10-11, 新華月報, 25期.

403 '思想改造與工業化,'　　　　　　人民, 1951. 10. 24.

　　　1952

404 '在蘇聯大使館慶祝中蘇友好同盟互助條約兩週年宴會上講話,'
　　　　　　　　　　　　　　　　　世界知識, 20期, 1958. 10. 20.

405 '論反對貪污浪費,' (摘錄)　　　新華月報, 27期.

406 毛澤東選集第一, 二, 三卷

1953

407 '人民政協第一屆全國委員會第四次會議'的指示,'　　人民, 1953.2.8.
　　新華月報

408 '弔唁斯大林電,'　　　　　　　　　　1953.3.6, 41期.

409 '最偉大的友誼,'　　　　　　　　　　1953.3.10, 42期.

410 '對青年團工作方向的指示,'　　　　　1953.6.30, 46期; 思想萬歲, 頁14.

411 '關於增強黨的團結的決議,'　　　　　1953.12.24, 原文未發表, 見七屆中
　　　　　　　　　　　　　　　　　　　央委員會第四次全體會議的公
　　　　　　　　　　　　　　　　　　　報, 新華月報, 53期.

1954

412 浪淘沙 (北戴河)　　　　　　　　　　1954, 夏 (?)

413 '中華人民共和國第一屆全國人民代表大會第一次會議開幕詞,'
　　　　　　　　　　　　　　　　　　　人民, 1954.9.16; 新華月報, 60期.

414 '關於"紅樓夢"研究問題的信,'　　　　1954.10.16, 人民, 1967.5.27.
1955

415 '在中國共產黨緊急會議上的開幕詞,'　1955.3, 全文未發表, 見新華月報,
　　　　　　　　　　　　　　　　　　　67期; 摘錄見思想萬歲, 頁10.

416 '"關於胡風反革命集團的第二批材料"的按語,'　人民, 1955.5.24; 語錄,
　　　　　　　　　　　　　　　　　　　頁162; 思想萬歲, 頁11.

417 '"關於胡風反革命集團的第三批材料"的按語,' 人民, 1955.6.10; 思想萬歲,頁12.

418 '關於農業合作化問題,'　　　　　　　1955.7.31, 人民, 1955.10.17.

419 '中國農村社會主義'的高潮,' (序言, 按語) 1955.12.27, 人民, 1956.1.12; 選讀, 甲, 下.
1956

420 '在中央召開的關於知識分子問題會議上的講話,'　1956.1.20, 思想萬歲, 頁13.

421 '論十大關係,'　1956.4 政治局擴大會議上講演, 見劉少奇報告, 人民手冊,
　　　　　　　　　　　　　　　　　　　1959, 頁21; 不知名集, 頁19-28.

422 水調歌頭 (游泳)　　　　　　　　　　1956.5.

423 '中共第八次全國代表大會開幕詞,'　　1956.9.15, 中國共產黨第八屆全國代表
　　　　　　　　　　　　　　　　　　　大會文獻, 北京, 1956, 頁9-10; 社會主
　　　　　　　　　　　　　　　　　　　義教育課程的閱讀文件彙編, 第
　　　　　　　　　　　　　　　　　　　一編, 下, 頁1121-1124; 人民, 1956.9.16.

424 '紀念孫中山先生誕生九十週年,' 1956.11.12, 人民, 1956.11.12, 1966.11.13.

425 '在中共中央第二次全體會議上的發言.'　　　人民, 1956. 11. 16.

1957
426 '致臧克家等關於詩的一封信.'　　1957. 1. 12, 思想萬歲, 頁14.
427 '就正確處理人民內部矛盾的問題講了話.'　　1957. 2. 27, 人民, 1957. 3. 3.
　　　　　　　　　　　　　　　　　　　全文見人民, 1957. 6. 19.
428 '在中國共產黨宣傳工作會議上的講話.'　　1957. 3. 12, 選讀, 甲, 下.
429 蝶戀花 (貝爾李淑一)　　　　　　　　　1957. 5. 11.
430 '歡迎伏羅希羅夫主席宴會上的講話.'　1957. 4. 17, 社會主義教育課程閱讀
　　　　　　　　　　　　　　　　文件彙編, 第一編, 下, 頁, 1135-7.
431 '事情正在起變化.'　　　　　1957. 5, 思想萬歲, 頁15.
432 '接見新民主主義青年團第三次全國代表大會全體代表的講話.' 1957. 5. 25,
　　　　　　　　　　　　　　　　　新華半月刊, 12號.
433 '文匯報的資產階級方向應當批判.'　　人民, 1957. 7. 1.
434 '一九五七年夏季的形勢.'
　　　　　　　　　　　1957. 7, 思想萬歲, 頁16.
435 '在中共中央第三次全會上講話.'　　　人民, 1957. 10. 10.
436 '在莫斯科機場的演說.'　　　　　　人民, 1957. 11. 3.
437 '在十月革命四十週年會議上講演.'　　人民, 1957. 11. 7.
438 '在蘇共中央主席團招待會講演.'　　　人民, 1957. 11. 19.
439 '對中國學生講話.'　　　　　　　人民, 1957. 11. 19.
　　　(以上四篇刊載於毛主席在蘇聯的言論. 人民日報社, 1957.)

1958
440 '就辦報問題給廣西區黨委的一封信.'　　1958. 1. 12, 思想萬歲, 頁19.
441 '在最高國務會議上的講話.' (摘錄)　　1958. 1. 28, 反黨集團, 頁1.
442 '關於"紅專"問題的指示.'　　　　　1958. 1. 31. 思想萬歲, 頁17.
443 '工作方法六十條.' (草案)　　　　　1958. 1. 31, 不知名集, 頁29-38.
444 '關於半工半讀的指示.'　　　　　　1958. 2,　思想萬歲, 頁17.
445 '關於民族問題的指示.'　　　　　　1958. 3,　思想萬歲, 頁18.
446 '介紹一個合作社.'　　　　　　　　紅旗, 1期, 1958. 4. 15; 選讀, 甲, 下.
447 '在中共八大第二次會議上講話.'　　　人民, 1958. 5. 25.
448 '在軍委擴大會議小組長座談會上講話.' (摘錄)　1958. 6. 28,
　　　　　　　　　　　　　　　　　反黨集團, 頁3-5.
449 律詩 (送瘟神)　　　　　　　　　　1958. 6. 30.
450 '給張聞天的信.'　　　　　　　　1958. 8. 2, 反黨集團, 頁14-5.

451 '視查天津大學時所作的指示,' 1958. 8. 13, 思想萬歲, 頁18.

452 '關於枚乘"七發",' 1958. 8. 16, 反黨集團, 頁15-6.

453 '在十五次最高國務會議上精辟分析國內外形勢,' 1958. 9. 8
人民, 1958. 9. 9.

454 '視查武漢大學時所作的指示,' 1958. 9. 12, 思想萬歲, 頁18.

455 '視查湖北鋼鐵生產時所作的指示,' 1958. 9 思想萬歲, 頁18.

456 '與新華社記者談話,' 1958. 9. 29, 紅旗, 10期, 1958. 10. 16;
人民 1958. 10. 1.

457 '中共中央政治局武昌會議上的講話,' 1958. 12. 1, 語錄, 頁65. 全文未發表.

1959

458 '給福斯特同志的信,' 1959. 1. 17, 思想萬歲, 頁19.

459 '在中央政治局(擴大)鄭州會議上的講話,' 1959. 2 反黨集團, 頁5.

460 '在第二次鄭州會議上的講話,' 1959. 3 反黨集團, 頁6.

461 '在第十六次最高國務會議上談到國際形勢, 國內形勢, 并談到西藏問
題,' 人民, 1959. 4. 6.

462 律詩 (回韶山) 1959. 6:

463 律詩 (廬山) 1959. 7. 1.

反黨集團

464 '廬山會議前後的談話,' 1959. 7. 10, 8. 16, 頁11-2.

465 '對彭德懷一九五九年七月十四日"意見書"的批判,' 1959. 7, 頁6.

466 '關於一封信的評論,' (李仲雲"意見書"的評論) 1959. 7. 26, 頁13.

467 '關於印發三篇文章的按語,' (公社問題駁赫魯曉夫)
1959. 7. 29, 頁14.

468 '給王稼祥的信,' (人民公社問題駁赫魯曉夫) 1959. 8. 1, 頁14.

469 '在八屆八中全會上的講話,' 1959. 8. 2, 頁16-7.

470 '對"湖南平江縣談鎖'公社稻竹大隊幾十個食堂散伙又恢復的
情況," 一文的按語,' 1959. 8. 5, 頁17.

471 '對"王國藩社的情況-真很好"和"目前農村中閒話較多的是
那些人"二文的批語,' 1958. 8. 6, 頁18.

472 '對"安徽省委書記處書記張愷帆下令解散無為縣食堂的報告"
的批語,' 1959. 8. 10, 頁18.

473 '對"遼寧省執行中央反右傾指示的報告"的批語,' 1959. 8. 12, 頁19.

474 '對 "馬克思主義者應當如何正確地對待革命群衆運動" 一文的批語,'
1959.8.15, 頁19-20.

475 '經驗主義還是馬克思列寧主義" 一書的前言,' 1959.8.15, 頁20.

476 '機關槍和迫擊炮的來歷及其它,' 1959.8.16, 頁20-1.

477 '給 "詩刊" 編輯部的第二封信,' 1959.9.1, 頁21-2.

478 '在中共中央軍委擴大會議上和外事會議上的講話,' 1959.9.11, 頁22-4.

479 '發展養豬事業的一封信,' 1959.10.11, 思想萬歲, 頁21-2.

480 '給生產隊長的一封信,' 1959.11.29, 思想萬歲, 頁19-21.

1960

481 '對日本文學代表團談話,' 1960.6.21, 竹內 實, '毛沢東主席との一時間半,' 新日本文學, 1960.9月號, 頁95-102.

482 毛澤東選集 第四卷

1961

483 七絕 (為女民兵題照) 1961.2.

484 律詩 (贈友人) 1961.

485 '給江西共產主義勞動大學的一封信,' 1961.8.1, 思想萬歲, 頁22.

486 七絕 (廬山仙人洞) 1961.9.9.

487 律詩 (和郭沫若) 1961.9.17.

488 卜算子 (梅) 1961.11.

1962

489 '關於民主集中制問題的講話,' 1962.1.30, 思想萬歲, 頁22-5.

490 '在八屆十中全會上的講話,' 1962.9.24, 反黨集團, 頁24-7.

491 '中共八屆十中全會通過, 進一步鞏固人民公社集體經濟發展農業生產,' 人民, 1962.9.29.

492 '對柯慶施同志報告的批示,' 1962.12.12, 思想萬歲, 頁25.

493 律詩 (冬雲) 1962.12.26.

1963

494 滿江紅 (和郭沫若) 1963.1.9.

495 '人的正確思想是從那裡來的?' 人民出版社, 1963.5.

496 '支持美國黑人反對美帝國主義種族歧視的正義鬥爭聲明,' 人民, 1963.8.9.

497 '反對美國—吳庭艷集團侵畧越南南方和屠殺越南南方人民的聲明,' 人民, 1963.8.30.

498 ‘關於文學藝術的一個批示.’ 1963.9, 思想萬歲. 頁 26.
499 ‘關於文學藝術的一個批示.’ 1963.12.12, 人民, 1967.5.28.
500 ‘中央關於加強互相學習克服固步自封驕傲自滿的指示.’ (摘錄)
　　　　1963.12.13, 不知名集. 頁 4-7.

1964
501 ‘中國人民堅決支持巴拿馬人民的愛國主義鬥爭.’ 人民, 1964.1.13.
502 ‘中國人民支持日本人民偉大的愛國鬥爭.’ 人民, 1964.1.28.
503 ‘關於教育工作的春節指示.’ 1964.2.13, 思想萬歲. 頁 26-8.
504 ‘毛澤東語錄.’ 1964.5.
505 ‘關於文學藝術的一個批示.’ 1964.6.27, 人民, 1967.5.28.
506 毛澤東著作選讀 1964.7.9.
507 ‘關於文學藝術的一個批示.’ 1964.8, 思想萬歲. 頁 26.
508 ‘關於支持剛果 (利奧波維爾) 人民反對美國侵畧的聲明.’
　　　　1964.11.28, 新華月刊 242 期.
509 ‘接見尼泊爾教育代表團時關於教育問題的談話.’ 思想萬歲. 頁 28-9.
510 ‘對 “關於學習解放軍加強政治工作的指示.” 的批示.’ 思想萬歲. 頁 30.
1965
511 ‘社會主義教育二十三條.’
　　　　1965.1.14, 人民, 1967.3.31; 福建出版, 1965.1.18.
512 ‘對徐寅生同志的 “關於如何打乒乓球”一文的批示.’ 1965.1, 思想萬歲. 頁 31.
513 ‘對陳正人同志的蹲點報告的批示.’ 1965.1.29, 思想萬歲. 頁 31.
514 ‘政治局全國工作會議上的講話.’ 1965.1 (未發表) 見人民, 1966.6.3.
515 ‘與斯諾的談話.’ 1965.1 (英文) 倫敦星期時報, 華盛頓郵報, 1965.2.14.
516 水調歌頭 (訪井崗山) 1965 春夏之交, 竹內 實 ‘毛沢東 の詩’ 期日新聞夕刊, 1967.1.19.
517 ‘支持多米尼加人民反對美國武裝侵畧的聲明.’ 人民, 1965.5.12.
518 ‘對衞生工作的指示.’ 1965.6, 不知名集. 頁 9.
519 ‘與法國文化部長馬洛的談話.’ 1965.8, (法文), André Malraux, Antimemoires.
　　　　Paris: Gallimard, 1967, 頁 522-53.
520 ‘在杭州的講話.’ 1965.12.21, 思想萬歲. 頁 31-4; 不知名集. 頁 1-3.
1966
521 ‘給林彪同志的信 —— 對軍委後勤總部 “關於進一步搞好部隊農業的報告,”
　　　　的批示.’ 1966.5.7, 思想萬歲. 頁 34-5.
522 ‘中共中央的通知.’ 1966.5.16, 紅旗, 1967.7 期, 1967.5.20.

523 '在一次會議上的講話.'　　　　1966.7.21. 不知名集. 頁8-9.
524 '在會見大區書記和中央文革小組成員時的講話.'　1966.7.22. 思想萬歲. 頁43-4.
525 '給清華附中紅衛兵的一封信.'　　1966.8.1, 思想萬歲. 頁35-6.
526 '炮打司令部,'　(大字報)　　　1966.8.5. 人民, 1967.8.5.
527 '中共第八屆十一次中全會關於文化大革命的決定,'　(十六條)
　　　　　　　　　　　　　　1966.8.8. 人民, 1966.8.9.

思想萬歲
528 '在八屆十一中全會開幕式上的講話.'　　　1966.8.8, 頁37-8.
529 '在擴大中央工作會議上的講話.'　　　1966.8下旬(?), 頁38-40.
530 '在中央工作會議上的講話.'　　　1966.8.23, 頁40.
531 '對青島, 長沙, 西安問題的指示.'　　　1966.9.7, 頁42.
532 '對陳伯達同志"兩個月來運動的總結"的批示.' 1966.10.24, 頁42.
533 '在滙報會議上的講話.'　　　1966.10.24, 頁44-6; 不知名集, 頁10;
　　　　　　　　　　　　　摘錄見反黨集團, 頁27.
534 '在中央工作會議上的講話.'　　　1966.10.25. 思想萬歲. 頁40-2.
535 '致阿爾巴尼亞勞動黨第五次代表大會賀電,' 紅旗 1966.15期, 1966.12.13.

1967
不知名集
536 '在中央文革會議上講話.'　　　1967.1.8, 頁11.
537 '在中央文革會議上講話.'　　　1967.1.9, 頁11-2.
538 '給林彪同志的指示.'　　　1967.1(?), 頁12, 13.
539 '在中央常委會上的四點指示,'　1967.1(?), 頁12.
540 '對廣播局奪權的指示.' (王力同志傳達)　1967.1, 頁12.
541 '在軍委擴大會議上的講話,' (周總理傳達) 1967.1.27, 頁13.
542 '對人民解放軍的指示,' (葉劍英同志傳達) 1967.1.27, 頁13-4.
543 '和周恩來總理談奪權問題,'　　　1967　頁14.
544 '電阮友壽主席祝賀越南民族解放陣線七週年,' 人民, 1967.12.19.

補遺

545 `中共中央關於反對敵人五次"圍剿"的總結決議,' (遵義會議, 1935年1月 8日政治局會議通過)　　毛澤東選集上冊,中共晉冀魯豫中央局編印, 1948, 并見 中國革命史參考資料,第三集,中國人 民大學中國革命史教研室編輯,1957.

546 贈彭德懷 (五絕)　　香港友聯研究所,彭德懷案件專輯,1968,封底.

547 毛澤東選集　　除 258-62 已列者, 尚有

548 　　蘇中出版社 第一卷　1945

549 　　膠東新華書店第五卷　1946

550 　　晉冀魯豫中央局編　1948　　第五卷,第六卷,有人建議在`九大'以前出版 見中共中央文件. 中發 (67) 358, 新疆天山烽 火. 1968.1.15. 頁 1.

551 論中國革命　　東北軍區政治部出版　　1948

552 毛澤東文選　　渤海新華書店　　1948

553 `1957年3月6日在九省市宣傳文教部長座談會上的談話,' (全文 未發表)　　見人民 1968.9.1.

554 `對人民日報的批評,' 1957.4 (全文未發表)　　見人民 1968.9.1.

555 `文滙報在一個時期內的資產階級方向,' (人民日報編輯部) 1957.6.14　　見人民 1968.9.1.

556 `關於人民日報的一次談話.'　1958.1　　見人民 1968.9.1.

557 `關於辦好報紙的指示,' (全文未發表)　　見人民 1968.9.1.

558

559 `給日本工人朋友們的題詞.' 1962.9.18 `1964年1月的一次談話,' (全文未發表)　　見人民 1968.9.1.

560 `論教育革命,' (全文未見) see Union Research Institute, CCP Documents of the Great Proletarian Cultural Revolution 1966-1967 Hong Kong, 1968, p. 635.